Japanese Schooling and Identity Investment Overseas

This book is about education, ideology, power and identity investment and concerns an influential East Asian expatriate community. Specifically, it seeks to understand particular ways in which the Japanese white-collar elite live as a closed and self-referentially defined in-group, despite the manifestly multicultural ethos of their Singaporean domicile. The study attends to issues regarding schooling, unity, diversity and community based on grounded anthropological observations. Specific observations centre around the particularities of Japanese nation-state schooling practices set in cosmopolitan Singapore, a contrastingly non-Japanese setting. The insights therein are made possible by way of seeing education as an ideological domain and powerful discursive platform. Using this framework, cultural and identity-related practices are viewed dynamically and appreciated for their fluidic reflection of identity praxes.

Readers will gain fresh insights into the role of education and ideology in reproducing asymmetry and the value of sociohistorical analyses in surfacing hidden power relations. Researchers, educators and decision makers will appreciate the transparency of grounded ethnographic observation yielding insights into practices which imbricate inclusion-exclusion and privilege-marginalization debates within a neoliberal hegemony. Students of the social politics of education and the cultural politics of language, ideology and identity will find the book a provocative read.

Glenn Toh teaches in Nanyang Technological University, Singapore. He has written books and articles on language, ideology, power and education and continues to maintain an ongoing interest in current developments in the area.

Routledge Research in International and Comparative Education

This is a series that offers a global platform to engage scholars in continuous academic debate on key challenges and the latest thinking on issues in the fast-growing field of International and Comparative Education.

Titles in the series include:

50 Years of US Study Abroad Students
Japan as the Gateway to Asia and Beyond
Sarah R. Asada

Informal Learning and Literacy among Maasai Women
Education, Emancipation and Empowerment
Taeko Takayanagi

Parental Involvement Across European Education Systems
Critical Perspectives
Edited by Angelika Paseka and Delma Byrne

Transculturalism and Teacher Capacity
Professional Readiness in the Globalised Age
Niranjan Casinader

Residential Schools and Indigenous Peoples
From Genocide via Education to the Possibilities for Processes of Truth, Restitution, Reconciliation, and Reclamation
Edited by Stephen James Minton

Transnational Perspectives on Curriculum History
Edited by Gary McCulloch, Ivor Goodson, and Mariano González-Delgado

Japanese Schooling and Identity Investment Overseas
Exploring the Cultural Politics of "Japaneseness" in Singapore
Glenn Toh

Considering Inclusive Development across Global Educational Contexts
How Critical and Progressive Movements can Inform Education
Christopher J. Johnstone

For more information about this series, please visit: https://www.routledge.com/Routledge-Research-in-International-and-Comparative-Education/book-series/RRICE

Japanese Schooling and Identity Investment Overseas

Exploring the Cultural Politics of "Japaneseness" in Singapore

Glenn Toh

Routledge
Taylor & Francis Group
LONDON AND NEW YORK

First published 2021
by Routledge
2 Park Square, Milton Park, Abingdon, Oxon OX14 4RN

and by Routledge
52 Vanderbilt Avenue, New York, NY 10017

Routledge is an imprint of the Taylor & Francis Group, an informa business

British Library Cataloguing-in-Publication Data
A catalogue record for this book is available from the British Library

Library of Congress Cataloging-in-Publication Data
Names: Toh, Glenn, author.
Title: Japanese schooling and identity investment overseas : exploring the cultural politics of Japaneseness in Singapore / Glenn Toh.
Identifiers: LCCN 2020019090 (print) | LCCN 2020019091 (ebook) | ISBN 9780367538668 (hardback) | ISBN 9781003083559 (ebook)
Subjects: LCSH: Japanese--Education--Singapore. | Elite (Social sciences)--Education--Singapore. | Japanese--Ethnic identity.
Classification: LCC LC3189.S55 T65 2021 (print) | LCC LC3189.S55 (ebook) | DDC 371.0095957--dc23
LC record available at https://lccn.loc.gov/2020019090
LC ebook record available at https://lccn.loc.gov/2020019091

ISBN: 978-0-367-53866-8 (hbk)
ISBN: 978-1-003-08355-9 (ebk)

Typeset in Times New Roman
by Taylor & Francis Books

To Sakiko, Nobuyoshi and Megumi

Contents

Tables

Acknowledgements

I take this opportunity to acknowledge the role that people of wisdom and solid principle have had in my career as teacher and academic. These are respected educators who have given the better part of their lives to promoting the sound principles of fairness, equity and uprightness. I name with esteem Professors Masaki Oda, Robert Phillipson, Andy Kirkpatrick among the top people who have helped me become the educator that I am. I thank Professors Angel Lin, Ryuko Kubota, Nathanael Rudolph, Damian Rivers, Paul McBride, Kingsley Bolton and Darryl Hocking who have readily shared their thoughts, works, wisdom and passion with me at key and crucial moments. My deep appreciation also goes to Katie Peace and Jacy Hui of Routledge Singapore and the two anonymous reviewers who provided their thoughtful suggestions. Last but not least, I thank the love of my life, Sakiko, who apart from raising a Christ-centered family, is also a wonderful mother-mentor to our two children.

List of abbreviations

AIS	Australian International School
ASEAN	Association of Southeast Asian Nations
CPE	Committee of Private Education
EDB	Economic Development Board
EAP	English for Academic Purposes
EFL	English as a Foreign Language
ELF	English as a Lingua Franca
FTA	Free Trade Agreement
GDP	Gross Domestic Product
HDB	Housing and Development Board
IBDP	International Baccalaureate Diploma Programme
IBPYP	International Baccalaureate Primary Years Programme
IGCSE	International General Certificate of Secondary Education
JSEPA	Japan-Singapore Economic Agreement for a New Age Partnership
MOFA Japan	Ministry of Foreign Affairs Japan
NPP	Neighborhood Police Post
OFS	Overseas Family School
OHQ	Operational Headquarters
OWIS	One World International School
PEI	Private Education Institution
SAS	Singapore American School
SCAP	Supreme Commander for the Allied Powers
TEFL	Teaching English as a Foreign Language
TESOL	Teaching English to Speakers of Other Languages
TSLN	Thinking Schools Learning Nation
UWCSEA	United World College of Southeast Asia

1 Japanese culture and overseas schooling

Critiquing academic miscreance and pretentions to objectivity and generalizability

This is a book about Japanese schooling and cultural and identity investment. It sets out to address two central concerns: (1) investment in (and enactments of) Japanese identity among Japanese people living away from the Japanese homeland, a recognizable domain where a cultural and political discourse of homogeneity is affirmed in an ideologically powerful manner; and (2) outworkings of the (performative) nature of Japanese identity in an English-speaking cosmopolitan setting outside of Japan, such outworkings being part of a reproduction of particularized forms of Japaneseness deemed to be crucial for the assertion and preservation of the same. Set in the cosmopolitan city state of Singapore where the Japanese population numbers 30,000, the book examines the diversity of ways in which Japanese identity is marked, staked, asserted and enacted among Singapore's Japanese residents. Of particular interest are the ways in which education, especially language education, is viewed as a form of investment (Darvin & Norton, 2015), particularly one which is strongly indexical of identity, its imbrications on socially imaginable futures, and its implications for the reproduction of social forms which are identifiable with particular constructions of Japaneseness.

The fulfilment of these objectives mandates a performative, interactive as well as co-constructed view of identity and identity investment, which needs to be contrasted with one that regards identity as static, pre-determined or one that fails to acknowledge its inherent constructedness, situatedness and negotiability. Such a fluid view of identity duly recognizes the increasingly deterritorialized, unbounded, yet power-laden nature of socialization. Recognizing these aspects of socialization gives rise to the hope and possibility that in any given situation, a broader range of vested identity positionings can be negotiated and extended, 'spurred [presently] by technology and characterized by mobility' (Darvin & Norton, 2015, p. 36). As for the key notion of investment, Darvin & Norton (2015) are helpful in recognizing that a dynamic co-constructed identity model is one which situates investment at important confluences of ongoing ontological and epistemological struggles, where power, ideology and capital intersect, often unsettlingly, with performances of identity.

In terms of my own positioning, I approach the writing of this book conscious of my professional role as a reflexive educator but also one who is a parent with two children educated entirely in the Japanese school system. In so doing, I am made all the more conscious of the importance of acknowledging the challenges and complexities inhering my vested interests (and vulnerabilities) in my habitation of both identity roles. I am also aware of the constructed and constituted nature of the multiple subjective positionings that mark the negotiation (and outworking) of such interests. Nonetheless, I remain positively challenged by the potential for deeper and more revealing insights that can be gained from these multiple negotiated subject positionings, not least in terms of the possibilities available for problematizing the dictates of pre-determined role identities.

As a critically reflexive professional, I recognize that I have available for me tools and affordances that allow me to delve probingly into power and social asymmetries that come in the way of greater opportunities for fairness and equity. As parent and member of the parenting fold in the Japanese school my children go to, I admit (to) the emic perspectives available to me as I seek conscientiously to understand the grounded realities of the ways in which a system of schooling is planned and administered, perspectives which might otherwise be unavailable in my role as critical professional. Such possibilities and the benefits to be gained from them can (and indeed must) only work towards achieving transformative ideals and humanizing outcomes (see Freire, 1985; 2000; Dale & Hyslop-Margison, 2010; McLaren, 2015).

Giving due attention to matters of accountability, contextual and historical importance

In terms of accountability, it is important that the circumstances leading to the writing of this book are made clear to readers, not only for reasons to do with authenticity and ethnographic rigor, but so that readers are appropriately ushered and allowed into the historicity, narrativity and eventuality of the critical reflections that follow. Moreover, it is these same eventualities which account for the textual and narrated nature of the ethnography that characterizes much of the discussion, here centered on issues of investments in and assertions of Japaneseness in an overseas location.

In relating as I do the unfolding of events that compose and catalyze my human and professional praxis, I am conscious of a helpful observation by noted critical educator, Paulo Freire, which is that:

> seemingly trivial incidents are, in fact, very important because they involve our whole lives, our cultures … Culture extends history to the praxis of people. These trivial incidents, then, have proven to be fundamental to me, and the more I experience them, the more they help me to keep in touch with myself, while learning and reflecting.… We do not generalize without basing our generalizations on particulars.… Whatever universality there is … derives from the vigor and force of its locale. (Freire, 1985, p. 182)

The locale in its force and vigor in this case is the Singapore I was born in, and where I have now resettled after an absence of more than a decade teaching overseas. The seemingly trivial incidents are ones which unfold within the contextual realities of this locale. Aspects of my own resettlement back in Singapore after a period of nine years teaching in Japan have been documented in Toh (2019). Inside this account were details related to my avowed positioning as language educator and parent of my two children, both born overseas but on that occasion (as is now still the case as I write), enrolled in one of the Japanese-medium schools in Singapore, on account of our relocation.

Accounting for the events leading up to the present (concerns and book)

In attending to the abovementioned concerns, I am aware (convinced) of the need for a broader organizing problematic (see Simon & Dippo, 1986, for the role of the problematic in critical ethnographic studies) as part of characterizing and giving meaning to the narrative data. The way in which I set out to capture and harmonize this storied data is to have them organized around extant, exigent professional (and variously, ethical and moral) concerns relating to the production and enactment of critical discourse, the sustenance of critical academic practice and ultimately the steep challenge of (to) criticality itself (see e.g. Hall, 1997; McVeigh, 2002; 2006; Murphey, 2004; Aspinall, 2011; Stewart & Miyahara, 2011; Rivers, 2013; 2015; Toh, 2016a; 2018). These concerns relate particularly to education in Japan as it presents itself as, and proves to be, the formidable subject I seek to address. In turn, these professional and ethical concerns are for me relatable to frameworks and conversations elaborating identity and identity investments, ways of experiencing, meaning and being meaningful, and ultimately, ways of being, behaving and becoming (see e.g. Simon & Dippo, 1986; Pierce, 1995; Goosseff, 2010; 2014; Darvin & Norton, 2015; Rudolph, 2016; Rudolph, et al., 2018).

The beginnings of this present discussion came as part of a journal manuscript, which was rejected at the point of its submission to a team of four journal editors, describing an experience of Japanese schooling in Singapore and the ideological implications surrounding the inequities uncovered thereof. The manuscript was written in response to a call for papers for a special edition of a journal which published articles on different aspects of English language teaching and applied linguistics. The call for papers required potential contributions to discuss language, ideology, dominance and critical practice with particular attention to neoliberal forces at work in education. Like what has since been published in Chapter 4 of Toh (2019), this manuscript sought through the groundedness of narrative inquiry to better understand by way of ideological deconstruction the nature of ideologized Japaneseness (or *nihonjinron* – see Chapter 2 for more detailed treatment of this important topic) as it was enacted in a storied instance of overseas Japanese schooling, the way it was administered, and what it revealed about Japanese attitudes towards internationalization and language education.

The original abstract and the editors' response to the manuscript are appended here as part of my accountability to readers for the manner in which the concerns I address in this present book were formed and developed. Details of the lived (hi)story and contextual landscape on which this manuscript was based which are recounted in Toh (2019) are discussed here in relation to the teaching and learning of English in Chapter 6. Briefly, the manuscript concerned the manner in which an encounter with two English teachers in the Japanese elementary school in question led to deeper critical reflections on ways in which ideology is liable to influence the 'production and reproduction of social forms', particularly through 'what people do' (Simon & Dippo, 1986, p. 198; also see Chapter 6).

In the following two sections, the abstract of the manuscript and the full response are first provided. This is followed by a reflexive commentary addressing critical academic practice, challenges to (and for) criticality in Japanese education, and their imbrications on professional and ethical issues concerning identity, experience, meaning making and humanization in education.

The abstract of the original manuscript

> This article concerns an area of Japanese English language education that is not commonly brought to notice in scholarly literature – that of the sorts of assumptions and ideologies that are reified in the teaching of English to younger children in Japanese international schools located outside of Japan – precisely the particularized (and recalcitrant) type of setting that is in full exposure to the neoliberal, mercantilist and exclusivist ideologies which characterize the aggressive expansion of Japanese companies and multinationals overseas. Set in a Japanese international school in Singapore's urban metropolis, the article will critically examine institutional domains, artefacts and practices – including curriculum and school-based and school-sponsored activities – to understand the manner in which the English language program is skewed ideologically to affirm and legitimate Japanese nationalistic, culturist and neoliberal agendas.

The response

> Dear Glenn
>
> Here is our response (which I've written in consultation with my co-editors):
>
> After reading this essay, we all revisited the abstract in an effort to understand why we were so disappointed with the discussion as it had unfolded. We find there no reference to the aggrieved parent who begins to loom so large in the second part of this essay or, for that matter, the incident (the peremptory resignation of an English teacher at the school that the author's children attended) that constitutes the single example of *ninhonjinron* that mediates the teaching of English in a Japanese school in Singapore. The prompt for these reflections on English language teaching and *ninhonjinron* could have been

reduced to ***a relatively brief anecdote*** that might have led to a sustained analysis of the complex ways in which English language teaching inside/outside of Japan is mediated by notions of a Japanese national identity. Unfortunately, this kind of analysis doesn't eventuate, and the ***deeply felt*** personal situation that is at the heart of this essay finally appears to be too ***deeply felt*** and personal to warrant the kind of reflections to which it gives rise. This is a pity, as the essay is otherwise well written and clearly structured, and it evinces a wealth of knowledge about the complex intersections between a Japanese national identity, globalisation or internationalisation and the teaching and learning of English as a lingua franca.

Our view is that this writing is not publishable in its current form, as it runs the risk of being interpreted as a vendetta directed at the institutions mentioned in the essay. There are, however, other aspects of the style of the essay that ought to be addressed. We are not necessarily taking issue with the author's characterisation of *ninhonjinron* – he knows far more about this aspect of Japanese culture than we do - but we think it would have been appropriate to present this concept ***in a more tentative way***. What happens, instead, is that we are presented with definitive ***generalisations*** about Japanese nationalism ***made by an outsider***, which (for all the scholarly material assembled to support the ***generalisations*** made) run the risk of repeating the essentialism that the essay is supposedly opening up to critique. The teaching of English in Japanese educational settings may indeed be mediated by *ninhonjinro,* (sic) but the paradoxes and complexities to which this kind of practice gives rise might still be characterised relationally, ***as an in-between space***, however flawed and contradictory it might be with respect to the claims that are usually made about the positive role that English plays as a lingua franca in a globalising world.

To sum up: the essay might have used the specific situation that is at its heart as ***a small window*** on the status of English as an international language, helping readers to reach ***a more differentiated view*** of the role that English actually plays within the contemporary world. To accomplish this, we suspect that the author would have needed to draw on ***a wider range of experiences***, including the time that he has spent as an English language teacher in Japan, than he does here. Despite the claim made in the essay that it is written from the standpoint of his combined 'subjectivities as an experienced language educator of Singaporean-Chinese extract' who is married 'to a Japanese spouse', the essay finally amounts to a complaint by a parent, albeit one backed up by his extensive reading. We are sorry to reach this conclusion, as the abstract – as we've indicated – seemed to be very promising.

(Lead Editor of Special Edition of Journal, 2018, bold italics added)

Drawing (on) lessons from the response as backgrounding for subsequent discussion on criticality – a logically storied concatenation toward praxis

I begin this section acutely aware of an observation found in Freire (2014), which amply qualifies the narrativities and reflexivities of human creativity and praxis:

> a poem, a song, a sculpture, a painting, a book, a piece of music, a fact or deed, an occurrence, never just have one reason to explain them. An event, a fact, a deed of love or hatred, a poem, a book, are always found wrapped in thick webs, tapestries, frameworks, and touched by manifold *whys*, of which some are more proximate to the occurrence or creation. (Freire, 2014, p. 110)

Moreover, in staying true to the fact that history can be extended into praxis (Freire, 1985), specific situations at the heart of different eventualities can be turned into rigorous critique, again, in keeping faith with the problematic which I outlined earlier.

These observations from Freire (1985) will become even more significant in subsequent chapters, where seemingly trivial incidents, history and praxis trace a pattern of important motifs in the discussion of Japanese schooling in Singapore. If the above response may count as one of Freire's (1985, p. 182) 'seemingly trivial incidents' and if indeed '[c]ulture extends history to the praxis of people', such extension into praxis must take place despite (or because of) examples of minimalizing or trivializing representations of situations placed some time at the heart of professional critique. In the above case, the example of trivialization comes by way of the diminishingly 'small window' referred to by the lead editor.

Assaying the production, construction and apprehension of knowledge and meaning transparently

In an evolving manner of things, the above response first came across to me as one that was very worrying. Its worrisome aspect was something which I found difficult to explain initially after what was a rather disturbing first reading. The reasons behind this discomfiture, I felt sure, went far beyond the face-threatening manner in which the response was written (see Paltridge, 2017, for a study of reviewing practices and face-threatening reviewer behaviors).

Upon careful reflection, I was able to conclude that what I found discomfiting were that (1) the stealth attempts to question or undermine the centrality of grounded experience in knowledge construction and creation (see Freire, 1985; 2014; Simon & Dippo, 1986; Canagarajah, 2005; Goosseff, 2014) were (2) framed innocently as impeccable suggestions offered in the guise of balance, detachment and differentiation ('in a more tentative way', 'as an in-between space', 'a more differentiated view'; and even or notwithstanding 'a wider range of experiences'). However, this pedantic attempt at 'balance' and 'objectivity': (a) betrayed a clichéd manner in which the force, adjectivity and reality of lived meanings (Goosseff, 2014; Freire, 2014) could be decentered, dissipated or diluted; (b) reified discourses which '[put]constraints on what [could] be said' (Williams, 2010, p. 142); (c) legitimated 'notions that establish[ed] how things should be done' (Williams, 2010, p. 144). All of these concerns became the more worrying bearing in mind that the response was tendered as a piece of writing that sought to be accepted and trusted as serious academic critique.

The lack of nuancing or gradation of meanings came across for me as reminiscent of the sort of reviews I would have read of critical work in the 1990s, which was during a time when understandings of criticality were in my experience not as finely calibrated. Such limitations in understanding of criticality were symptomatized by: (1) reductionist treatment of knowledge and meaning making, not as constituted, situated and intersectional in character but as monolithic hermetic sealed either-or processes; and (2) equally reductionist understandings of researcher identity, with little evidence of understanding that researcher identity evolved alongside in the exploratory work of research as praxis (Norton & Early, 2011). For me, these concerns suggested the operations of ideologized forms of control and oppression which fed typically on the bounded and circumscribed understandings of positivist meaning making (Freire, 1985; 2000).

Surfacing and contesting fixities in meaning and outmoded practices

To consider the matter in another way, one can draw on Simon and Dippo's (1986, p. 197) observations that a well-articulated problematic reveals 'social practices as produced and regulated forms of action and meaning' and begins with 'a focus on [exposing] *ordered sets* of social practices' (italics added). In this regard, the way in which particularized social (academic meaning making) practices are fleshed out in the above response proves useful precisely to the formulation of the relevant problematic itself. Such kinds of display make an 'academic' response of this kind and the social practices it exposes very amendable to the type of critical ethnography sought for in Simon and Dippo (1986). Its pedantic assumptions, and the controlling practices it permits, attract the articulation of a finely-tuned problematic useful for exposing the reductionist positivist nature of pieces similar to it. In Chapters 5 and 6 it will be seen as much that certain particularized social behaviors demonstrating the influence of patterned or ingrained beliefs are equally attractive to the articulation of similar types of problematics. This latter point will become relevant in later discussion (see Chapters 5 and 6), when the matter of habituated and/or patterned behaviors comes up for notice.

In a concatenating manner of events, the above response opened up a way to highlight the culpable influence of ideologies and beliefs, in this case, in bringing to bear the production and elaboration of certain detractive forms of ('academic') practice (see Toh, 2018 for a detailed study on the influence of ideology on pejorative manuscript reviews). This became an important realization which led me to do a literature search, in hopes of getting a better understanding of the ways in which the workings of ideology can influence the construction, appropriation and sometimes, perversion, of knowledge and meaning. The value of this interesting search showed itself in the revelation of an ironic parallel. This parallel is demonstrated in the way hackneyed practices and paradigms are relied upon to protect an outmoded status quo. In both the rejected manuscript which surfaced outmoded regimes of power and control in Japanese schooling in Singapore, and the response to it which sought the guise of outmoded positivist practices, the status quo is upheld unabashedly.

Thus, problematics set up to investigate one type of situation in outmoded social practice can well be adapted to investigate other parallel situations, all the more if the areas involve uncovering problems to do with the mollycoddling of 'fixit[ies] in meaning' (Williams, 2010, p. 141).

Managerializing while mollycoddling the outmoded

The above editors' response and the uncovering of particularized beliefs and practices relating to journal reviewing (again, see Toh, 2018 on journal reviewing and ideology) can yield one further benefit. Both are useful as timely reminders, since there will be ways in which a book like this would be vulnerable to similar forms or per(mutations) of reception from detractors or defenders of the status quo. But this, in a sense, is all along to be expected, especially when practices which help perpetuate the exercise of power are problematized, questioned and exposed for what they really are. Discourses find their way into social practice while the hegemony of managerial discourses 'can have an impact on the operation of work' (Williams, 2010, p. 144). Certain managerial and managerialist discourses while they implicate the subjectivities of students, teachers, writers and workers (Williams, 2010) are recognizably or notoriously difficult to write back against for reasons to do with their situation in organizations and other powerful domains, academic journals not excluded.

Similarly inequitable paradigms enjoy their staying power on account of the formidable hegemonic backings they receive. As noted in Williams (2010), '[t]he effects of discourses set constraints on what can be said' (p. 142), to the extent that 'statement[s are] conditioned by prior discourse which influences the meaning that [they are] capable of achieving' (p. 143). For writers in particular, writing back against dominant discourses and their operationalized practices for the purposes of restoring equity often involves having to adopt a refuse-to-go-away attitude of chipping patiently away, perhaps not at their minions, collaborators and their sometime back alley tactics, but more justifiably, at the flawed and fallacious nature of the assumptions they lean on.

Perceiving or failing to perceive a hierarchy of meanings, or falling (gunning) for extremities in meaning

Part of the fallacious nature of flawed or misplaced assumptions is attributed in Goosseff (2014) to the fact that common knowledge and assumptions are not equally prioritized among different individuals, editors and reviewers included. Such differences strongly suggest 'a hierarchy of meanings' or a prioritization of meanings, and more worryingly, the real possibility that meanings can even 'fall under [a] threshold of awareness' (p. 706). More familiarly, one is perhaps reminded of the saying that common knowledge (common sense) may not be that common, at the end of a proverbial day. Pithy but basically uninformative or dis-informative conclusions like 'aggrieved parent', 'vendetta', 'complaint by a parent' are symptoms of the operation of such a hierarchy of meanings. My point, in this respect, is a poignant one. Japaneseness or *nihonjinron* which is that much prioritized in this book is precisely an area that may be dismissed owing to this bespoken 'hierarchy [of understanding] of meanings' (Goosseff, 2014, p. 706). In some instances, Japaneseness or *nihonjinron* may not even achieve a basic threshold of meaningfulness, expert readers notwithstanding (not spared). My reason for such pessimism has to do with the hidden presence of dissembled ideologies which mask the inner workings of power asymmetries (see Befu, 2001; Lie, 2001; Lebra, 2004; McVeigh, 2006; Makino, 2002; Qi, 2014). From lived experience (see Toh, 2014; 2016; 2018), discussions involving sincere but serious questionings of practices relating to Japaneseness can be misunderstood or subverted. Such misunderstanding and subversion stem as innocuously as might be the case from 'meaning [simply] not perceived' (Goosseff, 2014, p. 706), if looked upon kindly, or meaning under-perceived or misperceived, if looked upon less hopefully.

In any of such worrying instances, one can resort to an earlier study of Goosseff's (2010, p. 146) where the writer draws on the Kantian idea that 'the knowing subject can never transcend his experience towards knowledge of things as they are in themselves' (sic). In certain extreme cases of oblivion, 'self-reference is [or becomes] the source of all knowledge' (p. 146). Elaborating, Goosseff's understanding of sense making is that it naturally obeys 'not so much the observed' (so much for attentive readers and intensive reading, and telling children to be and to do the same) but more so 'the inner world of entities' (p. 149). (More on the relevance of the inner world of entities can be found in Chapter 2 when Japaneseness or *nihonjinron* is examined in greater detail). Commenting on the matter of structurally determined meaning, Goosseff highlights a point that will prove very important, not just for the way in which critical commentaries (here concerning Japan and Japaneseness) may be perceived by an informed (amenable) and not-so-informed (not-so-amenable) readership, but also for the subsequent discussions (in Chapters 5 and 6) concerning how perceptions of an outside world (for the Japanese living in Singapore) are ultimately very much internally referential in nature.

Internal referencing in meaning recognition and specification

To explain the way in which meaning is internally referenced, Goosseff (2010) turns to the theory of autopoiesis as described by theoretical biologists Humberto Maturana and Francisco Varela. I intend, in this section, to discuss autopoiesis in fair detail for reasons to do with its potential as an approach to understanding ways of knowing and meaning or ways in which knowledge and meaning are perceived and responded to. In relation to present concerns, autopoiesis potentially facilitates the drawing of a parallel between the manner in which Japanese domiciled in Singapore are able to make sense of the non-Japanese Singaporean environment, and the sometime equally autopoietic nature of the manner in which different readers of critiques on this very topic would make sense of the insights provided by these critiques.

Goosseff (2010) begins his description of autopoiesis by referring to the concept of *organization* as the basic design of living creatures, albeit one that is not observable from the outside. The idea of *internal dynamics* therefore captures the internal processes, which by nature, are subject to the living creature's organizational design. The latter implies too that living systems are only able to react 'within themselves to themselves', giving rise to what is termed *organizational closure* (p. 146). The idea of organizational closure, moreover, resonates with the abovementioned Kantian claim that knowing subjects are not able to transcend experience or perceive anything independent of it.

Turning to Maturana and Varela's (1980) observation that 'perception should not be viewed as a grasping of an external reality [as such], but rather as a specification of one' (cited in Goosseff, 2010, p. 146), specifications are then seen to be 'internal constructions and are [thereby] determined by the organization of [a] system' (p. 146). It can thus be concluded that '[d]ifferent organizations with different internal dynamics will make and experience different "specifications"' (Goosseff, 2010, p. 146) in situations when open interaction or *structural coupling* with an external environment takes place. Interestingly with regard to subsequent discussion, one is able to learn the following:

> The function of a living entity is to keep itself alive by responding appropriately to environmental triggers in a way that is faithful to itself by obeying its organization. But how does the entity know what to do, when it meets a perturbation because of outside triggers. (sic) System-specific, the perturbation is [in fact] an inside response to the trigger, awakening assignments of meaning. Some are experienced as *dangerous*; others as *desirable*. A more limited range of possible meanings indicates more instinctual behaviour, *but instincts need "fixed" very predictable environments to be effective.*
>
> (Goosseff, 2010, p. 147, italics added)

With respect to subsequent discussion on Japaneseness (in Chapter 2), it will be observed that Japaneseness works like a constituted form of internal organization that is capable of influencing the way in which external changes can be (come) internally specified. The latter is possible given Japaneseness as a form of internal organization which comes into play in situations of interaction or structural coupling. Culturally and ideologically, Japaneseness can be said of itself to be autopoietic, in its self-creating, self-affirming, self-perceiving and self-ordering character (see especially Befu, 2001; Lebra, 2004; Makino, 2002). Additionally, with respect to the above italicized portions, I will, by way of understandings of autopoiesis just outlined, argue that a foreign non-Japanese Singaporean environment is not one that is as easily predictable to Japanese stationed in Singapore as would be a setting that uniquely specifies the familiarities of their homeland. I will, moreover, observe that critiques of Japaneseness are especially challenging to readers not used to the 'perturbation' of candid or perhaps 'deeply felt' questioning. Such critiques may be perceived or construed autopoietically in ways that only the internal organization of the said readers would definitively permit. Such permission vis-à-vis 'an entity's handling of unpredictable diversities of structural coupling processes' (given new environments, new unfamiliar information), internally and autopoietically determined as it is, is thought by Goosseff (2010, p. 148) to be in proportion to 'the complexity of the brain'.

To sum up this section, one practical illustration will prove useful by way of applying the theory of autopoiesis. To illustrate, Goosseff (2010) is able to conclude the following about, for example, the roar of a crowd at a sports match: 'according to autopoiesis, there are no sounds that are [actually the] property of the crowd. Instead, the sounds I hear are properties of me' (p. 146). Such being the case, following the theory of autopoiesis, it becomes highly plausible that much of the range of possible reactions to discussions on *nihonjinron* can be paralleled with not just: (1) the internal and closed aspects of *nihonjinron* itself discussed vis-à-vis Japanese insularity (see Befu, 2001; Lie, 2001; Toh 2019), but also (2) the whole idea of organizational closure (Goosseff, 2010; also see Peters & Roberts, 2012, for a conceptualization of ideological closedness and Toh, 2019, for its application in relation to *nihonjinron*). In the case of the response dealt with earlier, and applying what Goosseff (2010) has outlined about autopoiesis, the editors' reaction to a critique of *nihonjinron* in the manuscript is one that displays the internal operations of organization, or more specifically, organizational closure, to the (external) world of the contents.

Anatomizing 'generalizability': miscreance and mischief through the management and subversion of meaning

Concerning the making, apprehension, and occasionally, the subversion of meaning, it is appropriate at this point to reiterate the manner in which I have sought early on in this chapter to recognize the need for an overarching problematic. Such a problematic needs to be one that is adequate for addressing questions concerning ways of making and managing meaning, identity and identity-related investments, and ultimately, ways of being, behaving and becoming (see Rudolph, 2016; Rudolph et al., 2018). The articulated problematic then serves as a framing and organizing strategy for the gathering together of narratives on which understandings of autopoiesis and internal specification, just now discussed, will help to shed light.

Subverting or undermining adjectivity in experience through pretentions to objectivity and generalizability

What can be professionally very worrying is the possibility (or likelihood) that certain references or pretentions to generalizable meanings, or seemingly objective calls to the same, are liable to conceal social and power relations that are in reality oppressive (Friere, 1985; 2000). It is therefore important to be able to locate 'the specificity of social practices [as] central to understanding how oppressive relations "work" (how they happen)' (Simon & Dippo, 1986, p. 198). This particular preoccupation with generalizability and more mythically, objectivity, largely involves the sedimentation of viewpoints which take 'existing forms of social life and social consciousness as obvious, natural, and taken for granted' (Simon & Dippo, 1986, p. 198). Goosseff (2014) provides a timely reminder in this regard:

> All neutral (objective) language originally once had (unspoken or under the threshold of awareness) adjectives as all empirical descriptions *originate from experience.* It is safe to say that experience without meaning cannot exist and language without adjective does not describe experience. That makes (scientific) objectivity *a linguistic construct, a regulative idea.* (p. 706, italics added)

Ironically, even accusations of over-generalization – like in 'for all the scholarly material assembled to support the ***generalisations*** made' (Lead Editor, sic, 2018) – can in fact reveal the presence or concealment of this very preoccupation with generalization or regulation, which are of course rhetorical constructs (following Goosseff, 2014). This same preoccupation in turn symptomizes the possibility of either a careless or a myopic oversight of the specifics or adjectivity of experience (see Goosseff, 2014). These specifics are precisely those which provide the very opportunity for generalizable 'truths' to come across (deceivingly, or credulously if indicative of the workings of naiveté) as what they are mistakenly thought to be. Or, if universals and generalizations are a way of smoke-screening storied specificities, insinuations of the very same are equally responsible for the dissimulation (blindsiding and hoodwinking) of locatable details from which precious and priceless lessons can be drawn in situ. With this in mind, it will be seen in subsequent discussion that popularized and generalized assertions or reifications of Japaneseness through the sedimentation of institutionally situated (ensconced) myths, habits or scripted practices, can serve as a way of blindsiding unwary participants and victims to the color of real-life experience, particularly in the case of the Japanese moving to Singapore. For these people, this blindsiding can take place at the expense of their uniquely experiencing what it means to move to a new country and the fresh (but regrettably not eye-opening) realities relocation has to offer (see Chapters 5 and 6).

Generalizations, and more so, accusations of the same, must be interrogated for the specifics of experience they (attempt to) manage, dissemble or parry away.

Recontextualization and reappropriation of meaning

Of course, the reference to over-generalization, in some respects a Freudian slip on the part of the editors, betrays a self-same pre-disposition to entering the (social and textual) trapdoor of generalizability. Not unexpectedly, this is followed by the very same allegation directed at the manuscript (see Toh, 2018). Acting like what Fairclough (2005) calls a 'filtering device' for selective inclusion or exclusion of meanings (more on inclusion and exclusion hereafter), the response lends itself to reappropriating the critique of Japanese schooling. In this way, the matter becomes recontextualized as a neutered and generalized observation, and therefore rendered (renditioned) as not worth reader attention. This again is suggestive of underlying ideology at work – in the way in which the deprecation and fragmentation of richly grounded and contextualized experience ('small window'; 'relatively brief anecdote') contributes to: (1) its diminution, repudiation, de-emphasis, disengagement, assimilation and co-optation; and (2) the concealment or dissimulation of its epistemological and ontological origins in lived and elaborated experience (see Thompson, 1987; Eagleton, 1991; Goosseff, 2010; 2014).

The crudity of renaming, recontextualization, reappropriation, sweeping generalization, in 'dredge-net like' fashion (Toh, 2003b, p. 568), can be used a tool to neutralize or render inane, arguments grown out of the very forces of the locale, as Freire (1985) is clearly wary of. Such neutralization can prove to be a very dehumanizing way of silencing local knowledge and experience (see engaging debate in Kumaravadivelu, 2003a; Toh, 2003a; Berns, 2003; Brutt-Griffler, 2003; Leki, 2003; Kumaravadivelu, 2003b; Toh, 2003b, where crudely totalizing pronouncements are up-ended and burlesqued for what they are). As will be seen for the Japanese people in question, unique aspects of the experience of relocation to cosmopolitan Singapore, is similarly liable to be overwhelmingly reappropriated. Powerful assertions and enactments of discourses of Japaneseness are often both directly and indirectly foisted on Singapore's Japanese residents (see Chapters 5 and 6). Pretentions to generality and generalizability are precisely a way of banishing and disqualifying the use of adjectives (Goosseff, 2014, p. 706), except those inanely generalized ones permitted by the pretenders.

Marginalizing localized experience

In this respect, Canagarajah (2005) is sharp in his observations that the reflexive practice so crucial in enlightened (human and professional) praxis can only be well served by a fresh and grounded 'awareness of nonlocal discourses' while still 'enjoying a local subjectivity' (p. 15). Such accommodation enables 'a dual consciousness that provides a critical vantage point [especially] for … intercultural engagement' (p. 15). In so observing, Canagarajah is able to highlight the fact that certain aspects of Western scholarship have been hopelessly unable to imagine local ecological and relational factors. The prime(d) knee-jerk (perhaps Freudian) reaction to such inability is to treat local specificities as matters that need to be reappropriated as (and through) uniformed generalization, or as something simply non-generalizable, and therefore aberrant. Both are equally oppressive acts to marginalize, jettison and repudiate.

Echoing Freire (1985), Canagarajah (2005) notes indeed that '[g]eneralization, systematization, and model building involve a certain amount of abstraction that *filters out the variability of experience* in diverse contexts' (p. 5, italics added). Such acts of filtering out variable experience are also to conveniently forget that modernist knowledge is invariably 'also a form of local knowledge – local to communities in Europe', quite easily 'accountable for in terms of 17th century socio-historic conditions in Europe' (p. 6). So-called 'global knowledge' is paradoxically traceable to local or even parochial origins, if '*all* knowledge producing activities are [ultimately] context-bound' (p. 6, italics in original), and if (not) also deeply felt (Lead Editor, 2018). One recalls the manner in which Lillis and Turner (2001) describe Sir Isaac Newton's palpably impassioned arguments before highly critical scientific audiences. If there is so much truth in Lillis and Turner's (2001) observations about Newton's deep personal commitment to his craft, then the demand for detachment and transparency in the discourse of scientific writing is ultimately about reifying a myth, something which needs to be considered problematic (Lillis & Turner, 2001, p. 64). Even Newton himself was obliged to create 'a style of argumentation' just in order that his work would come across as acceptable to the illustrious and venerable members of the Royal Society.

Still or nevertheless, it was by virtue of this type of editors' response (and perhaps those years ago, my own part in the abovementioned debate in the *World Englishes* forum) that I felt professionally and, ever more so, *morally*, obliged to revisit the literature on ways in which the workings of ideology can influence the construction or destruction of knowledge and meaning making. The latter's situatedness in grounded and realized experience (Goosseff, 2014) is often cleverly disguised or dissimulated by way of a reification of sweeping totalities seemingly as objective 'truth'. Such deference or homage to objective 'truth' and totality are in turn given to a form of reductionism that is unthinkingly pre-disposed towards simplistic monoliths and/or dichotomies.

This is very worrying if or as it occurs once too often in academia. For instance, in terms of identity positioning, the reference to my being subjectively positioned as an (unqualified) outsider reveals a preoccupation with naively dichotomous insider-outsider polarities which shuts off (down) the sort of nuancing and negotiation (not so) commonly expected of people in academia. This is a case of falling into *nihonjinron*'s Venus flytrap. In it, academia exhibits the very same credulity for reductionist insider-outsider dichotomies that *nihonjinron*, much like the flytrap, tempts and traps inelegant and unsuspicious insects into – as a way to classify, deprecate and exclude (see Befu, 2001; Stewart & Miyahara, 2011; Rivers, 2013; 2019; Kubota & Fujimoto, 2013). In contrast, nuance, creativity and imagination thrive in spaces which are 'related to a critical view of the concepts of repeated action and routines' (Nadal-Burgues, 2014, p. 807), or in this case clumsily reductionist dichotomizations.

Reductionism as a form of oppression and marginalization

Once duly exposed, the attempt to silence grounded experience of the locale as well as to problematize a bona fide (but yet reflexive) identity positioning ('Despite the claim … of his combined 'subjectivities as an experienced language educator of Singaporean-Chinese extract' who is married 'to a Japanese spouse') became an unfortunate reminder of the way in which reductionist forms of *nihonjinron* (see Chapter 2) reify one truth forms of identity (Japaneseness) which operate, in like fashion, to deny the specifics of history, personality, locality and variety (see Stewart & Miyahara, 2011; Rivers, 2013; Kubota & Fujimoto, 2013). Such depersonalizing discourses tend to be blatant, dispensing with hackneyed dalliances, whether such dalliances are to do with anomalously clichéd 'in-between space[s]', 'differentiated view[s]' or equivocatingly 'more tentative way[s]' (Lead Editor, 2018). If dominant oppressive ideologies do not waste any time indulging in such dalliances, there appears to be little sense for critiques of the same to be thus pretentiously or hypocritically dainty-footed (or pedantic). The very thought that people can be browbeaten into politeness and cautiousness is a form of crassness or distastefulness in ordinary situations, but actually a form of disinformation or self-delusion in academia (see later discussion on Japanese forms of politeness in Chapter 2).

In sum, what is now helpful to me as I enter in earnest into dealing with present concerns is this historically verifiable realization that forms of deprecation of the uniqueness of subject positioning, locally-situated, locally-realized, locally-identifiable, ecologically-negotiated experience (and meanings thereof) can happen readily by way of totalizing and assimilating discourses. For good reason therefore, I treat my subject matter ever conscious (and suspicious) of threats and bluffs that are not only borne of oppressive ideologies and insular mindsets, but which have an uncanny way in which they can mimic or shadow some form of powerful incumbent truth (myth). Such mimicking is often ventriloquist- or parrot-like, yet always smug, pedantic, limiting, restraining and silencing. I resonate readily with Simon and Dippo's (1986, p. 197) observation that '[p]ower operates not just on people but through them', meaning also that 'what is [at any given time or circumstance] legitimated and available in the way of particular practices in the domains of body, language, and activity *is not arbitrary*' (italics added).

The non-arbitrary and non-accidental nature of such legitimation of particular and indulgent practices must be understood 'materially and historically' (Simon & Dippo, 1986, p. 197), as I will hereafter seek to do. The far-from-random work(ing) of ideology in sanctioning and non-sanctioning, legitimation and delegitimation, in and of itself, is already a good and sobering lesson to learn (from). Yet certainly not apart from this lesson, I remain, as I write, also (gain)fully reminded that responses to manuscripts are after all highly situated, sometimes imprecise and/or partisan documents (Toh, 2018). Admittedly fresh from my own engagement with the contents of Toh (2018) which methodically documents the same partisan and ideological aspects of journal reviews, reviewer behaviors, practices and bluffs, and their part in the construction (contortion or suppression) of knowledge, my own professional instincts allow me to see the above editors' response as part of a historical segment (albeit one which involves an unfortunate display of faux pas in a professional context). This history can now in good part be further extended by way of the written realizations of a new book-length critique, yet again, of Japaneseness and its extensions into education.

Happily therefore, and to concur with Freire (1985), these present eventualities and realizations are also a way for me to express my humble commitment to highlighting critical issues, certainly not in a weak(ened) or 'more tentative way' (Lead Editor, 2018) as would be terribly ill advised, but in ways that appropriately reflect the force and vigor of their very locale.

Final comments for this section on possible misperception or miscreance

Returning finally to the problematic outlined at the beginning of the chapter, my point of carefully narrating and reflecting on the abovementioned events, as I trust will be appreciated, is not only to demonstrate how easily criticality and critical discourse can be misconstrued or run roughshod over (as if only possible in learned or quasi-learned circles – see Alderson, 2009; Rivers, 2015; 2019; Toh, 2018). It is also to highlight a case in point of how illustrative a grounded phenomenon like the editors' response in question can be of the power of experience and the realization of meanings thereof, or simply the absence of such realization. In relation to the latter, I now examine how easily the work of decentering or critiquing dominant practices can be misunderstood or misperceived, here with reference to a lack of 'awareness of meaning', where meaning happens to fall 'under the threshold of awareness' (Goosseff, 2014, p. 706), or where it is subject to a willful exploitation of its extremities, under the guise of being 'balanced'. Both of these failures make it necessary for critical discussions like the ones which will follow in this book to be preceded by a detailed exposé of possible miscreances resulting from opportunistic exploitations or perjuring of meaning.

Two of Goosseff's (2014) more recent examples of the way meaning is perceived or perjured can be used to drive home my point. When similar but not identical objects are observed, in Goosseff's (2014) case, open versus closed scissors, or more simply, two pebbles, miscreance takes places when these differences are *exaggerated* beyond reasonable fairness, and when the blame for this exaggeration is then placed on the one who cares enough to point out the differences. Goosseff (2014) also highlights the case of two boys' encounter of the same dog and how this clearly reflects likely differences in the way they are 'aware of the world' (p. 706). My own conclusion from this latter illustration is that there could well be a general lack of recognition on the part of some that assertions and exertions of Japaneseness or *nihonjinron* can be that much hegemonic and therefore oppressive in outcome (McVeigh, 2002;

2006), as I will seek to argue (see Chapters 5 and 6). To return to the illustration, one or both boys may respond or react positively or negatively to the dog, depending on '[w]hat the dog personally means to them' where 'the meaning in the boys not within the dog, determines how they will respond' (p. 706). Like Goosseff (2014), I make no apology as I turn, once again, to narrations of grounded experiences relating to the workings of *nihonjinron* ideology (see Toh, 2014; 2016; 2019), in the hope that the same will be meaningful to readers, particularly with respect to the matters concerning Japanese education and identity in cosmopolitan Singapore, outlined at the beginning of this chapter.

Finding resonance and support in humanizing motifs

In attending to these concerns and conscious of the part to be played by my own praxis, I bear in mind Freire's (1985) observation that histories often find their further extension and elaboration in praxis. As a parent of two children educated in the Japanese system, the writing of this book is part of an unfolding landscape which now enables me to seek a better understanding of the ways in which Japanese people in Singapore envision and administer their lives and futures, through insights gained from the way children are educated. In this bid, I am helped by Simon and Dippo's (1986, following Sartre (1963)) use of the term 'project'. For Simon and Dippo (1986, citing Sartre, 1963), a project speaks of an activity which is 'determined both by *real* and *present* conditions' as well as by 'certain conditions still to come which it [the project] is trying to *bring into being*' (p. 196, italics added). The authors make known that it is their 'interest in how people are *implicated* in the *regulation and alteration* of the terms of *how they live together* and how they *define what is possible and desirable* for *themselves and others*', that has helped them to understand what the idea of 'project' means for studies in critical anthropology as their area of focus (Simon & Dippo, 1986, p. 196, italics added). For me, the italicized portions identify important thematic, moral and critical concerns or motifs which will resonate with my own arguments, especially those regarding the humanization of teaching and learning as an expression and aspiration of hope (see Freire, 2000; Dale & Hyslop-Margison, 2010). In my praxis, both humanization and hope are attributes which help to make possible genuine investments in identity and self-representation, as well as in better ways to experience, signify and express oneself. Moreover, for nuance and creativity to be reinforced in Simon and Dippo's (1986) understanding of project activity, one is reminded by Nadal-Burgues (2014, p. 807) that 'creative possibilities in projects' adopt a critical view of reductionism, repetition and routine. These creative possibilities also recognize that 'spaces of creativity' admit the 'mak[ing of] appropriate judgements' as well as 'subjective projections' (p. 817). In such a view of creativity, rhetorical openness, as opposed to rhetorical closure in which 'various meanings [converge] into a single one', is said to only be the tiniest of first steps (Nadal-Burgues, 2014).

Insofar as creativity in projects opens up space for human judgement and agency, and insofar as 'high levels of project indeterminacy' creates opportunities for 'intensive creativity' (p. 817), I am necessarily inclined to view determinacy and smugness with doubt and suspicion.

In attending to these aspects of praxis therefore, I invoke an organizing framework that will give meaning to the narrative data to be examined. This framework will help to relate the storied data with: (1) issues concerning access, equity and humanization; (2) problems to do with reductionism, fixity and a lack of nuancing in thought; and (3) aspects of critical discussions which answer the call to criticality when dealing with (1) and (2). Helping to further such critical praxis is William's (2010) reminder that a 'central feature of the knowledge economy is that where[ever] information is limited in the sense that it is fixed and given' (as will be clear in subsequent discussions of essentialist conceptualizations of Japaneseness), it remains possible for aspects of new knowledge to emerge from a 'learning by doing' (p. 141). In other words, in fulfilling the need to critically question a constricting fixity of beliefs and practices, learning by doing, learning by telling or learning by writing, are all useful strategies for knowledge creation. They can also be used as ways to redress inequities resulting from the silencing of voice. For Freire (1985, p. 89), liberating actions are not about going to 'another part of the world' to 'normalize it' according to a particular 'way of viewing reality'. Neither are they about manipulation, mechanical transfer, depositing, handing over or cultural invasion (p. 89). These terms are a denial of 'true action and reflection' while insinuating 'actions which transform people into "things" and negate their existence as beings who transform the world' (p. 89).

To say as much therefore, I am obliged think, write and tell with a strong consciousness that true education, as it is for Freire (1985), involves 'educational action of a liberating nature' (p. 91) and 'incarnates [a] permanent search of people *together with others* for their becoming more fully human in the world in which they exist' (p. 90, italics added). In this regard, the discussions I enter into are in no small part motivated by the hope that situations where the prevalence of dominant ideologies and hegemonies perpetuate inequitable and outmoded practices as well as misperceived or dehumanized meanings can be exposed to achieve greater fairness and equity. Education, as Freire (1985) sees it, is a response to the call to be more fully human (see Freire, 1985; 2000; Dale & Hyslop-Margison, 2010).

Chapter content

Following this introductory chapter, the next (Chapter 2) sets out to better understand the manner in which Japanese people administer and manage their lives within the safety of their homeland. This is seen to work as a way of appreciating who and how the Japanese are, if preferably left to themselves (and if this is possible in these overwhelmingly panoptic and heady days of globalization), before they take leave of Japan's watery shores to venture overseas (Befu, 2009). In this chapter, *nihonjinron*, or tenets of Japaneseness, is seen to function in Japanese society like a civil religion (Befu, 2001). The internally oriented trajectories of *nihonjinron* operate self-referentially in situations where Japanese people find themselves having to adapt to life in non-Japanese environments. The reality of this challenge remains true notwithstanding the fact that Japan's putative identity as a mono-cultural nation has lately had to cope with challenges to do with immigration and the presence of (and a certain degree of reliance on) foreigners on Japanese soil.

Singapore, the island nation which is (temporary) home to some 30,000 Japanese domiciles then becomes the subject of discussion in Chapter 3, especially where it concerns the open, cosmopolitan and globalized character the nation state seeks unwaveringly to display on the world stage, and somewhat boasts of, internationally. Modern Singapore's journey to nationhood is traced in the contents of this chapter. Its former and less glamorous identity as a British colony is contrasted in this chapter with the rapid economic expansion it experienced in the post-war and post-independence years of the 1950s, 1960s and 1970s. In these years of struggle with unemployment and poverty before the turn towards industrialization and economic growth, Singapore looks northwards to Japan, not only as major source of foreign investment but also for transfer of technical expertise and knowhow. Japan, as Asia's then only industrialized country, becomes a major contributor to Singapore's rapid growth as an independent nation, which accounts for the recognizable presence of the Japanese population and the wide range of businesses and services to serve the needs and wants of its members.

Chapter 4 then traces the specific histories of the Japanese population in Singapore, dating back to the mid-1800s after the arrival of the first Japanese settlers who were in the main traders, doctors and dentists, but not without a significant number of prostitutes and brothel keepers being part of the growing population size. Japan's attention southwards is examined in relation to *nanshin ron* (southward advancement), the Japanese government's push to have its people think in terms of fostering strategic contacts with Southeast Asia as a potential area for economic ties and expansion. *Nanshin ron*'s advocacy for southward advancement is seen in the chapter to take on particularly belligerent meanings during the Second World War when Japan fatefully occupied Singapore for a period of three years and eight months from 1942 to 1945. The eventfully busy period after the war saw the mass repatriation of the defeated Japanese forces, followed not long after by the gradual return of Japanese businesses to Singapore. Post-war independent Singapore is seen to be courting and welcoming the presence of Japanese corporations, Japanese expertise and Japanese expatriates, not least from the enthusiasm witnessed in its 'Learn from Japan' drive. As a result of such government policy, a distinct if rather sheltered and privileged community of Japanese businessmen and executives and their families steadily increased in size. In part due to the terms of their expatriate postings to Singapore, and in part due to the powerful influence of conservative ideologies governing the prosecution of big business, many of these businessmen and executives had little occasion to engage socially and locally outside of their well-defined business circles. Largely deprived of opportunities to interact locally, something innocently explained away as part and parcel of being a member of the Japanese business elite, relocating to Singapore became only like being away on an extended business trip. Bearing in mind the importance of paying close attention to both particularities and practices at points of contact between actors of different cultural histories (Qi, 2014), the chapter ends with descriptions of the Japanese community in Singapore, their distinctiveness as a community, the ecologies and discourses which help to reify them putatively as a group as well as discourse-community (Maxwell et al., 2019), and the ways different quasi-group members relate to each other and to local Singaporeans.

The discussion in the next chapter (Chapter 5) turns its attention to narrative and interpretative data relating to Japanese-medium schooling in Singapore. A detailed description of four Japanese institutions directly associated with Japanese education in Singapore sets the contextual background against which subsequent developments are seen to unfold. These storied enactments provide understandings of the way their cultural and political dimensions are both indexical and symptomatic of ways in which Japanese people imagine, approach, apprehend or otherwise adjust to life outside of their homeland. Of sufficient importance in the interpretative storytelling (see Flory & Iglesias, 2010) that takes place in this chapter is the matter of the way perspectival viewpoints are seen to bear on perceptions of order, borders and boundaries. The discussion draws from the dynamic treatment of order, borders and boundaries in Crang (2000) and Thrift (2007), foregrounding the work of philosopher and psychoanalyst Michel de Certeau, particularly de Certeau's 'Walking in the City'. Apportionment, enactment, perception and appropriation of space become relevant to ways in which operations of space are revealed to be expressions of 'unwritten geographies' (Crang, 2000, p. 136). In relation to Japanese domiciled in Singapore, such geographies are seen to be translatable into instantiations of visibility or invisibility, inclusion or exclusion, placement or displacement, power or disempowerment, strength or helplessness and other indices of existence, identity and experience. The critical reflections in (and on) the stories told are subsequently recognized in this chapter to be important for understanding what Japanese perceptions of internationalization and multiculturalism mean (or augur) for cross-border and cross-cultural interactions in non-Japanese dominant domains, in this case, Singapore. Furthermore, observations of particularized enactments of identity, community and communality reveal the tendency to adhere, defer or resort to certain forms of patterned behaviors which are reflective of the influence of ingrained beliefs symptomizing the workings of ideologies relating back to *nihonjinron*.

Following Chapter 5, Chapter 6 provides insights into the way English is taught and treated in a particular Japanese elementary school in Singapore. This critically oriented discussion traces the outcomes of three ecologically significant aspects of reality that bear on the type of education the school has to offer. The first aspect concerns the fact that the school has been set up to educate children of Japanese expatriates employed by Japanese firms and multinational corporations, a reminder that their presence and the companies they work for are a major reason for the school's continued existence in Singapore. The second aspect is with regard to the fact that an education based exclusively on the Japanese state curriculum suggests that certain statist and/or nationalistic aspects of education are felt to be in need of reaffirmation when it comes to the schooling of a younger generation in a foreign context. Such reaffirmation may in turn be viewed as a way of counteracting perceivably un-Japanese influences that come with the very forces of globalization that make it necessary for Japanese expatriate families to move and live overseas, in the first place. The third aspect relates to the teaching and learning of English and how, against the mercantile and pecuniary motivations of the first and the nationalistic if inward-looking motivations of the second, the teaching of English is realized singularly (if reductively) in the manner of its curricular, pedagogical and administrative practices. One notable facet of such reductive particularity highlighted is the lack of critical attention given to the choice of content materials that reflect essentialist portrayals of people and cultures, in a largely disinforming fashion. The adoption of such a reductionist culturalist one-language one-culture approach to the teaching of English is traced in this chapter to a protectionist agenda that seeks to legitimate elitist Japanese expatriate identities. In this connection, observations are made in the chapter that having a Japanese institution teach English from the first year of elementary school is rarely usual, while the social differentiation that comes with having one's child learn English overseas (see Adams & Agbenyega, 2019) is one that suggests elitist privilege not enjoyed by Japanese workers who are not sent away on much-coveted overseas postings with their families. The early introduction of English to Japanese expatriate children is highlighted as a kind of betrayal of convention, especially by those who revere the preservation of Japaneseness as an alibi for remaining staunchly monolingual. It is consequently noted that the way English is taught must be very much part of the maintenance if not the production of Japaneseness, meaning that students have to be treated perennially as deficit *learners* as opposed to being potential *users* of the language (see Iino & Murata, 2016; Toh, 2019). The chapter ends with an epistemological exploration of the notions of *critique* and *design* and ways in which they can be part of a praxis of action and reflection made necessarily urgent by the challenges of prevailing ideological discourses influencing the teaching and learning of English particular to the given situation (Freire, 2000; Lillis, 2003).

Chapter 7, the final chapter, returns to the observation in Freire (1985) that lived histories find their extension and elaboration in praxis, such praxis in the case of this book being an integral part of the extension and elaboration of a confluence of events traceable to my nine-year sojourn in Japan, my return to Singapore with family and to matters inspiring my quest to understand the way Japanese residing in Singapore seek to envision and administer their lives and children's futures. In connection with the latter concern, specific aspects of Goosseff's (2010) description of autopoiesis are revisited as part of gathering together insights gained in preceding chapters on identity investments of Japanese domiciled in Singapore and their particularized outworkings in a Singaporean setting. These identity investments are seen to be heavily influenced by the shortness (three to five years) of Japanese expatriate postings, such shortness in lease (or leash) affecting too the way expatriate children are schooled in a curriculum that serves veritably as a tool and technology of Japaneseness itself. Chapter 7, in this regard, once again returns to the broader organizing problematic on the nature of criticality as a way of appropriating narrative data and addressing concerns over inequality, oppression, domination and hackneyed didacticism found within such data. The ramifications of these concerns over criticality are seen in this final section to extend into the production and appropriation of critical discourses that seek to affirm moral, ethical, humanizing and transformative ideals, not only within education per se, but also in the quality of human interaction across cultural and national borders as well as other rhetorically borne and discursively enforced ways of governing and cataloging people.

References

Adams, M., & Agbenyega, J. (2019). Futurescaping: school choice of internationally mobile global middle class families temporarily residing in Malaysia. *Discourse: Studies in the Cultural Politics of Education*, 40(5), 647–665. doi:10.1080/01596306.2019.1576266

Alderson, J. C. (2009). The micropolitics of research and publication. In J. C. Alderson (Ed.), *The politics of language education: individuals and institutions* (pp. 222–236). Bristol: Multilingual Matters.

Aspinall, R. (2011). Globalization and English language education policy in Japan: external risk and internal inertia. In D. B. Willis & J. Rappleye (Eds.), *Reimagining Japanese education: borders, transfers, circulations, and the comparative* (pp. 127–146). Oxford: Symposium.

Befu, H. (2001). *Hegemony of homogeneity*. Melbourne: Transpacific Press.

Befu, H. (2009). Concepts of Japan, Japanese culture and the Japanese. In Y. Sugimoto (Ed.), *The Cambridge companion to modern Japanese culture* (pp. 21–37). Cambridge: Cambridge University Press.

Berns, M. (2003). Comment 1. *World Englishes*, 22(4), 559–560. https://doi.org/10.1111/j.1467-971X.2003.00319.x

Brutt-Griffler, J. (2003). Comment 2. *World Englishes*, 22(4), 561–562. https://doi.org/10.1111/j.1467-971X.2003.00320.x

Canagarajah, A. S. (2005). Reconstructing local knowledge, reconfiguring language studies. In A. S. Canagarajah (Ed.), *Reclaiming the local in language policy and practice* (pp. 5–24). New York: Routledge.

Crang, M. (2000). Relics, places and unwritten geographies in the work of Michel de Certeau. In M. Crang & N. Thrift (Eds.), *Thinking space* (pp. 136–153). London: Routledge.

Dale, J., & Hyslop-Margison, E. (2010). *Paulo Freire: teaching for freedom and transformation*. Dordrecht: Springer.

Darvin, R., & Norton, B. (2015). Identity and a model of investment in applied linguistics. *Annual Review of Applied Linguistics*, 35, 35–56. https://doi.org/10.1017/S0267190514000191

Eagleton, T. (1991). *Ideology: an introduction*. London: Verso.

Fairclough, N. (2005). Critical discourse analysis in transdisciplinary research. In R. Wodak & P. Chilton (Eds.), *A new agenda in (critical) discourse analysis* (pp. 53–70). Amsterdam: John Benjamins.

Flory, M., & Iglesias, O. (2010). Once upon a time: the role of rhetoric and narratives in management research and practice. *Journal of Organization Change Management*, 23(2), 113–119. https://doi.org/10.1108/09534811011031274

Freire, P. (1985). *The politics of education: culture, power, and liberation*. Westport CT: Bergin and Garvey.

Freire, P. (2000). *Pedagogy of the oppressed* (30th anniversary edition). New York: Bloomsbury.

Freire, P. (2014). *Pedagogy of hope: reliving pedagogy of the oppressed* [Bloomsbury Revelations Edition]. London: Bloomsbury.

Goosseff, K. A. (2010). Autopoiesis and meaning: a biological approach to Bakhtin's superaddressee. *Journal of Organizational Change Management*, 23(2), 145–151. https://doi.org/10.1108/09534811011031319

Goosseff, K. A. (2014). Only narratives can reflect the experience of objectivity; effective persuasion. *Journal of Organizational Change Management*, 27(5), 703–709. https://doi.org/10.1108/JOCM-09-2014-0167

Hall, I. (1997). *Cartels of the mind: Japan's intellectual closed shop*. New York: W. W. Norton.

Iino, M., & Murata, K. (2016). Dynamics of ELF communication in an English-medium academic context in Japan: from EFL learners to ELF users. In K. Murata (Ed.), *Exploring ELF in Japanese academic and business contexts: conceptualization, research and pedagogic implications* (pp. 111–131). London: Routledge.

Kubota, R., & Fujimoto, D. (2013). Racialized native speakers: voices of Japanese American English language professionals. In S. A. Houghton & D. J. Rivers (Eds.), *Native speakerism in foreign language education: intergroup dynamics in Japan* (pp. 196–206). Clevedon: Multilingual Matters.

Kumaravadivelu, B. (2003a). A postmethod perspective on English language teaching. *World Englishes*, 22(4), 539–550. https://doi.org/10.1111/j.1467-971X.2003.00317.x

Kumaravadivelu, B. (2003b). Response 1. *World Englishes*, 22(4), 565–567. https://doi.org/10.1111/j.1467-971X.2003.00322.x

Lebra, T. S. (2004). *The Japanese self in cultural logic*. Honolulu: University of Hawai'i.

Leki, I. (2003). Comment 3. *World Englishes*, 22(4), 563–564. https://doi.org/10.1111/j.1467-971X.2003.00321.x

Lie, J. (2001). *Multiethnic Japan*. Cambridge: Harvard University Press.

Lillis, T. (2003). Student writing as 'academic literacies': drawing on Bakhtin to move from critique to design. *Language and Education*, 17(3), 192–207. https://doi.org/10.1080/09500780308666848

Lillis, T., & Turner, J. (2001). Student writing in higher education: contemporary confusion and traditional concerns. *Teaching in Higher Education*, 6(1), 57–68. https://doi.org/10.1080/13562510020029608

Makino, S. (2002). Uchi and soto as cultural and linguistic metaphors. In R. T. Donahue (Ed.), *Exploring Japaneseness: on Japanese enactments of culture and consciousness* (pp. 29–66). Westport: Ablex.

Maxwell, C., Yemini, M., Koh, A., & Agbaria, A. (2019). The plurality of the global middle class(es) and their school choices – moving the 'field' forward empirically and theoretically. *Discourse: Studies in the Cultural Politics of Education*, 40(5), 609–615. https://doi.org/10.1080/01596306.2019.1602305

McLaren, P. (2015). Reflections on Paulo Freire, critical pedagogy, and the current crisis of capitalism. In M. A. Peters & T. Besley (Eds.), *Paulo Freire: the global legacy* (pp. 17–38). New York: Peter Lang.

McVeigh, B. (2002). *Japanese higher education as myth*. New York: M. E. Sharpe.

McVeigh, B. (2006). *The state bearing gifts: deception and disaffection in Japanese higher education*. Lanham: Lexington Books.

Murphey, T. (2004). Participaiton, (dis-)identification, and Japanese university entrance exams. *TESOL Quarterly*, 38(4), 700–710. doi:10.2307/3588286

Nadal-Burgues, N. (2014). Project specification: creativity and rhetoric in scientific research. *Journal of Organizational Change Management*, 27(5), 807–818. https://doi.org/10.1108/JOCM-09-2014-0176

Norton, B., & Early, M. (2011). Researcher identity, narrative inquiry, and language teaching research. *TESOL Quarterly*, 45(3), 415–439. https://doi.org/10.5054/tq.2011.261161

Paltridge, B. (2017). *The discourse of peer review: reviewing submissions to academic journals*. London: Palgrave Macmillan.

Peters, M. A., & Roberts, P. (2012). *The virtues of openness: education, science, and scholarship in the digital age*. Boulder: Paradigm Publishers.

Pierce, B. N. (1995). Social identity, investment, and language learning. *TESOL Quarterly*, 29(1), 9–31. https://doi.org/10.2307/3587803

Qi, J. (2014). Surveillance and normalization: policies and pedagogies of Japanese language education for immigrant children. In M. Pereyra & B. Franklin (Eds.), *Systems of reason and the politics of schooling: school reform and sciences of education in the tradition of Thomas S. Popkewitz* (pp. 235–247). New York: Routledge.

Rivers, D. J. (2013). Institutionalized native speakerism: voices of dissent and act of resistance. In S. A. Houghton & D. J. Rivers (Eds.), *Native speakerism in foreign language education: intergroup dynamics in Japan* (pp. 75–91). Clevedon: Multilingual Matters.

Rivers, D. J. (2015). The authorities of autonomy and English-only: serving whose interests? In D. J. Rivers (Ed.), *Resistance to the known: counter-conduct in language education*. London: Palgrave Macmillan.

Rivers, D. J. (2019). Walking on glass: reconciling experience and expectation within Japan. *Journal of Language, Identity and Education*, 18(6), 377–388. https://doi.org/10.1080/15348458.2019.1674149

Rudolph, N. (2016). Negotiating borders of being and becoming in and beyond the English language teaching classroom: two university student narratives from Japan. *Asian Englishes*, 18(1), 2–18. https://doi.org/10.1080/13488678.2015.1132110

Rudolph, N., Yazan, B., & Rudolph, J. (2018). Negotiating 'ares,' 'cans,' and 'shoulds' of being and becoming in English language teaching: two teacher accounts from one Japanese university. *Asian Englishes*, 21(1), 22–37. https://doi.org/10.1080/13488678.2018.1471639

Simon, R. I., & Dippo, D. (1986). On critical ethnographic work. *Anthropology and Education Quarterly*, 17(4), 195–202. https://doi.org/10.1525/aeq.1986.17.4.04x0613o

Stewart, A., & Miyahara, M. (2011). Parallel universes: globalization and identity in English language teaching at a Japanese university. In P. Seargeant (Ed.), *English in Japan in the era of globalization* (pp. 60–79). New York: Palgrave Macmillan.
Thompson, J. B. (1987). Language and ideology: a framework for analysis. *The Sociological Review*, 35(3), 516–536. https://doi.org/10.1111%2Fj.1467-954X.1987.tb00554.x
Thrift, N. (2007). *Non-representational theory: space, politics, affect*. London: Routledge.
Toh, G. (2003a). Toward a more critical orientation to ELT in Southeast Asia. *World Englishes*, 22(4), 551–558. https://doi.org/10.1111/j.1467-971X.2003.00318.x
Toh, G. (2003b). Response 2. *World Englishes*, 22(4), 568–569. https://doi.org/10.1111/j.1467-971X.2003.00323.x
Toh, G. (2014). English for content instruction in a Japanese higher education setting: examining challenges, contradictions and anomalies. *Language and Education*, 28 (4), 299–318. https://doi.org/10.1080/09500782.2013.857348
Toh, G. (2016). *English as medium of instruction in Japanese higher education: Presumption, mirage or bluff?* Cham: Palgrave-McMillan.
Toh, G. (2018). Anatomizing and extrapolating from 'Do Not Publish' as oppression, silencing, and denial. *Critical Inquiry in Language Studies*, 15(4), 258–281. https://doi.org/10.1080/15427587.2018.1460846
Toh, G. (2019). *Effecting change in English language teaching: exposing collaborators and culprits in Japan*. Cham: Palgrave Macmillan.
Williams, G. (2010). *The knowledge economy, language and culture*. Bristol: Multilingual Matters.

2 The Japanese in Japan (and overseas)

Singapore is a former British colony and (now an) independent cosmopolitan city state with a local population of ethnic Malays, Chinese, Indians and Eurasians apart from a sizeable presence of expatriates and immigrants from America, Europe and the Asia-Pacific. Japan, in contrast, has been spoken of as being principally a mono-cultural nation, but one which has lately been confronted with onerous matters with regard to low birth rate, immigration and border fluidities (Douglass & Roberts, 2003; Willis & Rappleye, 2011; Rudolph, 2018). Foreign immigration and the presence of non-Japanese have been viewed in a manner which scholars consider to be ambiguous or even hostile by both government and general populace alike. This palpably negative attitude towards foreigners and immigration has to a good extent been attributed to ideologies relating to reifications of Japaneseness and Japanese uniqueness (see Befu, 2001; Lie, 2003; Douglass & Roberts, 2003; Lebra, 2004; Willis & Rappleye, 2011; Rudolph, 2018). Conceptualizations of Japaneseness can be found widely discussed in an albeit controversial genre of literature known, both to its loyal stalwarts and the harshest of critics alike, as *nihonjinron* (principles or tenets of Japaneseness) literature (Befu, 2001; Lie, 2003). Japaneseness as it is represented in such literature, particularly 'what it means and how it is realized', is considered to be '[a]t center stage in Japanese studies', particularly with regard to those aspects concerned with Japanese nationalism and identity (Donahue, 2002a, p. ix). *Nihonjinron* literature and its reifications and exemplifications of Japaneseness is believed to exert a significant influence on perceptions and understandings of matters considered extraneous to Japanese society, including foreign peoples, languages, cultures, and even non-locally made products. According to Lie (2003), there exists by way of *nihonjinron*-inspired belief, a hierarchy which accords superior status to people and things that are Western and inferior status to people and things of Asian, particularly Southeast Asian, origin. Japan's postwar economic successes have furthermore allowed the Japanese to distinguish 'Japan from its poor Asian counterparts' (Lie, 2003, p. 79). Within this hierarchical mindset, the Japanese are said to regard Westerners as representing an upper class that signifies superiority, while Asians (again, especially East and Southeast Asians) are said to stand for a lower class which denotes cultural inferiority (Lie, 2003). Such relations of class, as Lie (2003) points out, is liable to be 'transposed onto the world system of national hierarchies where Japan, quite obviously, stands near the top' (p. 79).

The literature itself is held to be important 'not only for the Japanese themselves', putatively as an affirmation of self and identity, 'but also for area-study specialists, including those in intercultural communication who seek greater understanding of the Japanese, their culture, and society' (Donahue, 2002a, p. ix). According to Donahue (2002a, p. xiii), *ninonjinron*, which is considered to be both a national ideology as well as an intellectual pursuit, has, over the years, gained a degree of 'notoriety for some of its extreme claims for Japanese cultural uniqueness'. Befu (2001), moreover, notes that *nihonjinron* functions in Japanese society like a civil religion or even a national sport. Its veracity in the Japanese psyche also means that even 'contrary evidence does not shake [a] believer's faith in it', which also explains 'why … [the] Japanese accept [it] as an ideology when it [apparently] does not truthfully reflect reality' (Befu, 1984, p. 70). Aspinall's (2003, p. 111, italics added) resonance with this viewpoint is seen in his observation that *nihonjinron* has in the main been 'aimed at a domestic audience and has never been received well by foreign scholars (except possibly as a *source of amusement*)'. This observation is reinforced by Aspinall's (2003) comment that *nihonjinron* may in fact only be 'a body of pseudo-sociological and -psychological theory dedicated to showing the uniqueness of the Japanese race' (p. 111), alluding to aspects of bigotry that could be instrumental to its legitimation. In this regard, Lie (2003) observes that 'many descriptions of Japanese difference or uniqueness are problematic' to the point that most are, for all practical purposes, 'empirically false or unverifiable' (p. 86). Despite the subjective nature of such expressions of (superior forms of) uniqueness, generic claims to Japanese superiority continue to be made, quite frequently in a pointedly indirect (oxymoronic as this may sound) manner, as noted by Lie (2003): '[o]ften stated as asides, these utterances effectively mask essentially the same sentiment as those who are ethnocentric and even chauvinistic' (p. 79).

In this respect, one is reminded of an observation by Peter Mayo, a long-time commentator of the work of Paulo Freire, who notes the famed educator's deep conviction that popular consciousness is characteristically 'permeated by ideology' (Mayo, 2008, p. 54), which appears to be the case with *nihonjinron*.

Nihonjinron's veracity and actuality within a Japanese ethos

Concerning *nihonjinron* purveyed beliefs, the veracity of these beliefs in the Japanese psyche and *nihonjinron*'s surrogate functions as a civil religion are liable to give rise to essentialized ways in which they are enacted in real life situations. The following account of the manner in which Japaneseness is spoken about by a senior educator heading a Japanese kindergarten established in Singapore to cater to the children of Japanese families is an example of such particularity. The aim and mission of the type of early-childhood education that the kindergarten has been set up in Singapore to provide is 'the socialization of children into Japanese culture, customs, and lives', and according to Chew and Thang (2006, p. 252), the same is done 'with the underlying implication that … early childhood education in Japan' involves an element of 'cultural determinism' (p. 241).

Notwithstanding this deterministic element, Chew and Thang (2006) observe that the institution in question is not entirely 'an independent entity' but one which must engage in a negotiated form of socialization between 'its own set of *internal* ethics and the *external* environment', in this case, its very physical 'situation in Singapore' (p. 242, italics added, see next section on *uchi* and *soto*). In the following extract, it is revealed that Singapore's equatorial location and tropical climate is deemed to be a hindrance for the instilling of an authentic (or sanctioned) form of Japaneseness, where Japaneseness is associated essentially with an affinity with, or closeness to, nature. While Singapore is mainly made up of urban built-up spaces, the particularity of the actual concern is over the belief that 'the essence of being a Japanese' is related to nature as it is realized in (or conflated with) the four seasons and a benignly mild temperate climate:

> But Japanese are Japanese from the very day they are born.… I think nature must play a very important role [in our socialization of the children]. In Singapore, there is nothing but heat all year round.… This is very different in Japan where we have clear seasonal changes.
>
> (Senior Educator, cited in Chew & Thang, 2006, p. 248)

The 'active incorporation of a relationship with nature' (Clammer, 2000, p. 215) and the conflation of nature with Japan's four seasons reifies a particular understanding of nature that overlooks the luxuriant natural environment thriving in the form of equatorial rainforests found in stretches of Singapore's nature reserves. Nature can only be nature if it is naturalized according to Japanese climatic rhythms, or so it is implied. This type of oversight can be considered ideological as long as Singapore's tropical climate is seen as an obstacle to the engenderment of the particular form of Japaneseness that is being spoken about:

> This proves to be a challenge when relating to the children what season is all about (sic); and especially, there are different nuances in the season that could only be understood through experiencing them (sic).… For example, when snow is not merely just snow, there are different types of snow … and even heat in Japan has different levels of hotness. So we try to teach the children for example through songs. We have different songs for different seasons.
>
> (Senior Educator, cited in Chew & Thang, 2006, p. 248–249)

Apart from the four seasons and the uniqueness of the way heat or cold is to be experienced, another motif of Japaneseness that is reified for its associations with nature is the identity of one's feelings with flowers or '*hana no kokoro*' (Chew & Thang, 2006, p. 249).

> We try to develop the 'flower heart' ... in the child. You know, how a Japanese child would draw the picture of a flower, completing it with a smiling face; and the child is able to feel like the flower. But I don't think the Singaporean child does that, right?
>
> (Senior Educator, cited in Chew & Thang, 2006, p, 249)

As a 'sensitivity to nature and seasons' is said to constitute the essence of being a Japanese person, Singapore's tropical climate is seen as something that needs to be compensated for, on pain of the compromising loss of this very essence (Chew & Thang, 2006, p. 249). The kindergarten therefore makes every effort to compensate for the absence of the natural influence of the four seasons in the Japanese children's experience of life. An excursion in the month of May is called a 'spring outing' because it is supposed to parallel spring in Japan. A corner of the campus is designated as a corner where items to do with each season are displayed to evoke the mood of a particular season, cherry blossoms (artificial ones) for spring, maple leaves (also artificial) for the autumn. For the winter season, special arrangements are made for All Nippon Airways to fly in a snowman from Japan, 'so that the children [can actually] feel for themselves what a real snowman is like' (Chew & Thang, 2006, p. 249).

As might be apparent from such descriptions, in terms of its veracity and pervasiveness, *nihonjinron* and the actual 'belief in the truth of the uniqueness of Japanese culture is [and remains] conscious and salient in the minds of [the] Japanese' (Befu, 1984, p. 70). Serving as a set of 'normative imperatives for their behavior', *nihonjinron* 'constitutes an ideology which orients and guides the attitudes and thinking of the common people' (Befu, 1984, p. 70). Its importance is such that educational institutions located outside of Japan take very seriously their role to solemnly inculcate what they believe are qualities or traits of Japaneseness into pupils entrusted to their watch. In cosmopolitan Singapore, it may not be entirely expedient for this sort of socialization into Japanese culture to take place so blatantly to an extent that this might in some way risk being regarded as a form of chauvinism. It is entirely possible that the preoccupation with nature and with Japan's four seasons as they are so diametrically contrasted with Singapore's hot equatorial climate is a politely euphemistic or circumlocutory way of using natural differences (such as are beyond human control, ostensibly at least – see next paragraph) to draw subtle attention to Japanese uniqueness. Japanese are different because they are *naturally* or *by nature* different. If this is true, nature becomes used as a way of demarcating physical space and reifying cultural space (see Crang, 2000; Thrift, 2007; Gulson, 2007; see also discussion on the performativity of space in Chapter 5) to the end that Japaneseness can be enacted and asserted in an overseas environment.

Even so, Befu (2009) cautions that such a way of sensitizing young learners to nature and the four seasons by the senior educator would actually be a very 'culturally constituted' (p. 22) and 'culturally defined' (p. 22) version of seasonality in Japan. According to Befu (2009), evocations of 'spring with cherry blossoms, a summer of sweltering heat, autumn with beautiful foliage colors and a bitterly cold winter' are in fact biased in favor of central Japan where indeed, 'the power to create such cultural narratives has historically resided' (p. 22). In reifying such a particularized cultural narrative, the senior educator would also be naturalizing evocations of the Kansai (Kyoto, Osaka) and Kanto (Tokyo) regions, as being representative of an entire Japan. For locations like Okinawa and Hokkaido which experience different seasonal patterns, Befu (2009, p. 22) points out that the 'seasonal changes [so typified] are only partially true at best'. In this way, it is a culturally particularized version of seasonality that selectively reifies the centrality of the Kanto and Kansai regions that the kindergarten pupils are exposed to.

Uchi and *soto* as key cultural concepts to understanding Japaneseness

Two key ideas, *uchi* and *soto*, which are thought to imbue the Japanese cultural psyche, are seen by Donahue (2002a, p. xi) as core motifs which help constitute and capture 'the fabric of Japanese society'. An important aspect of Japanese culture and worldview is said to be capturable within an *uchi* and *soto* (inside versus outside) framework which helps to specify the manner in which life phenomena are understood and schematized spatially (Donahue, 2002a). Here again, the influence of *nihonjinron* is to be noticed. Its largely self-referential nature contributes to a framing of social relations as spatial juxtapositions expressed within an *uchi* and *soto* binary, one that carries metaphorical and symbolic extensions (Donahue, 2002a). While *uchi* connotes for the Japanese a sense of security and reassurance that comes with being found within protected spaces, *soto* speaks of an unfamiliarity evoking an absence of security or assurance, always to be associated with the outside (as well as with outsiders).

A plethora of *ninhonjinron* literature continues to distil for readers virtues and qualities that are thought to be unique to Japanese insiders. The Japanese people are averred to as having 'a positively characterized Japanese personality' derived from the country's 'natural scenery [thought] to be the most beautiful in the world' (Befu, 2001, p. 131). Patriotism, a quintessential respect for harmony, group loyalty, sensitivity and empathy with nature are powerful traits which are said to meld into an implicit style of communication, which is considered to be one of the virtuous attributes of the Japanese people (Befu, 2001). Such implicitness and the ability to 'anticipate or conjure the intentions of another' or *sasshi no bunka* (guessing culture) is described in Makino (2002, p. 37) as an aspect of Japanese culture which involves '*uchi-soto* relations unique to [the] Japanese'. Anticipatory sensitivity assumes and lauds one's ability to think ahead along the same insider patterns as the rest of fellow insiders. Internal homogeneity extends accordingly to homogeneity and conformism in thought as well as in behavior.

By naturalizing relations and experience as matters that pertain invariably to insider-outsider positionings (Makino, 2002; Lebra, 2004), *nihonjinron* succeeds in legitimating a morality that accepts the suspicion and/or exclusion of anything that is deemed unJapanese. Offering a historical reason, Edwin Reischauer, Harvard Japanologist and former American Ambassador to Japan, notes that the clear line between *uchi and soto* exists because a person was 'by race, language, culture and nation either fully Japanese or not a Japanese at all', as if among themselves, the Japanese 'formed a sort of gigantic modern tribe' (Reischauer, 1988, p. 396). Basing his argument on the ineluctable manner in which 'feelings about race, culture, and nation' have been merged together to make Japanese attitudes toward race 'all the stronger', Reischauer (1988, pp. 396–397) notes that the strength of such attitudes would be 'almost as if [the Japanese] regarded themselves as a different species from the rest of humanity'. Indeed, until recently, 'all the people in the world who spoke the distinctive Japanese language and lived in the distinctive Japanese way resided in Japan, and there was virtually no one else in the country' (Reischauer, 1988, p. 396). Given this aspect of history, the *uchi-soto* insider-outsider binary in turn foments other relational metaphors which implicate symmetry and asymmetry, inclusion and exclusion, truth and falsehood, genuineness and ingenuity. Examples of these metaphors include: *honne* (real wishes) as opposed to *tatemae* (stated reasons); *ninjo* (humane feeling) as opposed to *giri* (social obligation) (Makino, 2002).

The significance of insider versus outsider relations will be explored later when it will become apparent how they can be played out in the practical outworkings of Institutions A, B, C and D (all Japanese institutions operating in Singapore) in Chapter 5, and in the actions and behaviors of those representing them. Suffice to say at this stage that the influence of *nihonjinron* is not to be missed in education, which as Reischauer (1988) points out, 'has been the chief tool in shaping national uniformity' (p. 217), while reinforcing 'the conformist nature of society' (p. 200). Indeed, since the latter part of the 1980s, revisions of the national curriculum have seen more emphases being placed on 'inculcating Japanese children with a greater sense of patriotism and self-awareness of their "Japanese-ness"', not least of all through an increasingly conservative stance towards textbook screening (Rose, 2006, p. 134). In similar vein, Lebra (2004) notes that when children raised (or sometimes born) outside Japan return to the country, there is a felt need to have them re-Japanized according to behaviors expected of them. The latter point is a relevant one as later chapters (see Chapters 5 and 6) concern the education of Japanese children in a Japanese school located outside of Japan.

Rudolph (2018) meanwhile attests to the difficulties Japanese students face when they are challenged to think beyond essentialized discourses of Japaneseness and 'being and becoming in Japanese society' (p. 157). In his description of these difficulties, Rudolph (2018) examines reflections from students after they have been enrolled for nearly two semesters in an elective on Japan and globalization where they were given the opportunity to explore and grapple with issues concerning identity, globalization and discourses of Japaneseness. Student reflections revealed the way in which they wrestled with matters to do with hybridity and diversity in Japanese society:

> Student 15 noted, for instance, that 'I strongly noticed that people have their own identity, idea, and belief even they are categorized as Japanese,' as did Student 7, who argued, 'We Japanese have to understand there is not only one way to everything.' Student 5 concurred, stating, 'There're a lot of Japanese people whose backgrounds are unique and who have international backgrounds and family.' Student 3 noted, 'I had never thought that people who look internationals could be born and raised in Japan, so I just used to use English to communicate with those people, but now I've noticed that each person has different backgrounds, so I started to think first.'.... Students expressed sensitivity to the creation and maintenance of borders of identity in Japanese society, as characterized by Student 17: 'Japanese people are unconsciously draw a line between 'you' and 'me.' Although this is not only Japan.' Student 6 took issue with such lines, believing that, 'I can say we cannot easily say what is "inside" or "outside."'
>
> (Rudolph, 2018, p. 165)

Given the general tendency for young people to look to an inward muse for the gaining of social acceptance (despite enlightened attempts toward the contrary as is reflected in Rudolph's (2018) account), Ishikawa (2011, p. 214) notes that it is not surprising that 'an inward-looking tendency [has] reportedly [been lately] emerging' among Japanese young people. Taken to a parochial extreme, such a tendency can give rise to the idea of studying abroad (or *ryugaku*) as being about 'enroll[ing] temporarily in another university in another region' (Lebra, 2004, p. 268), like when a student from Tokyo moves to Kyoto for studies. Such an example begs the question of whether concerns over *uchi* and *soto* are indicative of concerns over homogeneity as such, or over the less discussed matter of parochialism.

Internationalization, dealings with the outside and its detractors

Japanese conceptualizations of internationalization or *kokusaika* were forged in the period when Japan found itself on the wrong side of blame-mongering with respect to trade imbalances with Western countries, notably, the United States (Kubota, 2002), an issue which continues to be relevant as the second decade of the new millennium draws to a close (Smith & Carter, 2019). Japanese internationalization must, of necessity, be viewed alongside another powerful counter discourse which expresses what McVeigh (2006) describes as the 'gravitational pull of nationalism' (p. 148).

Within Japan and particularly among the Japanese elite, worrying concerns over internationalization are often discussed alongside those over globalization, with internationalization being the term that is seen to be more commonly used in discourses attributable to the education ministry and globalization being used more in non-governmental parlance (Hashimoto, 2000; 2007; see Yamagami & Tollefson, 2011). Noted anthropologist, Harumi Befu, according to Lebra (2004), has lobbied for Japan and the Japanese to be generally more attentive to 'what is happening outside Japan' while 'disappointment or irritation with Japan's refusal to globalize' has been linked to a reluctance 'even on the part of overseas Japanese' to be more outward-looking (p. 264). Possibly because internationalization for the Japanese was forged rather traumatically over contentions resulting from trade and currency disputes with other (principally western) nations (Kubota, 2002), a discourse of resistance or 'globalization-as-threat', as is captured in Yamagami and Tollefson (2011, p. 26), is thought to be mobilized as a felt part of the need to maintain Japanese identity.

'Globalization-as threat' discourse is characterized by a wariness of 'deep and troubling danger[s] to fundamental aspects of the narrative of Japanese national identity' (Yamagami & Tollefson, 2011, p. 28). Of particular concern, as readers are told, is the felt assailment of Japanese national identity, 'particularly the (alleged) homogeneity of Japan (shared beliefs, values and attitudes)' together with fears of a loss of a 'sense of personal safety and security' (Yamagami & Tollefson, 2011, p. 28). As a consequence, one is told that Japanese politicians on both sides of the Diet have been heard to be speaking ominously and populistically about concerns over the presence of foreigners and the crime and disease they are thought to bring into Japanese shores (see Yamagami & Tollefson, 2011). While dramatically hyperbolic, Yamagami and Tollefson (2011, p. 30) nonetheless recognize the tensile chord that such politicized rhetoric about foreigners on Japanese soil would strike with the voting public. Such discordant rhetoric typically leads to 'discussions of measures to eliminate them', with '[p]revention at the water's edge' being a familiar slogan which calls to mind images of Japan's insular geography (Yamagami & Tollefson, 2011, p. 30). The country's treatment of Brazilians of Japanese descent (the Nikkei) comes across as an example of insularity at work.

When Japan like many other countries was struck by the 2008 economic recession, the government set up a scheme for Brazilians of Japanese descent to leave the country and return permanently to South America by offering each person $3000 ($2000 for family members), in exchange for which, each recipient of this money would have to undertake to never return to Japan (Yamagami & Tollefson, 2011). Apparently, the presence of the Nikkei was not (about) internationalization. Mostly honest-to-goodness hardworking blue collar workers, the home-sending or jettisoning of the Nikkei soon after the economic crisis was suggestive of the possibility that internationalization was not only a White phenomenon as such (see Rivers, 2013; Kubota & Fujimoto, 2013), but also a white collar phenomenon at that. The significance of this observation becomes all the more apparent in subsequent discussion on Japanese institutions which play a role in Japanese schooling in Singapore, where white collar elitism is legitimated by way of activities and practices that naturalize the same.

Another aspect of the struggle is to do with what Makino (2002) observes about *miren*, a term which describes a centripetal psychology which creates 'lingering attachment to someone/something of the ... past' (p. 35). Where *miren* impinges on Japanese attitudes towards internationalization is also where Makino draws attention to the tendency among Japanese to be 'very hesitant about becoming a pioneer into *terra incognita*', which indexes 'a total *soto* space' (p. 36). Citing the example of the successful moon landing in 1969 by the Americans as 'an embodiment of American frontier spirit or spirit of looking forward into the future', Makino (p. 36) notes that the Japanese 'would rather stay in *terra cognita*, a familiar space of *uchi*'. The acuteness of Makino's observation, as will be seen, both sheds light and casts shadows on the manner in which Japanese expatriates and their families are seen to cope with life in a putatively *soto* situation like Singapore's (see Chapters 5 and 6).

Nihonjinron and English language learning in Japan

Scholars note that the teaching and learning of English among the Japanese is strongly prefaced with a particularized version of internationalization that rests on *nihonjinron* influenced beliefs. These influences can be traced to a line of reasoning that unfolds in the following manner. There is an expressed belief in the need for the rest of the world to better understand Japan, resulting in a need for Japanese culture to be explained particularly to those foreigners with whom the Japanese have business or diplomatic dealings. These dealings as well as other forms of interaction with non-Japanese parties are part of challenges that have arisen as a result of 'Japan's economic development ... [and also] trade imbalances between Japan and Western nations', making the avoidance of 'further economic conflict and possible world isolation' an important priority (Kubota, 2002, pp. 16–17). The kinds of foreigners that the Japanese interact with are assumed in this regard to be English-speaking, particularly those from the industrialized West. This assumption is, in large part, attributable to a lingering preoccupation with Japan's 'post-World War II military subordination ... to the USA and its allies' (Kubota, 2002, p. 17). Befu (2001) notes advisedly that to the Japanese mind, cultures of the industrialized West continue to be held as superior to Japanese culture, while the languages and cultures of the rest of Asia are thought to be inferior. Reischauer (1988) in similar vein describes the way Chinese and Koreans are discriminated against while '[p]rejudice against Southeast and South Asians' appears 'even stronger' (p. 398).

With regard to the learning of English, it is conceived of as a part of the need to acquire 'the communication mode of the West', paradoxically, for the purpose of expressing and explaining 'unambiguously Japanese points of view' (Kubota, 2002, p. 17), towards the goal of 'making the outside world know and understand Japan' (Ishikawa, 2011, p. 212). Accordingly, the teaching of English is not without its ideological dimension in the form of a manifestly nationalistic agenda that not only seeks to prevent the much-feared erosion of Japanese identity, but also to purposefully convey 'Japan's unique traditions and way of life to other people in the world' (Kubota, 2002, p. 18). The response to this much-feared loss of national values and traditions comes in the form of concerted efforts on the part of policy makers to remove English from the core of Japanese identity while tolerating its role as supposedly 'the most powerful language in the world' (Yamagami & Tollefson, 2011, p. 22). The strategy adopted to this end is for English is to be identified with outsiders, or more specifically, its White native speakers (Rivers, 2013), as a way of having it jettisoned from any form of association with Japanese identity. Put in practice, such a policy conceptualization entails having Japanese students learn the language while at the same time maintain sufficient distance from it through cultural dis-identification, what Hashimoto (2000) recognizes as a deliberate 'Japananization' of learners of English. Having Japanese students learn English, given the nationalistic nature of internationalization, involves, in a convoluted way, strong investments in nationalism. These strong nationalistic investments, according to Burgess et al. (2010), are translated into 'the cultivation of patriotism in schools', which features as 'an ongoing theme in Japanese educational reform' (p. 465). A more ironic or contrarian version of these nationalistic investments even promotes the view that 'Japanese people who have poor English skills should not be ashamed of that fact, but rather, should be proud of it' (Aspinall, 2003, p. 104). This latter viewpoint has been traced to a fear that is frequently expressed in the following supposition: 'If the majority of Japanese people overcome the problems they are currently having with English and become fluent in the language, will that not change fundamentally the identity of the Japanese nation?' (p. 104). This supposition may be sometime (re)phrased, but this time in the form of a warning that: 'those Japanese people who become too good at English pose a threat to their own and their nation's fundamental identity' (p. 104). Also quite aptly, seeing that the present discussion involves Singapore, '[i]f the population of Japan achieved the same level of fluency in English as, say, the population of Singapore, would that not fundamentally change Japan's identity as a nation?' (p. 114).

In this regard, prevailing rhetoric is seen to promote the 'continued development of Japanese language abilities' particularly among 'elementary school students' (Yamagami & Tollefson, 2011, p. 22). The practical reality then turns into one where 'no serious effort to teach elementary students to speak English well has [in earnest] been undertaken' (p. 22). Citing documents released by the education ministry, Yamagami and Tollefson draw attention to the coyly ambiguous nature of official discourse on the status of English in Japanese education: which is the admission that while English is generally not spoken well among the Japanese, the same too applies to their lack of mastery of Japanese. Considering this an 'odd suggestion', Yamagami and Tollefson note that Japanese citizens speaking 'neither English nor Japanese adequately' appears to be 'part of a discursive programme' to 'promote English within strict social limits' alongside a 'reinvigorated programme of Japanese national cultural identity' (p. 16). Such equivocation or double-talk resonates with an observation by McVeigh (2002a) that the promotion of English is in reality a specious undertaking that is, ironically, mobilized for the purpose of promoting (or fetishizing) a learner's Japaneseness. This view is similarly reflected in Seargeant (2009) who notes that the Japanese may harbor a 'deeply ingrained form of cultural conditioning' which is liable to lead them to 'insist on their uniqueness, and therefore have no interest in actually integrating with the international community' (2009, p. 55).

Seargeant's (2009) latter observation comes across as one that is perhaps worrying if one has to consider seriously matters relating to the relocation of Japanese nationals and their school-going children to environments overseas which are dissimilar to Japan's, for the purposes of employment. In the case of the present discussion, cosmopolitan multilingual Singapore constitutes a fairly contrastive overseas environment, particularly one in which English is appropriated differently policy wise, as the language for trade, legislation, workplace interaction and education (see Bolton & Botha, 2017). In situations where border crossing experiences involve negotiating differences that inhere socio-cultural borderlands, fresh scholarly observations can complement existing ones (like those discussed above) to provide a better understanding of areas where official policy has continued to remain equivocal or contradictory. Of particular interest in this connection are the sorts of educational beliefs and practices enacted in the operations of Institution B, a Japanese elementary school based in Singapore, to which I will devote space in a later chapter. Meanwhile, I turn my attention back to *nihonjinron*, and the reality of its historically constituted nature as part of the backgrounding necessary for subsequent discussion.

The culpability of the high-hand of history and education in *nihonjinron* perpetuation

Even though it is commonly thought to be a phenomenon of the 1980s when dealings with foreigners brought on by politics and trade wars became reason for increased Japanese introspectiveness (Kubota, 2002), the roots of *nihonjinron* literature actually extend further back to the Meiji era when Japan embarked determinedly on its modernization program (Befu, 1984; 2001). The need for self-definition and self-identification became particularly urgent when the adoption of military, economic, political and educational practices of Western nations 'necessitated some mode of clearly separating Japanese from others at conscious level' (Befu, 1984, p. 69). Apart from lauding 'the superiority of Japanese culture over Chinese culture' (Befu, 2001, p. 124) and distinguishing Japan from the West, earlier forms of *nihonjinron* literature also sought to legitimate the 'bloated view that Japan in every respect was superior to the rest of the world', a view that 'continued until it burst in August 1945' (Befu, 2001, p. 135). With economic prosperity, however, *nihonjinron* has been seen to be experiencing a late resurgence with strong reassertions of its beliefs increasingly 'stated in laudatory, sometimes even hawkish, terms', and with its adherents holding fast to the triumphalist view of 'Japan as Number One' (Befu, 2001, pp. 123, 140). Reischauer (1988) notes admissibly that race 'loom [s] large in the self-image of the Japanese, who pride themselves on the "purity" of their blood' (p. 396). A resurgence of *nihonjinron* came about in the 1970s by way of the pride and increased confidence that followed economic prosperity (Befu, 2001).

The role of the Allied Occupation's turnaround in policy in the resurgence of hawkishness

The opportunity for such a resurgence of *nihonjinron* came about in large part from a change of policy of Japan's post-war occupiers. Not with any urge to disappointing loyal adherents of *nihonjinron*, the ideologies and self-referencing beliefs it promotes have been seen by critics as not being as pre-existent or ahistorical as might be assumed. The perpetuation or continued endurance of such beliefs as are reifying of the uniqueness of the peoples occupying the Japanese home islands can (actually) be traced fairly recently to Japan's seven-year occupation by the Allied forces after the final cessation of hostilities. The Allied forces, or more officially the Supreme Commander for the Allied Powers (SCAP), came to Japan in the person and office of General Douglas MacArthur. Arguably, the post-war experience of the Japanese people was just as much about having one's own country occupied by foreign powers as it was (quite challengingly) about 'increased exposure to alien peoples and cultures, most overwhelmingly to the United States' (Lebra, 2004, p. 264–265). Initially, SCAPs mission and vision was to democratize defeated Japan and free its citizenry from the tyrannies of erstwhile imperial oppression (Dower, 1999). It was also known that the Americans came with the intention to 'create an agrarian Japan, incapable of making war' by systematically reducing it to 'pastoral helplessness' (Ezrati, 1999, p. 142), a short-sighted policy which the Cold War would quickly change. Upon arrival, SCAP sought to dissolve powerful industrial conglomerates or *zaibatsu*, those conservative right-wing entities which controlled a significant part of the Japanese economy and supported the prosecution of Japan's war effort in the most hawkish of fashions (Dower, 1999). SCAP's initial agenda of 'demilitarization and democratization' included the banning of the rising sun flag and the national anthem (p. 223). This initial agenda would change with the advent of the Cold War and would pave the way for 'postwar Japan's conservative resurgence' (p. 226). Both the Korean War and the Cold War would quickly enough fuel the necessary paranoia that would bring about a policy turnaround, so called 'the "reverse course" in occupation policy' on the part of the Allied Powers (p. 560). By the end of 1948, circumstances had changed as drastically as to require the Americans to regard China and not Japan as the major threat of the day: 'China was "going communist" and [was] replacing Japan in American eyes as the major enemy in Asia' (p. 511). With Japan's wartime aggression against China that quickly forgotten, SCAP then proceeded to support the recruitment of five hundred former Japanese pilots by the Chinese Nationalist regime based in Taiwan 'for possible assistance in retaking the mainland' (p. 511).

In a turnaround of policy, charges against alleged Class A war criminals were dropped while the authorities embarked deliberately on suppressing the crimes they had supposedly committed, as a matter of political expedience (Dower, 1999; 2012). The fashion of deliberateness with which alleged war crimes were suppressed eventually led to the notable absence of a 'decisive break with the past in defeated Japan' (Dower, 2012, p. 124; also see Chapter 3). In the absence of this much-needed break, the relationship between the US and Japan would become one that would provide the latter, especially the conservative factions in its leadership, with the liberty to continue like matters were before the war. Conservative Japan was given the much-desired liberty and mandate to cultivate for the future a 'clear, fixed [and] almost myopic sense of security and national identity' (p. 120). In the meantime, under the (oversight of) the Allied Powers, changes to old bureaucratic structures were cosmetic and not significant. The wartime bureaucracy or the '1940 system' remained the 'bedrock on which the Allied occupation of Japan rested – and it was a system that the Americans who controlled the occupation largely perpetuated' (Dower, 1999, p. 559), with obviously little objection from the Japanese.

> In the maw of defeat, confronted by a staggering *postwar* crisis, it seemed logical to most Japanese [too] to maintain these [bureaucratic and administrative] arrangements; and with the good grace of their American overlords, this is essentially what they did.
>
> (Dower, 1999, p. 559, italics original)

Rather ironically therefore,

> Much of what later became identified as the 'Japanese model' and was then shrouded in a vapor of rhetoric about Confucian values was simply a carry-over of arrangements that had been spawned by the recent war.
>
> (Dower, 1999, p. 559; see Chapter 3 for more about the 'Japanese model')

Dower (1999), furthermore, notes that Japanese postwar planners, on their part, were either supportive of, or coldly pragmatic about, maintaining the '1940 system' as such, 'not because they were secret samurai, but because they believed this was a rational way to promote maximum economic growth' (p. 560).

In this respect, the Allied Occupation in no small part helped to revive the socio-political climate conducive to the perpetuation of a conservative political ethos that has, time and again, betrayed its hawkish tendencies. It is (not) ironical, therefore, that the United States has not ceased to urge 'Japan to build up its military forces' in its periodic grumbles 'about Japan's "free ride" in defense at the American taxpayer's expense' (Reischauer, 1988, p. 369), even though this dispute is said to seldom reach 'serious proportions'.

Neither is it to be unexpected that domestic critics have registered their doubts over the reliability of American commitment to Japan, saying that 'the United States might risk New York in a nuclear war for the sake of London, but not for Tokyo', with racial feelings entering quite clearly into such judgements (Reischauer, 1988, p. 368). According to Reischauer, after repeated reassurances that America would make no 'sudden shift on China without first informing Tokyo' (p. 368), the US-China rapprochement came as quite a betrayal to the Japanese, as was when 'Washington suddenly placed an embargo on the export of soybeans to Japan, which are critical to the Japanese diet' (p. 369).

The collaboration of schooling in the maintenance of ritualized politeness

Japanese behavior, which is strongly marked and guided by what McVeigh (2002b) describes as 'an ethnomorality of civility' as a sine qua non of decency and good form, is actually revealed to be mandated and schooled (or contrived) behavior, definitely not to be confused with attributions of 'timeless "tradition"' (p. 133). Such confusion could happen if civility itself is mistakenly attributed to 'premodern, feudalistic "traditional values"' rather than on the reality of a 'very modern "bureaucratic ethos" implicated in nation-state construction' (p. 133). In other words, the politeness and civility that often pass off as timeless tradition are in reality an artifact of sociopolitical and economic management (or contrivance). McVeigh points out that this 'patina of "tradition" provides current forms of civility with legitimacy' while polite and formalized sociolinguistic practices 'are [in reality only] an "aestheticization" of the state/capital nexus' (p. 133). *Aisatsu*, which is the most common term for this form of ethnomorality, is said to elaborately cover 'an entire range of sociolinguistic practices, from perfunctory greetings to complex ceremonials' (p. 122). In terms of importance in Japanese society, *aisatsu* is comparable to an 'invisible institution tied to Japaneseness' itself, as it provides the Japanese with a 'sense of "we-ness"', and in this sense 'interlinks national identity with capitalism and statism' (p. 133).

The capitalistic economics of *aisatsu* is supported by the 'learning [of] official Japaneseness' within the auspices of state-sponsored schooling (McVeigh, 2002b, p. 125). As behavior that is both taught and learnt in schools, schools can be regarded as 'a key site in which individuals are socialized' into becoming thoughtful moral beings (p. 125). Such a kind of thoughtfulness, otherwise known as *omoiyari*, is tied to 'love of family, friends, patriotism, and respect for law', and where it pertains to pleasant manners, refinement and empathy, is taught alongside the germane value of belongingness (p. 126). In this way, schooling itself, in answering the call to promote an ethnomorality of civility linkable to the running of the 'machinery of capitalism, nationalism and statism in modern Japan' (p. 121), becomes precisely an intrinsic and constitutive component of the same machinery. Politeness, civility and consideration and the schooling that is mobilized to engender their legitimacy are therefore not 'innocent' cultural phenomena as such, but are imbued with hidden hegemonies which make them constituents of broader economic and statist agendas. The significance of this aspect of Japaneseness will become apparent in the description of a Japanese schooling situation as part of the discussion on education and ideology in Chapter 5. The bigotries of *nihonjinron* and its state sponsored parochialisms will similarly be considered, in light of the fact that the schooling situation in question concerns the education of Japanese children growing up in cosmopolitan Singapore where their parents are sent for work.

'National language' or kokugo as a product of language ideology

Consonant with notions of ideologies which reify 'insider-ship' (or '–hood') and group solidarity are language ideologies which reify the myth of communicability or intelligibility among putative insiders. Doerr (2014) notes that coeval with the formation of the modern nation state was the emergence of an ideology contending that 'all Japanese people should be able to understand each other's utterances' within a larger controlling framework which assumes that 'Japanese people constitute a single entity and that the Japanese language is one unit of language and thus all Japanese speakers should be able to communicate with each other perfectly' (Doerr, 2014).

The discourse of communicability and intelligibility, the promotion of *kokugo*, and the notion that 'Japan, the Japanese language and Japanese people are bounded units' (Doerr, 2014, p. 72) are in fact reifications of language ideologies traceable to political agendas concerned with the forging of a national spirit. Such language ideologies in turn signal an attempt to introduce an added moral dimension to the discourse of communicability and intelligibility through *kokugo* (Doerr, 2014). In this regard, a normative *kokugo* came to be reified though war, colonization (of Korea and Taiwan), imperialism (through the creation of the East Asia Co-prosperity Sphere during the Second World War), democratization and the forging of a national spirit (after the end of the Second World War). Thus, *kokugo*, of itself, needs to be looked upon as a historically layered, ideologically constituted, economically situated and politically motivated construct, created and curated for the purpose of prospering the nation state (Doerr, 2014). Aspinall (2003, p. 113) observes that the persistence of such hegemonies are a result of 'unquestioning attitude[s] to the "naturalness" of the relationship between people and the nation they are born in', with such attitudes remaining in place ordinarily through a 'taken on faith' basis. On this basis, nationality is said to be 'an essential component of self-identity'; one nation state is said to have 'only one language'; the culture of one nation is said to be 'inherently different from that of another' (p. 113). Meanwhile, 'the division of the planet's surface into separate national units is the most natural thing in the world', or so it should be thought (p. 113).

The reality of course is that rhetorically or mythically constructed aspects of *kokugo* are not apart from the fact that *kokugo* was after all a derivation of 'the linguistic variety used by Tokyo's educated class' and was constructed in the (political) interests of specific groups affiliated to Tokyo as 'the center of politics and the economy' of the country (Doerr, 2014, p. 65). Along with 'intelligibility' or 'unintelligibility', Doerr (2014, p. 66) is able to conclude that terms 'such as Japan, Japanese people, the Japanese language, language, dialect, common language, standard language, *kokugo* and native speaker' are all derived from 'notions constructed via ideologies of modern nation-state building and maintenance' and should accordingly be recognized as such. Such recognition is necessary as way to avoid buying credulously into the idea that the entire nation of Japan is homogeneous and that people should therefore comprehend each other's utterances perfectly.

While Doerr's (2014) latter observations will be especially helpful when it comes to attempts at understanding the self-referential nature of internally constructed and appropriated meanings discussed in the next section, Aspinall (2003, p. 114) offers a sobering assessment over what would in fact be nationalistic concerns 'with using language education to increase the 'pride' of Japanese people in their country. According to Aspinall (p. 114), similar agendas in history education led 'to serious problems between Japan and its Asian neighbours, countries that still have memories of an era when "Japanese pride" held very ominous connotations indeed'.

Internally constructed meanings, autopoietic aspects and explanations of *nihonjinron*

Observations from Goosseff (2010) concerning autopoiesis bear revisiting here with respect to *nihonjinron*. The reason has to do with how autopoiesis provides an understanding of the way new information is known and characterized as being internally construed and specified in living beings (see points made earlier in Chapter 1).

> The function of a living entity is to keep itself alive by responding appropriately to environmental triggers in a way that is *faithful to itself* by obeying its organization. But how does the entity know what to do, when it meets a perturbation because of outside triggers. (sic) System-specific, the perturbation is [in fact] an inside response to the trigger, awakening assignments of meaning. Some are experienced as *dangerous*; others as *desirable*. A more limited range of possible meanings indicates more instinctual behaviour, *but instincts need 'fixed' very predictable environments to be effective.*
>
> (Goosseff, 2010, p. 147, italics added)

In autopoietic terms, *nihonjinron* is a way of considering Japaneseness as being faithful to itself. The Japanese professor mentioned in Rudolph et al. (2018, p. 10) asserts rather categorically that Japanese people are the veritable offspring of a 'soft, moist, humid climate' and are consequently 'more tolerant, and malleable' in terms of inbuilt character. In the language of autopoiesis, this inbuilt character is reminiscent of the way an organism is able to meet any form of external perturbation as an inside response to an outside trigger in the awakening of meaning specifications. The fact that such tolerance and malleability, as is thought to be the case by the Japanese professor, may also be attributable to autopoiesis is relevant here. The Japanese professor's perturbation constitutes an internally specified response, which is that western people are specified as being assertive and absolutist in their ways (see Rudolph et al., 2018).

> With meaning processed (learned), entities start to develop a unique identity. The more freedom the entity gets by its organization to construct meaning, the more it individualizes and develops a 'personal' identity. Identity is in a sense a self made (sic) dynamic construction of meaning. *More evolved systems do not so much obey their organization anymore but their identity.* Still autopoietic entities obey meaning in the same way … it must all lead to the maintenance of their autopoiesis. For identities to develop, they need an ongoing structural coupling (relationships) with other identities.
>
> (Goosseff, 2010, p. 148, italics added)

As can be seen from the above description, autopoiesis does have strong implications for identity by way of the manner in which meaning is processed and learned, as it also does for the freedom of the entity to construct meaning, by way of its internal organization. These observations are important as it is Japanese identity that is being discussed or at stake, especially as autopoiesis reveals that identity is ultimately self-made and or self-done-to, and is closely linked to an entity's freedom and also relationships.

These are key observations vis-à-vis *nihonjinron*, more so if it proves itself to be variously influential in an entity's freedom to relate, and therefore to develop. These observations, moreover, have equally important implications for the (de)humanizing forms of education spoken about in Freire, where action, reflection and conscientization depend on how *external* triggers through experiential instances of structural coupling are *internally* appropriated (1985, 2000). Ultimately, if human '[r]esponses that reestablish internal dynamic equilibrium are [actually] learned' (Goosseff, 2010, p. 148), then education (and approaches to the same) must be held responsible for the (re)establishment of such internal equilibriums, whether toward humanizing ends or otherwise (Goosseff, 2010, p. 148). Moreover, group(ish) behavior in social (especially *uchi* type) domains, which is a concern in *nihonjinron*, is implicated in such internal sense making, as can be seen in the following observation by Goosseff (2010). The maintenance of *seken* (acceptability in public eye or public society) is especially relevant in relation to the need to behave in a manner that is conforming and acceptable to larger society (Makino, 2002).

> Systems which create social domains in which reacting to one another becomes a major characteristic of that species (*group* behavior/group dynamics/relationships), especially need these internal processes of sense making.
>
> (Goosseff, 2010, p. 148, italics added)

In this way, in situations where behaviors acceptable within a schema of Japaneseness are to be 'monitored' for public approval, autopoiesis becomes relevant in regulating group behavior, first within each person, and further to this, within the group as well. While Goosseff (2010) is able to highlight helpful links between autopoiesis and its implications for successful communication, particularly in relation to the construct(ions) of a (super)addressee, autopoiesis can just as surely be linked to education as well as the enactment of group and public behavior, in this case, by way of its imbrications on the freedom to think, act and develop an identity.

Nihonjinron imaginaries and effects on the imagination and practice

In sentimental moments of yearning or insecurity or when faced with external changes, the familiarities of *nihonjinron* can be turned to as a (reassuring) reification of what Appadurai describes as imaginations of 'relatively stable communities and networks, of kinship, of friendship, of work and of leisure, as well as of birth' (Appadurai, 1990a, p. 297). Arguably, as will be seen in Chapter 5, such imaginations and/or yearnings for security may become more real among those who are residing overseas. The imagined communities and networks are virtually a reification of what was first mentioned in Chapter 1 concerning obedience to 'an inner world of entities' (Goosseff, 2010, p. 149). At other times, Japanese so inclined to the security (blanket) of such imagined forms may have to tell themselves to be more accepting of change, the fact of the matter being that 'the warp of these stabilities is everywhere shot through with the woof of human motion, as more persons and groups deal with the realities of having to move' (Appadurai, 1990a, p. 297). This would likely be the case with the Japanese expatriate employees in Singapore, their spouses and schooling children in tow.

In real life, this bespoken type of imagination, whether of illusory or elusively stable communities and networks or otherwise, cannot remain capsuled within timeless realms of fancy, fantasy or escape. Neither should it remain as an idle pass time of privileged or passive fantasizers. Instead, as noted in Appadurai (1990b), this type of imagination is often materially translatable into 'an organized field of social practices' or more practically, 'a form of work (both in the sense of labor and of culturally organized practice)' as well as 'a form of negotiation between sites of agency' (p. 5). In this case, the power of the imagination extends materially to its being 'central to all forms of agency' (p. 5). The benefits of such an understanding of the imagination as an organized field of social and culturally situated practice will become clear in subsequent examinations of the practical outworkings of the English curriculum in the Japanese elementary school in question and the sorts of *nihonjinron*-led cultural imaginaries, mental images or mentalities that feed and sustain them. Suffice to acknowledge now that the imagination as is understood in Appadurai (1990b) has its way of staying on to find its roost (or haunt, as the case may be) in observable manifestations of tangible and sedimented practice. In simple terms, what one group chooses to imagine or entertain in its imagination translates into what its representatives (puppets included) will be carrying out on very account of the same sort of fancying or imagination.

It stands to reason, therefore, that what transpires as imaginaries within the cranial impulses (i.e. heads) of such rich and fertile forms of imagination may be better understood if the outworked and enacted practices thereof are exposed for keen observation and ideological deconstruction (in Chapters 5 and 6).

Meanings held in abeyance as a frustration as well as a door of hope

It is understandably the case that when Japanese people, for whatever reason, move away from the comfort zones of the Japanese homeland into non-Japanese environments, contestations over cultural and language ideologies will take on unfamiliar dimensions. The unfamiliarity of these contestations serves as a reminder that 'linguistic resources travel[ing] across time, space and different regimes of indexicalities and organizations of repertoires' will be subject to new orders of the very same (Blommaert, 2003, p. 615). Where the present discussion is concerned, such new regimes and indexical frameworks are ones which can prove to be a serious challenge for those Japanese tending to be more deeply entrenched in identity conversations centered around the narrower circumscriptions of *nihonjinron*. This would be a perennially problematic issue that deserves (or demands) the attention it gets in this book.

If *nihonjinron* and its persistence involves a reliant dependence on understandings of knowledge and meaning that reify their fixity, a critique that sets out to question different underlying constructions and derivations of *nihonjinron* would undoubtedly involve a problematization of these very fixities. This would especially be the case if such an undertaking in problematization is going to be part of a stake in the engenderment of hope. If so, such forms of problematization would play their part in 'denying the discreetness of meaning' in ways in which 'new meaning becomes possible', a genuine recognition of the dynamic and multilayered qualities of meaning, as well as its constitution 'in and through … social praxis' (Williams, 2010, p. 141). Unless and until such problematization and recognition are given a chance to take place, regimes of authority responsible for acritical fixations of (on) particular(ized) meanings and subjectivizations will continue to pass off as ones which are neutral, unproblematic or mistakably benign. These forms of listlessness coupled with symptoms of systemic inertia and human apathy are strongly suggestive of the operations of hegemony in its subtlest of forms.

When the power and capacity to hope and imagine are held in abeyance, such a situation augurs badly for education, or at the very least, the sort of education where its providers are conscious, admissive and accommodating of its transformative value. The transformative potential of education, carrying with it hopes of ameliorating the deleterious effects of systematized oppression and systemic inertia, may only come to be acknowledged when a praxis of action and reflection so necessary for human conscientization and epistemological transformation is initially or finally set in motion (Freire, 2000). These are matters which will receive their due attention in Chapters 5 and 6. Meanwhile, the next two chapters describe the history of Singapore and that of the Japanese presence in Singapore as part of providing the necessary background to the discussions that follow.

References

Appadurai, A. (1990a). Disjuncture and difference in the global cultural economy. *Theory, Culture and Society*, 7(2–3), 295–310. https://doi.org/10.1177%2F026327690007002017

Appadurai, A. (1990b). Disjuncture and difference in the global cultural economy. *Public Culture*, 2, 1–24. https://doi.org/10.1215/08992363-2-2-1

Aspinall, R. W. (2003). Japanese nationalism and the reform of English language teaching. In R. Goodman & D. Phillips (Eds.), *Can the Japanese change their education system?* (pp. 103–118). Oxford: Symposium.

Befu, H. (1984). Civilization and culture: Japan in search of identity. *Senri Ethnological Studies*, 16, 59–75.

Befu, H. (2001). *Hegemony of homogeneity*. Melbourne: Transpacific Press.

Befu, H. (2009). Concepts of Japan, Japanese culture and the Japanese. In Y. Sugimoto (Ed.), *The Cambridge companion to modern Japanese culture* (pp. 21–37). Cambridge: Cambridge University Press.

Blommaert, J. (2003). Commentary: a sociolinguistics of globalization. *Journal of Sociolinguistics*, 7(4), 607–623. https://doi.org/10.1111/j.1467-9841.2003.00244.x

Bolton, K., & Botha, W. (2017). English as a medium of instruction in Singapore higher education. In B. Fenton-Smith, P. Humphreys & I. Walkinshaw (Eds.), *English medium instruction in higher education in Asia-Pacific: from policy to pedagogy* (pp. 133–152). Cham: Springer.

Burgess, C., Gibson, I., Klaphake, J., & Selzer, M. (2010). The 'Global 30' Project and Japanese higher education reform: an example of a 'closing in' or an 'opening up'? *Globalisation, Societies and Education*, 8(4), 461–475. doi:10.1080/14767724.2010.537931

Chew, D. K., & Thang, L. L. (2006). The Japanese kindergarten of Singapore: 'internalization' and 'internationalization'. In Y. H. Tsu (Ed.), *Japan and Singapore: a multidisciplinary approach* (pp. 240–258). Singapore: McGraw Hill Education.

Clammer, J. (2000). Received dreams: consumer capitalism, social process, and the management of the emotions in contemporary Japan. In J. S. Eases, T. Gill & H. Befu (Eds.), *Globalization and social change in contemporary Japan* (pp. 203–223). Melbourne: Transpacific.

Crang, M. (2000). Relics, places and unwritten geographies in the work of Michel de Certeau. In M. Crang & N. Thrift (Eds.), *Thinking space* (pp. 136–153). London: Routledge.

Doerr, N. M. (2014). On the necessity of 'being understood': rethinking the ideology of standardization in Japan. In S. Sato & N. M. Doerr (Eds.), *Rethinking language and culture in Japanese education: beyond the standard* (pp. 63–81). Bristol: Multilingual Matters.

Donahue, R. T. (2002a). Introduction. In R. T. Donahue (Ed.), *Exploring Japaneseness: on Japanese enactments of culture and consciousness* (pp. ix–xvi). Westport: Ablex.

Douglass, M., & Roberts, G. S. (2003). Japan in a global age of migration. In M. Douglass & G. S. Roberts (Eds.), *Japan and global migration: foreign workers and the advent of a multicultural society* (pp. 3–37). Honolulu: University of Hawai'i.

Dower, J. W. (1999). *Embracing defeat: Japan in the wake of World War II*. New York: W. W. Norton.

Dower, J. W. (2012). *Ways of forgetting, ways of remembering: Japan in the modern world*. New York: The New Press.

Ezrati, M. (1999). *Kawari: how Japan's economic and cultural transformation will alter the balance of power among nations*. Reading, MA: Perseus.

Freire, P. (1985). *The politics of education: culture, power, and liberation*. Westport CT: Bergin and Garvey.

Freire, P. (2000). *Pedagogy of the oppressed* (30th anniversary edition). New York: Bloomsbury.

Goosseff, K. A. (2010). Autopoiesis and meaning: a biological approach to Bakhtin's superaddressee. *Journal of Organizational Change Management*, 23(2), 145–151. https://doi.org/10.1108/09534811011031319

Gulson, K. N. (2007). Mobilizing space discourses: politics and educational policy change. In K. N. Gulson & C. Symes (Eds.), *Spatial theories of education: policy and geography matters* (pp. 37–56). New York: Routledge.

Hashimoto, K. (2000). 'Internationalisation' is 'Japanisation': Japan's foreign language education and national identity. *Journal of Intercultural Studies*, 21, 39–51. https://doi.org/10.1080/07256860050000786

Hashimoto, K. (2007). Japan's language policy and the 'Lost Decade'. In A. B. M. Tsui and J. W. Tollefson (Eds.), *Language policy, culture, and identity in Asian contexts* (pp. 25–36). Mahwah, NJ: Lawrence Erlbaum.

Ishikawa, M. (2011). Redefining internationalization in higher education: Global 30 and the making of global universities in Japan. In D. B. Willis & J. Rappleye (Eds.), *Reimagining Japanese education: borders, transfers, circulations, and the comparative* (pp. 193–224). Oxford: Symposium.

Kubota, R. (2002). The impact of globalization on language teaching in Japan. In D. Block & D. Cameron (Eds.), *Globalization and language teaching* (pp. 13–28). London: Routledge.

Kubota, R., & Fujimoto, D. (2013). Racialized native speakers: voices of Japanese American English language professionals. In S. A. Houghton & D. J. Rivers (Eds.), *Native-speakerism in Japan: intergroup dynamics in foreign language education* (pp. 196–206). Clevedon: Multilingual Matters.

Lebra, T. S. (2004). *The Japanese self in cultural logic*. Honolulu: University of Hawai'i Press.

Lie, J. (2003). The discourse of Japaneseness. In M. Douglass & G. S. Roberts (Eds.), *Japan and global migration: foreign workers and the advent of a multicultural society* (pp. 70–90). Honolulu: University of Hawai'i.

Makino, S. (2002). Uchi and soto as cultural and linguistic metaphors. In R. T. Donahue (Ed.), *Exploring Japaneseness: on Japanese enactments of culture and consciousness* (pp. 29–63). Westport: Ablex.

Mayo, P. (2008). Antonio Gramsci and Paulo Freire: some connections and contrasts. In C. A. Torres & P. Noguera (Eds.), *Social justice education for teachers: Paulo Freire and the possible dream* (pp. 51–68). Rotterdam: Sense Publishers.

McVeigh, B. (2002a). *Japanese higher education as myth*. Armonk, NY: ME Sharpe.

McVeigh, B. (2002b). *Aisatsu*: ritualized politeness as sociopolitical and economic management in Japan. In R. T. Donahue (Ed.), *Exploring Japaneseness on Japanese enactments of culture and consciousness* (pp. 121–145). Westport, CT: Ablex.

McVeigh, B. (2006). *The state bearing gifts: deception and disaffection in Japanese higher education*. Lanham: Lexington Books.
Reischauer, E. (1988). *The Japanese today: change and continuity*. Cambridge, MA: Harvard University Press.
Rivers, D. J. (2013). Institutionalized native speakerism: voice of dissent acts of resistance. In S. A. Houghton & D. J. Rivers (Eds.), *Native speakerism in Japan: intergroup dynamics in foreign language education* (pp. 75–91). Clevedon: Multilingual Matters.
Rose, C. (2006). The battle for hearts and minds: patriotic education in Japan in the 1990s and beyond. In N. Shimazu (Ed.), *Nationalisms in Japan* (pp. 131–153). London: Routledge.
Rudolph, N. (2018). Education for glocal interaction beyond essentialization and idealization: classroom explorations and negotiations. In A. F. Selvi & N. Rudolph (Eds.), *Conceptual shifts and contextualized practices in education for glocal interaction: issues and implications* (pp. 147–174). Singapore: Springer.
Rudolph, N., Yazan, B., & Rudolph, J. (2018). Negotiating 'ares,' 'cans,' and 'shoulds' of being and becoming in English language teaching: two teacher accounts from one Japanese university. *Asian Englishes*, 21(1), 22–37. doi:10.1080/13488678.2018.1471639
Seargeant, P. (2009). *The idea of English in Japan: ideology and the evolution of a global language*. Bristol: Multilingual Matters.
Smith, S., & Carter, R. (2019). Trump urges fairer trade with Japan at start of visit. Retrieved from https://sg.news.yahoo.com/trump-abe-burnish-ties-over-golf-sumo-steak-064726894.html on 28 May 2019.
Thrift, N. (2007). *Non-representational theory: space, politics, affect*. London: Routledge.
Willis, D. B., & Rappleye, J. (2011). Reimagining Japanese education in the global conversation: borders, transfers, circulations, and the comparative. In D. B. Willis & J. Rappleye (Eds.), *Reimagining Japanese education: borders, transfers, circulations, and the comparative* (pp. 15–49). Oxford: Symposium.
Williams, G. (2010). *The knowledge economy, language and culture*. Bristol: Multilingual Matters.
Yamagami, M., & Tollefson, J. (2011). Elite discourses of globalization in Japan: the role of English. In P. Seargeant (Ed.), *English in Japan in an era of globalization* (pp. 15–37). Houndmills: Palgrave Macmillan.

3 Singapore

Colonization, independence and industrialization

In this chapter, I will trace Singapore's modern history which dates from the time of its being founded as a British Colony by Sir Thomas Stamford Raffles, its rapid growth in population and as a center for entrepot trade, its independence from British rule not long after the end of the Second World War, its subsequent economic development as well as its rapid growth as a regional and international center for commerce and financial services. The chapter ends with a discussion of the Singapore education system and an overview of international school education in Singapore.

The founding of modern Singapore

Officially sanctioned discourse legitimates a history of modern Singapore (sometimes called the Singapore Story) that describes her beginnings as a bespoken fishing village or pirates' lair in the Malayan backwaters before a dramatic change of fortunes came by way of her being founded as a British colony in 1819 by Sir Thomas Stamford Raffles of the British East India Company. Most often credited with the prosperity of modern Singapore and still considered a revered hero in official histories, Raffles has also been portrayed as a controversial figure, with Turnbull (2009) noting that 'challengers of the Singapore Story [have] also sought to dislodge Raffles from his pedestal, sometimes reducing him to the status of a dubious adventurer' (p. 4). It has been argued that much of the success of the lately founded colony had actually to be shared among Singapore's first British Resident, Major (later Colonel) William Farquhar, John Crawfurd who was Singapore's second British Resident, the local Malay chiefs and the population of hard-working early immigrants (Turnbull, 2009). Turnbull notes the fact that much attention and credit have sometimes been given to the 'colonial government and to the expansion of British control' whereas it was perhaps 'the people themselves [who] were the most important factor in the making of modern Singapore' (p. 6). Arguing too that as the colonial period becomes gradually 'less prominent as the period itself shrinks in proportion to the longer expanse of Singapore's history' (Turnbull, 2009, p. 6), such attention and credit will become less prominent in discussions of early Singapore.

After the foundation period marked by the work of Raffles, Farquhar and Crawfurd, much of the momentum of Singapore's growth as a commercial hub was 'passed to the Asian and Western communities themselves' (Turnbull, 2009, p. 6). As Asian and Western merchants helped to establish Singapore's commercial institutions, the colony was quickly 'transformed from a precarious entrepot into the confident hub of an expanding regional economy' (p. 7). Beyond its initial role as an entrepot, Singapore came to be regarded as a gateway to British Malaya, 'a bridgehead from which the Malayan interior would be opened up to commercial agriculture and mining ventures', which would eventually become a major reason for Singapore's prosperity (Trocki, 2006, p. 38). Though in the minority as compared in number to the growing presence of Chinese, Malays, Indians, Siamese, Armenians, Arabs and Jews, political power and control was firmly vested in Singapore's European population: '[d]espite their small numbers, they possessed decisive military strength and unity of purpose; they also controlled the flow of capital' (p. 39). The social elite in Singapore were made up of the wealthy Europeans, owing to the belief among the British that power was heavily dependent on the portrayal and maintenance of prestige in public eye, which could only be achieved if the Europeans themselves kept up with their appearances of affluence. The visual and symbolic presentation of such contrasts meant too that at the time, 'Europeans and Asians lived in very different worlds' (p. 39).

Independence from British rule and warming of relations with Japan

From the time of its establishment as an entrepot, and particularly in the postwar years after its independence from British rule, Singapore's success story has been written about as one that has been predicated on claims to sound administration and political governance and their positive effects on a stable business environment and a disciplined workforce. In the area of Singapore's economic development, Japan has been recognized to have contributed greatly, especially after the period when the first internal government was set up in Singapore as a precursor to the colonial government's final departure (Shimizu & Hirakawa, 1999; Shimizu, 2008; Tsu, 2006). Tsu (2006), citing Mr. Wee Mon Cheng, Singapore's ambassador to Japan from 1973 to 1980, notes that Singapore placed great importance on its economic relationship with Japan, with the Singaporean ambassador being said to regard his particular role as one of economic diplomacy. Senior Singaporean officials including ministers made regular high-level visits to Japan and very high-ranking Japanese officials reciprocated with visits to Singapore, with 'one of their top priorities [being] to reaffirm the peaceful intention' of Japan's return to Singapore and to Southeast Asia (p. 12).

While the problem of interpreting Japan's wartime aggression continues to remain 'an ongoing source of angst within Northeast Asia', such a concern is not thought to be a 'significant feature of relations with Southeast Asia' (Smith, 2006, p. 180), particularly after Japan became a source of generous aid funding, providing massive aid programs for development (Smith, 2006).

In Southeast Asia, Japan has been regarded as more of being a 'strategic nonplayer' that 'does not factor into strategic calculations', or more stereotypically, as an 'economic giant' but a 'political/strategic dwarf' (p. 180). As for its contribution to sustained economic growth, Smith (p. 182) notes that Japan would soon enough 'become the greatest investor in Southeast Asia and one of the most important markets for Southeast Asian products'.

Japan's contribution to Singapore's postwar economic growth

There was, to be sure, a less peaceful time when the Japanese forces advanced into the then British colony in belligerence. After the fall of Singapore and during the period of the Japanese Occupation (from February 1942 to August 1945), there were large numbers of Singapore's inhabitants, 'notably the Chinese', who 'suffered terrible hardship' (Shimizu, 2008, p. 34). Renaming Singapore Syonan-to (Light of the South Island), the Japanese arrived with intentions of retaining the island 'as a permanent Japanese colony', given its location as well as strategic and economic importance (Turnbull, 2009, p. 202). Iconic symbols of British rule were removed, including the replacement of English signs with Japanese ones, while the statue of Sir Thomas Stamford Raffles was taken away from its pedestal in front of the Victoria Memorial Hall (Frost & Balasingamchow, 2009). Newspapers which were quickly put under the oversight of the propaganda department of the Japanese military were taken over as a key means for the new rulers to communicate with the local populace (Lee, 2005). Japanese national holidays became official holidays in Syonan-to and the local populace was expected to be visibly part of island-wide commemorations of Japanese victories and imperial events (Frost & Balasingamchow, 2009). Targeted by the Japanese Occupation administration for their anti-Japanese stance, a heavy levy was imposed on the Chinese population to raise revenue for administrative expenses as well as to make them atone for their prior hostility (Turnbull, 2009). The Malay, Indian and Eurasian communities were expected to conform to the new state, but the Japanese attitude to these groups were more varied and measured (Turnbull, 2009). The Malay community was largely left alone, the Eurasians were more strictly disciplined and subdued, while the Indian population was treated with greater consideration 'as allies' (p. 204), some employed as patrolmen and guards.

Return of the British colonial authorities after the war

After the Japanese surrender in August 1945, the British colonial authorities returned to Singapore, landing on the war-torn island in September of that year. Singapore was designated as the headquarters of the British Military Administration under Supreme Allied Commander, Lord Louis Mountbatten (Turnbull, 2009). Confronting the returning British were Singapore's 'mutilated landscape of wrecked military installations, tainted water supplies and makeshift "farms" sitting on any plot of land that would yield tapioca' (Frost & Balasingamchow, 2009,

p. 325). Just days after making landfall, the British announced that the Japanese wartime currency would not be honored, rendering the Japanese notes worthless and causing inflation to set in (Frost & Balasingamchow, 2009). Promptly taking charge of civil affairs, the supply of public utilities (water, electricity and gas) was restored, and schools were gradually reopened (Turnbull, 2009). While a war crimes commission was set up to deal with alleged atrocities at the hands of the occupiers (Turnbull, 2009), the returning British were also keen to exact war reparations from defeated Japan (Shimizu, 2008). With the outbreak of the Cold War in 1947, however, the American government made it a policy to provide assistance to Japan to rebuild its weakened economy as a way to make the defeated war-torn country a major bulwark of defense against the growing threat of Communism in the rest of Asia. This change of direction on the part of the American government meant that the British came under strong US pressure to renounce the right of Singapore and Malaya to claims for war reparations in order to reduce 'the financial burden on their former enemy' (Shimizu, 2008, p. 36). At the same time, Britain was given little choice but to accept American strategy in the Far East, in which Japan would eventually be rehabilitated through expansion of trade with Southeast Asia, despite the fact that Southeast Asia, especially Singapore and Malaya, was regarded by Britain as coming within its sphere of influence (Shimizu & Hirakawa, 1999). The US also adopted measures to minimize or even 'suppress certain aspects of Japan's war responsibility' which led to some degree of concealment of the 'true nature and full enormity of Japanese war crimes' (Dower, 2012, p. 123; also see discussion in Chapter 2). During (and largely because of) the Cold War, Japan and noncommunist Southeast Asia were seen to draw closer, under the aegis of America (Smith, 2006).

On their part, the returning British colonial authorities did try nevertheless to adopt 'strict measures against Japanese economic activities in Singapore' as well as the entry of Japanese nationals (Shimizu, 2008, p. 34). On account of these restrictions, it would take another ten years or so before economic relations between Japan and Singapore began to improve significantly, which was after the formation of Singapore's first internal government in the mid-1950s. According to Shimizu and Hirakawa (1999), the period from the late 1940s to the mid-1950s has generally been regarded as being somewhat of a 'void period' as far as Japan's economic relations with Singapore and the rest of Southeast Asia were concerned. Notwithstanding the reality of these restrictions, trade between Japan and Singapore was actually to resume within a fairly short time, which was as early as 1947, when private foreign trade took place on a restricted basis (Shimizu & Hirakawa, 1999; Tsu, 2006). Shimizu and Hirakawa (1999) argue that contrary to the commonly held view of the existence of the 'void period', Singapore was fairly early on regarded by Japan 'as the base for her economic return to Southeast Asia' particularly in connection with Japan's economic reconstruction efforts, while the Singapore government would come to value Japan 'as an indispensable partner for the country's industrialization' (p. 148), as well as for trade and investment (Smith, 2006).

Industrialization and Japan's role

At the time of the formation of Singapore's first internal government, which was an important political milestone in Singapore's postwar history, both the outgoing colonial government and the local government sought to take measures to eliminate poverty among the citizenry, which was one aspect of a set of measures taken to counter the incoming threat and tide of communism. Commerce and entrepot trade alone could not be any longer relied on to support a growing population and the government began to look to industrialization to provide the young nation with 'an alternative income stream' (Trocki, 2006, p. 149). To build the industrial sector, foreign 'and in particular Japanese' capital was much sought for (p. 149), while the government offered subsidies and other pioneer advantages to foreign investors.

As industrialization was slated to be one important strategy to foster economic stability, there was also a readiness on the part of the Singapore government to reach out for closer economic cooperation with Japan, for reasons to do with Japan being at that time the only industrialized nation in Asia (Shimizu, 2008). The Singapore government, as noted by Shimizu (2008), held high hopes that out of this cooperation would come increased Japanese input and investment into Singapore's new plans for industrialization. In October 1959, Singapore's finance ministry sought assistance from the Japanese Foreign Ministry and the Japan External Trade Organization (Jetro) to encourage Japanese firms to consider Singapore as a possible (or ideal) place for investment (Shimizu, 2008). In 1960, at the request of the Singapore government, a team of six experienced Japanese technical experts was sent by the Japanese government to make ready a detailed plan for the establishment of a new industrial estate to be located in the Jurong area in the western part of the island, which was at that time largely swampland. Soon to follow in the early part of the new decade was the opening of its Tokyo office by Singapore's Economic Development Board (EDB) in 1962. This office was set up for the purpose of making contact with influential people in the Japanese government and business and to woo Japanese investment (Shimizu, 2008). The EDB was responsible for regularly inviting Japanese experts and academics to deliver seminars and lectures to Singaporean managers and government officials, while numerous teams from Singapore were sent to Japan on study missions to tap on Japanese knowhow (Thang & Gan, 2003). On its part, Japan, too, demonstrated interest in having a stronger economic presence in a newly independent and fast-industrializing country, which was not apart from its quest to establish a presence in Southeast Asia out of which it would then be able to tap on the region's large natural resource base (Smith, 2006). The first Japanese investments in the manufacturing sector in the early 1960s were made in response to the Singapore government's new industrialization policy (Shimizu & Hirakawa, 1999). The 1960s marked the period of an 'investment boom' when large numbers of Japanese manufacturing firms set up their plants in Singapore (Shimizu & Hirakawa, 1999, p. 192), accompanied by the dispatch of senior management from parent firms in Japan (Mouer & Norris, 2009).

With the increased influx of capital from Japan as well as Western Europe, Asia and the United States, independent Singapore's dependence on the British declined (Turnbull, 2009). Multinational companies were welcomed for their provision of technical expertise and management skills, alongside their contribution to the expansion and diversification of Singapore's economy (Turnbull, 2009). In terms of economic development, Singapore's impressive growth rates in the years after independence, as noted by Turnbull, coincided with a time of international economic buoyancy, which enabled advanced technologies then common only in the industrialized countries to be brought to Singapore, providing employment and raising living standards.

Growth in volume and scope of Japanese investment

In the earlier years of Singapore's independence and industrialization efforts, Japan proved to be ready with its contributions, not just of foreign investment but also in areas like knowledge sharing and skills transfer. Shimizu and Hirakawa (1999) draw attention to the larger picture of American policy in this regard, where Japan's return to Singapore and other parts of Southeast Asia was guided by 'America's Far Eastern strategy, in which Japan was expected to act as the major industrial nation in Asia' (p. 211). With Japan in the role of being 'a constructive partner' (Smith, 2006, p. 183), Japan and Southeast Asia would thereby discover their 'common purposes in economic growth and [the] checking [of] the spread of communism' (p. 182). As restrictions began to be lifted gradually with regard to the entry of Japanese nationals, Japanese firms became more active in Singapore from the mid-1950s, with banks, insurance and trading companies, as well as shipping firms setting up representative offices or branches. As Singapore was to become 'the principal base for the activities of Japanese firms' (p. 211), there were actually many companies which began their operations in Singapore before their official dates of registration, as resident representatives were typically sent in advance to undertake business activities (Shimizu & Hirakawa, 1999).

As for businesses seeking to return to Singapore, stories of the way in which companies like Echigoya & Co reentered the Singapore market marked the slower and smaller beginnings of what would soon grow in volume and pace (Shimizu & Hirakawa, 1999). Echigoya & Co was the first Japanese company to make a return after the war. Closed in 1945, a local resident by the name of Mr. Hu contacted the former manager, Fukuda Kurahachi, expressing interest in importing silk goods and other Japanese products. Riding on this opportunity, Fukuda returned to Singapore at the end of 1954, even though this was at a time when British colonial policy was not to grant visas to Japanese who had resided in Singapore during the occupation period. Assisted by a Briton who was Fukuda's former customer and a director at the Immigration Department, Fukuda managed to remain in the colony. In July of the following year, permission was granted for Echigoya to reopen for business, which it did in November 1955, with Fukuda as general manager (Shimizu & Hirakawa, 1999).

While Britain as colonial power had reservations over Japan's return to Southeast Asia for fears that this might prove to be detrimental to British interests, a change of policy in the late 1950s meant that both the Singapore government and the outgoing colonial authorities, in their efforts to expand Singapore's economic base, would soon be looking to Japan for cooperation in the development of various pioneer industries (Shimizu & Hirakawa, 1999). In the meantime, an examination of names, credentials and institutions would have clearly showed that the growing Japanese community in Singapore in the later part of the 1960s included presidents, directors and senior managers of leading Japanese businesses, the most notable of which were companies involved in trading, shipping and finance.

Diversification in Japanese investments

Japanese investments into independent Singapore saw modest beginnings with the involvement of Japanese companies in the textiles and electronics sectors. Subsequently, to help solve problems due to high unemployment made urgent by the communist threat, the chief minister of Singapore's internal government sought the Japanese prime minister, Kishi Nobusuke, for investments in tuna canning, cement and fertilizer plants. This took place in 1957 when the Japanese prime minister visited Southeast Asia. This initial involvement was soon to be followed by the launching of ship building and ship repairing business ventures. In the 1960s, Japan was the largest ship building nation in the world (Shimizu, 2008). In tandem with a sharp increase in Japanese firms in the manufacturing and service sectors, one notable landmark in Japanese-Singaporean cooperation was when Ishikawajima-Harima Heavy Industries joined forces with Singapore's EDB to set up Jurong Shipyard Limited, which was a joint venture. Making advances into non-manufacturing sectors, Japanese commercial banks, insurance and securities companies were also set up alongside brand name Japanese supermarkets (Isetan and Yaohan) and leading department chain stores (Takashimaya and Sogo), which came into Singapore in the 1980s and 1990s (see Chapter 4 for a description of the range of Japanese businesses in Singapore). Providing much needed skilled talent and entrepreneurial leadership, there were some Japanese companies which established their regional headquarters in Singapore, creating jobs and transferring substantial amounts of their technical knowhow and work ethic to the local workforce (Balakrishnan, 2016).

On its part, the Singapore government has been welcoming of the Japanese presence, as relations between Japan and Singapore have regularly been spoken of as being 'exemplary', characterized 'by *shinrai* (trust) at the top political level and *kizuna* (bonds) between the peoples' (Balakrishnan, 2016, p. 3, italics original). The resultant presence of a sizable Japanese community (Shimizu & Hirakawa, 1999; Thang & Gan, 2003; Ben-Ari, 2006) and Singapore's importance as a major economic center for offshore manufacturing as well as business and financial services has, in the meantime, enabled two Japanese newspaper companies Nihon Keizai Shimbun, Inc. and Asahi Shimbun, Inc., to set up wholly owned subsidiaries on the island (Shimizu, 2008). In the 2019 Osaka G-20 (Group of 20) Summit hosted by Japan, Singapore, despite not being a member of G-20, was invited to take part in the summit as a guest of the 2019 Chair, Japan. Before leaving for Japan, Singapore's prime minister was interviewed by *Nikkei Asian Review*'s Singapore bureau chief about his country's relations with Japan (Lai, 2019). In the interview, the prime minister noted that Japanese construction giants like Obayashi and Kajima had played significant roles in building Singapore's infrastructure to a high standard of quality, such infrastructural projects including Singapore's mass rapid transit system as well as airport. According to the prime minister, Singapore and Japan enjoyed a firm and reliable partnership. Through this partnership, Singapore would be able to learn from Japan's experience in developing advanced technologies (Lai, 2019).

The 'Learn from Japan' drive and Singapore's admiration for the 'Japanese Model'

Japan's postwar successes and reputation as a 'rising superpower in the world economy' drew the attention of Singapore's leadership (Thang & Gan, 2003, p. 91). Potentially tangible benefits were seen to be gained from an economically strong Japan (Smith, 2006). Japan's quick recovery and success in economic reconstruction meant too that political leaders and industrialists from America and Southeast Asia would eventually become interested in the reasons for this success, which made for the beginnings of the 'Learn from Japan' drive (Thang & Gan, 2003). Before the bursting of Japan's economic bubble, the 21st century was going to be regarded as 'the Japanese century' (Mouer & Norris, 2009, p. 353). Looking at the matter more finely, Mouer and Norris (2009) point out that this drive to learn from Japan was one that was, in practice, centered mainly on interest in particular Japanese institutions that were thought to be capable of adding instrumental value to their running of overseas concerns. In different instances, learning from Japan meant that Japan was looked upon as a 'mentor' nation to Southeast Asians countries seeking to emulate its success, with neighboring Malaysia's 'Look East' policy being an example (Smith, 2006).

Thang and Gan (2003) note that, in 1973, the Singapore economy was badly affected by the oil crisis. When the Singapore government needed to shift the economy into high technology industries in the late 1970s, Japan was seen as a model to help realize this goal. With the 'Learn from Japan' drive reaching fervent pitch in the 1980s, the government turned to Japan for direction and inspiration. Malaysia in practically similar manner sought direction from what it saw as the 'uniqueness of the Japanese model' (Thang & Gan, 2003, p. 94). As leader, it was hoped that Japan would support the various 'Learn from Japan' initiatives 'with generous aid and technical assistance' (p. 92).

In terms of practical steps, learning from Japan involved first building a large base of local Singaporeans who would have a good working knowledge of Japan and the Japanese. These were the so-called Japan specialists who would 'help open up the Japanese market and enhance Singapore's bargaining strength in wooing increasing Japanese investments' (Thang & Gan, 2003, p. 94). In addition, efforts were devoted to learning about Japanese management styles and systems and to emulating Japanese work ethic and approaches to quality control for higher productivity. In its efforts to adopt Japanese management styles and systems, the modelling of Singapore's neighborhood policing system after the Japanese *koban* system of community policing was one example of the type of change that the government had wanted. The Neighborhood Police Post (NPP) system marked 'a new era of policing in Singapore, where the fundamental strategy of policing was shifted ... from a reactive, incident-centered mode of operation to community policing' (p. 101). On its part, the Japanese government provided assistance when the NPP system was being set up, sending their own team to train local police officers.

Two caveats: the situated constructions of the 'Japanese Model' and a politician's reservations

For Japan, providing Singapore and other Southeast Asian countries with packages of aid, mentorship and technical assistance apart from investments was a way of recognizing the mutual 'commercial and resource interdependency' between the two sides (Smith, 2006, p. 184). To be sure, there were other strategic factors involved in the provision of such amounts of assistance. The cohesion of Southeast Asian societies would have been part of the protection of the region's sea-lanes vital for the smooth delivery of oil from the Middle East to Japan. Japan's supply of oil, as pointed out in Smith (2006), is shipped through Southeast Asian waters. More controversially, citing political commentator Nishihara Masashi, Smith (2006) notes that 'a shored up and stable Southeast Asia' could yet prove to be important for the future balancing of China's might in the Asia-Pacific (p. 185); (see also Chapter 4's discussion on *nanshin ron* for further understandings of Japanese involvement in Southeast Asia).

For whatever mentorship or expertise Japan was seen as providing for the growth and prosperity of Southeast Asia, the so-called and well-regarded 'Japanese Model', as revealed in Chapter 2, was actually a by-product of Japan's postwar occupation by the Allied Forces. While Japan came under the command of the Supreme Commander for the Allied Powers (SCAP), much of the 'Japanese Model' (albeit couched in rhetoric affirming Confucian values) only came about because the carrying-over of pre-war conservative bureaucratic arrangements was determined by SCAP to be both expedient and necessary.

Dower (1999) argues that the sort of tribute and adoration given to the 'Japanese Model' makes it highly necessary for critical observations like the following to be made about the cultural and ideological mythologies that sustain its popularity:

> Such persistent and grandiose fixations on blood and culture demand attention in part because they are already *given* such inordinate attention in so many contemporary societies [Singapore in this respect being no exception]. (p. 558, italics original)

Dower (1999, p. 5558) reveals that the 'Japanese Model' is actually an offspring of a 'short, violent, innovative epoch', which, if properly understood, is one that 'proves [in reality] to be *a hybrid* Japanese-American model' (italics added). This model is, moreover, an artefact of history and subsequent exigencies embedded within an acute sense of vulnerability, the need for self-preservation, the lust for economic domination, and resultant macro- and micro-management (and manipulations) thereof:

> forged in war, intensified through defeat and occupation, and maintained over the decades out of abiding fear of national vulnerability and a widespread belief that Japan needed top-level planning and protection to achieve optimum economic growth. (Dower, 1999, p. 558)

Ultimately, according to Dower (1999), to properly understand the 'Japanese Model', it is necessary to recognize that Japan's 'bureaucratic capitalism [will remain] incomprehensible without understanding how victor and vanquished embraced Japan's [wartime] defeat *together*' (p. 558, italics added).

As another caveat where Singapore is concerned, the reference and deference to Japan as investor and mentor did not come about without the expression of some reservation from an older generation of leaders. Singapore's founding prime minister, Lee Kuan Yew was once quoted as registering his worries when asked his opinion about a more participative role for Japan's self-defense forces in overseas operations. The then prime minister, a Cambridge educated lawyer known for his well-articulated opinions, was reported as creating 'something of a minor controversy' when he said that giving the Japanese self-defense forces even a minor role would be 'tantamount to giving liquor chocolates to an alcoholic' (Smith, 2006, p. 179). While such a viewpoint was more to reflect the traumatic experience of people of the prime minister's generation, a newer generation of Southeast Asian leaders has been seen as being less similarly wary of Japanese involvement in the region. Smith (2006) notes that it is not a militarily strong or resurgent Japan that Southeast Asia now fears, but a Japan that is economically weak, given the fact that Southeast Asia continues to look to Japan for partnership (see next section on FTAs) in matters to do with trade and economic cooperation.

The signing of Singapore's Free Trade Agreement with Japan

Beyond Singapore's interest in learning from Japan as epitomized in the popular 'Learn from Japan' drive(s), the young city state's close relations with Japan would be marked indelibly by the signing of the Japan-Singapore Economic Agreement for a New Age Partnership (JSEPA), the very first bilateral Free Trade Agreement (FTA) ever signed between Asian countries (Terada, 2006).

Leading up to the signing of this historic agreement, conservative Japan had long been critical of FTAs, which it viewed as discriminatory against non-signatories, and which it treated as 'the last trade policy option' that it would take (Terada, 2006, p. 150). This meant that it was the Singapore side which had to play the catalyst's role in the bilateral negotiations. In contrast to Japan, Singapore sought to actively engage in trade liberalization negotiations as it (1) enjoyed a trade to gross domestic product (GDP) ratio that was (and continues to be) among the highest in the world; and (2) stood to benefit as FTAs would help secure its presence and status in Southeast Asia by the strengthening of ties, particularly, with major world economies as partners (Terada, 2006). In Japan's case, the major hurdle in any FTA negotiation was the question of domestic pressure to protect its agricultural sector. According to Terada, Singapore was 'one of the few nations that did not provoke resistance from the farming sector in Japan' (p. 163), which became a major reason for 'the speed of progress towards the completion of the FTA' (p. 162). Helping to smooth negotiations was also the fact that both countries had similar industrial structures and service sectors, enabling partnerships to be established in areas like financial services and information technology, while discounting the need to consider long-standing sensitivities presented by Japan's agricultural sector (Terada, 2006).

Apart from economic and strategic outcomes in balancing the influence of the US, China and Japan in the region, JSEPA has since proven to be a contributor to the growth of bilateral relations between Singapore and Japan, playing a vital role in supporting civil society level connections between both countries through educational exchanges, research collaborations, business interactions, apart from facilitating transfers of human resources, capital and information (Terada, 2006). The signing of JSEPA also provided the necessary stimuli for the trade liberalization movement in East Asia, increasing the momentum for FTA negotiations to take place between China and other Southeast Asian countries (Terada, 2006).

Singapore's education system: technology, competitiveness and meritocracy

Earlier sections of the chapter have sought to trace Singapore's beginnings as a British colony, its independence from British rule as well as its post-independence developmental phases in which Japan was seen to have played a major contributory role, especially in the area of the injection of expertise and investments. In the remaining parts of this chapter, I will highlight aspects of independent Singapore's education system and the overall fashion in which education is made to complement the country's ambitions to become a regional leader in the business, technology and finance sectors.

Singapore's education policies are guided by global changes and the need for the working population to remain highly skilled, competitive and technology savvy, and are characterized by the state's 'heavy involvement in all aspects of formal education' (Towndrow, 2001, p. 26). While meritocracy is a founding pillar in the highly structured and intensely competitive education system, policy makers are said to 'usually have very definite ideas about what it is that they would like to see at the end of a particular period of investment' in education (p. 27). The Singapore government's initiatives to promote excellence in education are couched in rhetoric that affirms their role in promoting the prosperity of the nation, the meaning of which is normally associated with 'widespread economic and social change' for the people (p. 29). Intense competition characterizes the manner in which both schools and individual students, while vying for the top positions, are thought to contribute to the 'entrenchment of social stratification' (p. 29), within which a culture of ranking both overtly and covertly contributes to the maintenance of a steeply hierarchical system among institutions and individuals. In 1997, the education ministry launched a blueprint for changes in the system called 'Thinking Schools, Learning Nation' (TSLN) that involved the introduction of a new curriculum. The TSLN curriculum emphasized critical thinking, IT skills and citizenship education in schools (Koh, 2004). In his critique of the TSLN, Koh comments that the blueprint was responsive to both global and local imperatives, 're-aligning educational change in response to the trajectories of (global) economic conditions' but also 'concomitantly framed by (local) sociopolitical and cultural-ideological needs' in what Koh regards as an 'an act of tactical globalisation' (p. 336).

Responsive to global trends in business, capitalism, science and technology, the government also made it a policy for the teaching of English 'to remain a priority in schools because it saw English as a (global) vital link to the world' (Koh, 2004, p. 337). This meant that the 'native tongue of the [erstwhile] colonial master' would be 'indigenised as a national language of Singapore' (p. 337). From 1987 onwards, every school in Singapore adopted English as the instructional medium as a matter of government policy, the reason for which was 'to connect Singapore to the rest of the world and [to] enable it to conduct business with the world at large' (Wang, 2001, p. 237). For the country to find its niche in the global economy, Singapore needed to shape itself into an 'information-technological, bio-scientific, knowledge-based, entrepreneurial, ever learning, borderless and yet cohesive nation', which was why policy makers were concerned that English standards had to be able to bear the load of these ambitious educational goals (p. 257).

Singapore's interest and involvement in international education

Singapore's physical location between the Asia-Pacific to the east, Australasia to the South, South Asia, the Middle East and Europe to the west, has been regarded as a geographically strategic one owing to its usefulness as a connecting point not only for commerce but also for cultural exchange. National resources and energies are channeled into having Singapore gain 'global recognition and prominence as an economic power-house and progressive city-state' (Lim & Tan, 2001, p. 177). With the state's involvement in all forms of formal education (Towndrow, 2001), the message to Singaporeans is that education initiatives must be centered pragmatically on maintaining and enhancing the country's 'competitive edge in the global stage' (Lim & Tan, 2001, p. 177). Sanderson (2002) makes the point that Singapore's history and prosperity are 'intimately related to its engagement with the outside world' meaning too that it would be 'hardly surprising … that the country exhibits a rich tapestry of experience with international education' (p. 88). Adopting a broad view of international education which could mean 'acquiring another language', 'completing part or all of studies overseas', 'education by correspondence', or 'education as aid', Sanderson (2002) notes that 'Singapore is not a newcomer to ideas associated with cross-border movements of ideas, institutions, teachers and students' (p. 88). Government initiatives have sought continually to 'develop a knowledge-based economy' with the aim of transforming the country into a global hub for the growth of knowledge-driven industries 'with world-class capabilities' (p. 94). In terms of understanding education in both its traditional and emergent spaces, Singapore is an example of a place or polity where international and transnational spaces, policy spaces and even cyberspace (see Waters & Brooks, 2011) are allowed to grow in tandem, part of a plurality of spaces in which new initiatives in education are explored.

With respect to the internationalization of education, values that Singapore's education ministry has sought to promote include 'intercultural awareness and engagement, competitive edge, and global citizenship' as part of seeking to 'meet the country's manpower and population requirements' and to 'promote Singapore as an international hub for education' (Daquila, 2013, p. 629). The promotion of these values indicates a general disposition (and climate) of acceptance with respect to the increasing openness of national borders, the consequent need for intercultural awareness and transformative experiences (Daquila, 2013), and a willingness to adapt policy wise to the same. Such openness is also in line with the country's adoption of an outward looking orientation in response to prevailing global forces, alongside an education system that constantly seeks to be more creative, collaborative, innovative, dynamic and internationally tradable (Daquila, 2013).

This general posture of openness may be held in contrast with descriptions of Japanese-medium education in Singapore, which are found in Chapters 5.

International schools in Singapore

As a regional nerve center for international education, Singapore is home and host to a variety and range of international schools providing schooling from elementary to high school levels as well as sixth form education. The registration of private education institutions (PEIs) under which international schools are classified comes within the purview of the Committee of Private Education (CPE), to which such institutions are responsible for good governance as well as sound curricular, pedagogical as well as teacher employment practices. In this section, I provide an overview of international schooling in Singapore as part of laying the groundwork for subsequent discussion on Japanese schooling in Chapter 5.

As there is no significant body of published articles on international school education and expatriate children studying in Singapore at present (see, for example, Starr et al., 2017), examining the websites of different schools is one way of gathering information about the types of schooling that are offered. International schools in Singapore range from ones which have been long established in Singapore to others which are relatively new, as well as ones which charge high tuition to ones which are more reasonably priced, with the cost of tuition often depending on the types of programs and range of facilities available. Official statistics on the exact number of international schools in Singapore are not available (see Ministry of Education, 2018), although the number of schools providing non-Singaporean school curricula can be estimated to be about 70 (Which School Advisor, 2019). While it is not the purpose of this section to examine Singapore's international schools in precise detail and still less to attempt any sort of empirical comparison between them and/or their systems, a representation of institutions teaching international (i.e. a non-Singaporean nation-state) curricula will provide an understanding of the types of schooling available for the children of the 189,600 or so expatriate employment pass holders (Lin, 2017). Demonstrating that international schools can be found right across the island city state, the schools featured in Tables 3.1 to 3.5 are each located in one of the five regions of Singapore where schools can be found: the north, northeast, east, west and central sectors. International schools cannot be found in the south, the central business district, which is dominated by modern skyscrapers and tall office buildings.

What can be learnt from a survey of the copious amounts of information available on international schooling is that expatriate families in Singapore have for them a range of choices to school their children. As would be appreciated, the wide range of the types of schooling available also speaks of the presence of a burgeoning global middle class clientele in Singapore or in the case of Maxwell et al.'s (2019) reckonings, in 'key global cities such as New York, London, Sydney, and Hong Kong, but also further afield in Stockholm, Melbourne, Kuala Lumpur' (p. 609). In keeping with the government's aims for the country to maintain its pole position as a regional education hub, Singapore has taken care to ensure that schooling for expatriate children are of a high standard. The government's Committee of Private Education (CPE) oversees the administration of the EduTrust Certification Scheme (EduTrust), which is a quality assurance scheme aimed at ensuring that private schools offer high quality education services while continually making improvements that lead to positive learning outcomes (SkillsFuture Singapore, n.d.; also see Chapter 5). The EduTrust scheme assesses private schools according to criteria like management commitment, corporate governance and administration, student protection

Table 3.1 Singapore American School (SAS)

Location	*North*
Year founded	1956
Enrolment, levels and curriculum	4,000 (actual); K-12; US High Schools Diploma; Advanced Placements
Mission and vision	To be a world leader in education, cultivating exceptional thinkers prepared for the future; to provide each student an exemplary American educational experience with an international perspective
Campus	35-acre campus, largest single campus K-12 school in the world; indoor air-conditioned rock climbing gym, natural rainforest used by science classes as living laboratory, theatres, auditorium, performing arts spaces, gyms, tennis courts, swimming pool, all-weather track, 1000-seat stadium, football, softball, baseball fields, health clinic
Impact and/or specialty	Major factor in expatriate families deciding to come to Singapore; contributes to the economic being of Singapore through spending by SAS families; one of the world's leading American international schools; provides an innovative education, personalized learning and extraordinary care.
Tuition	Singapore $40,000 to $50,000
Source reference	www.sas.edu.sg

Table 3.2 Australian International School (AIS)

Location	*Northeast*
Year founded	1993
Enrolment, levels and curriculum	2,600 (actual); K-12; IBDP, IBPYP, IGCSE, Australian HSC
Mission and vision	An institution which represents educational excellence in all aspects of its operations; committed fully to the notion of a holistic, rounded education, which emphasizes the arts and sports as well as academics as essential dimensions of each student's education; committed to teaching students to have a moral commitment to make the world a better place as reflective, caring, knowledgeable and principled people
Campus	Divided into three schools; swimming pool, visual arts, music, drama and technology classrooms, performance hall; early learning village, health center
Impact and/or specialty	The only southern hemisphere school in Singapore; involved in local community projects and projects in Vietnam and Cambodia; has sports exchanges with schools in Malaysia
Tuition	Singapore $34,000 to $42,000
Source reference	www.ais.com.sg

Table 3.3 Overseas Family School (OFS)

Location	*East*
Year founded	1991
Enrolment, levels and curriculum	3,000; K-12; IBDP, IGCSE
Mission and vision	To maintain a happy, safe and effective school environment for overseas families living in Singapore
Campus	110,000 square meters in size; running track, football and rugby field, basketball court, swimming pool, sports hall, auditorium, theatre, multi-purpose studios, health center
Impact and/or specialty	Provides a modern education in English for overseas families living in Singapore; maintains a 'worldwide family' approach to schooling
Tuition	Singapore $26,000 to $41,000
Source reference	www.ofs.edu.sg

Table 3.4 One World International School (OWIS)

Location	*West*
Year founded	2008
Enrolment, levels and curriculum	1,200 (Capacity), K-12, Montessori, Reggio Emilia, Cambridge IGCSE
Mission and vision	To develop inquiring, compassionate, reflective lifelong learners who respect all cultures and care for the world; to provide world class quality and affordable education to all students with an emphasis on values, collaboration, creativity and service to others
Campus	32,000 square meters in size; outdoor learning spaces, miniature rainforest, with enclosed sports area, basketball court, soccer field
Impact and/or specialty	A non-denominational, multi-cultural school catering for families looking for an international education; provides the benefits a smaller school can bring to each individual student; has a structured admissions policy to ensure that student body equitably represents a variety of nationalities
Tuition	Singapore $17,000 to $20,000
Source reference	www.owis.org

protocol, student support services, besides academic and assessment processes and monitoring (SkillsFuture Singapore, n.d.). Both the EduTrust and the CPE under whose auspices the scheme is administered are a way of demonstrating to parents of foreign students and Singapore's large and diverse expatriate community alike, that the choices of private schooling available in Singapore are ones which can be relied upon to produce favorable educational outcomes.

Table 3.5 United World College of Southeast Asia (UWC SEA)

Location	*Central (Dover Campus)*
Year founded	1971
Enrolment, levels and curriculum	5,500 (actual); K-12; IBDP, IGCSE
Mission and vision	To make education a force to unite people, nations and cultures for peace and a sustainable future; to educate individuals to embrace challenge and take responsibility for shaping a better world.
Campus	Two campuses; science laboratories, design and technology center, food technology facilities, specialist language and visual arts facilities, multiple performance spaces, age-specific music facilities, outdoor and indoor sports facilities, swimming pool, medical clinic
Impact and/or specialty	The college has a reputation for providing a challenging, holistic, values-based education with an emphasis on academic achievement, service to others, environmental stewardship, teamwork and leadership. Students are equipped to become compassionate, engaged global citizens who seek to make positive differences towards peace and a sustainable future. A diverse, united and caring college community focuses creatively on student learning through a dynamic, holistic program that supports individuals, their well-being and their readiness to cope with an uncertain future.
Tuition	Singapore $39,000 to $43,000
Source reference	www.uwcsea.edu.sg

Such favorable outcomes call to mind the way global middle-class parents afford themselves the opportunity to imagine and reimagine their children's futures, their so-called futurescaping as a multidimensional act of securing imagined futures (Adams & Agbenyega, 2019). Indeed, for these sorts of parents in Adams and Agbenyega (2019), education, mobility and language flows need not in reality be bounded strictly by nation-state landscapes and/or systems. Many seek to spare their children the pressures of learning in high-stakes nation-state systems while others look to having them study in the English medium from an early age. The boundedness of nation-state systems is a matter that will be followed up critically in Chapter 5 vis-à-vis the matter of schooling practices among Japanese families in Singapore, in keeping with Maxwell et al.'s (2019) call for 'empirical investigations and nuanced contextual analyses' of such or similar forms of schooling (p. 610).

Concluding remarks

As can reasonably be concluded from the important milestones marking its growth from being a newly founded British colony in 1819 to an independent nation, Singapore's development not just in purely economic terms but also in terms of its position as a global city state, proceeded at considerably swift pace in the decades after its first internal government was formed. As part of spearheading Singapore's industrialization efforts, the government turned to Japan, then Asia's only industrialized country, for assistance and expertise, on account of which was the influx of Japanese investments and businesses into the country.

Today, Singapore is home to a large representation of expatriate professionals and their dependents making up the diverse nature of the population, among whom are the Japanese businessmen and professionals and their families. It is to this particularly sizable community that I will turn my attention in the next chapter.

References

Adams, M., & Agbenyega, J. (2019). Futurescaping: school choice of internationally mobile global middle class families temporarily residing in Malaysia. *Discourse: Studies in the Cultural Politics of Education*, 40(5), 647–665. doi:10.1080/01596306.2019.1576266

Balakrishnan, V. (2016). Message from the Minister of Foreign Affairs of Singapore. In *History of friendship and cooperation: the 50th anniversary of Japan-Singapore diplomatic relations* (p. 3). Singapore: SG50 and JICA.

Ben-Ari, E. (2006). The culture of Japanese business in Singapore. In Y. H. Tsu (Ed.), *Japan and Singapore: a multidisciplinary approach* (pp. 219–239). Singapore: McGraw Hill Education.

Daquila, T. (2013). Internationalizing higher education in Singapore: government policies and the NUS experience. *Journal of Studies in International Education*, 17 (5), 629–647. https://doi.org/10.1177%2F1028315313499232

Dower, J. W. (1999). *Embracing defeat: Japan in the wake of World War* II. New York: W. W. Norton.

Dower, J. W. (2012). *Ways of forgetting, ways of remembering: Japan in the modern world*. New York: The New Press.

Frost, M. R., & Balasingamchow, Y. (2009). *Singapore: a biography*. Singapore: National Museum of Singapore.

Koh, A. (2004). Singapore education in 'new times': global/local imperatives. *Discourse: Studies in the Cultural Politics of Education*, 25(3), 335–349. https://doi.org/10.1080/0159630042000247917

Lai, L. (2019, 25 June). Singapore can work with Japan on ageing issues, smart cities: Prime Minister Lee Hsien Loong. *The Straits Times*. Retrieved from www.straitstimes.com/singapore/pm-spore-can-work-with-japan-on-ageing-issues-smart-cities on 2 July, 2019.

Lee, G. B. (2005). *The Syonan years: Singapore under Japanese rule, 1942–1945*. Singapore: Nation Archives.

Lim, L., & Tan, J. (2001). Addressing disability in educational reforms: a force for renewing the vision of Singapore 21. In J. Tan, S. Gopinathan & W. K. Ho (Eds.), *Challenges facing the Singapore education system today* (pp. 175–188). Singapore: McGraw Hill Education.

Lin, M. (2017, January 1). Expat number stable despite slowdown. *The Straits Times*. Retrieved from www.straitstimes.com/singapore/expat-numbers-stable-despite-slowdown on 23 June, 2019.

Maxwell, C., Yemini, M., Koh, A., & Agbaria, A. (2019). The plurality of the Global Middle Class(es) and their school choices – moving the 'field' forward empirically and theoretically. *Discourse: Studies in the Cultural Politics of Education*, 40(5), 609–615. https://doi.org/10.1080/01596306.2019.1602305

Ministry of Education (2018). *Education statistics digest 2018*. Singapore: Ministry of Education.

Mouer, R., & Norris, C. (2009). Exporting Japan's culture: from management style to manga. In Y. Sugimoto (Ed.), *The Cambridge companion to modern Japanese culture* (pp. 352–368). Cambridge: Cambridge University Press.

Sanderson, G. (2002). International education developments in Singapore. *International Education Journal*, 3(2), 85–103. http://hdl.handle.net/2328/3142

Shimizu, H. (2008). *Japanese firms in contemporary Singapore*. Singapore: National University of Singapore Press.

Shimizu, H., & Hirakawa, H. (1999). *Japan and Singapore in the world economy: Japan's economic advance into Singapore 1870–1965*. London: Routledge.

SkillsFutures Singapore (n.d.). Information for PEIs and students: private education institutions in Singapore. Retrieved from www.ssg.gov.sg/cpe/peis.html on 10 April, 2017.

Smith, A. L. (2006). Japan's relations with Southeast Asia: the strong silent type. In Y. Sato & S. Limaye (Eds.), *Japan in a dynamic Asia: coping with the new security challenges* (pp. 179–198). Lanham: Lexington.

Starr, R. L., Theng, A. J., Wong, K. M., Tong, N. J., Ibrahim, N. A., Chua, A. M., ... Peh, M. T. (2017). Third culture kids in the outer circle: the development of sociolinguistic knowledge among local and expatriate children in Singapore. *Language in Society*, 46(4), 507–546. https://doi-org.ezlibproxy1.ntu.edu.sg/10.1017/S0047404517000380

Terada, T. (2006). Japan-Singapore economic partnership agreement: origins and implications. In Y. H. Tsu (Ed.), *Japan and Singapore: a multidisciplinary approach* (pp. 149–185). Singapore: McGraw Hill Education.

Thang, L. L., & Gan, S. K. (2003). Deconstructing 'Japanisation': reflections from the 'Learn from Japan' campaign in Singapore. *New Zealand Journal of Asian Studies*, 5(1), 91–106.

Towndrow, P. (2001). The role of technology and technology training in shaping educational policy: the Singaporean experience. In J. Tan, S. Gopinathan & W. K. Ho (Eds.), *Challenges facing the Singapore education system today* (pp. 18–32). Singapore: Prentice Hall.

Trocki, C. A. (2006). *Singapore: wealth, power and the culture of control*. London: Routledge.

Tsu, Y. H. (2006). When 'advancing south' meets 'looking east'. In Y. H. Tsu (Ed.), *Japan and Singapore: a multidisciplinary approach* (pp. 1–19). Singapore: McGraw Hill Education.

Turnbull, C. M. (2009). *A history of modern Singapore, 1819–2005*. Singapore: National University of Singapore.

Wang, S. C. (2001). Which English for our schools? Some thoughts. In J. Tan, S. Gopinathan & W. K. Ho (Eds.), *Challenges facing the Singapore education system today* (pp. 257–263). Singapore: Prentice Hall.

Waters, J., & Brooks, R. (2011). International/transnational spaces of education. *Globalisation, Societies and Education*, 9(2). 155–160. https://doi.org/10.1080/14767724.2011.576933

Which School Advisor (2019). *Singapore school search* [Web page]. Retrieved from https://whichschooladvisor.com/singapore/school-search on 23 June, 2019.

4 Singapore's Japanese presence

Businesses, institutions and symbolisms

History reveals that the first Japanese arrivals in Singapore, consisting mostly of government officials and intellectuals on their way to distant Europe on diplomatic missions, date back to the mid-1800s (Tsu, 2006b). The first known arrival of a Japanese settler was about 40 years after Singapore was founded as a British colony. After the arrival of Yamamoto Otokichi in 1862, other Japanese settlers came in small but still noticeable numbers, forming a migrant community on the island in the period between 1862 and 1890 (Tsu, 2006b). By the turn of the twentieth century, there were already more than 1,400 individuals in the bustling British colony (Lee, 2005). Besides Singapore, many settled in the other cities of British Malaya notably in Kuala Lumpur and Penang. While the earliest settlers were women from Japan's (especially Kyushu's) poorer regions who worked in brothels (they were known as the *karayuki san*), there were subsequently other settlers who worked in the main as traders, bankers, import-exporters, shipping agents, hoteliers, restauranteurs, geishas, drapers, photographers, doctors, dentists, nurses among other occupations (Tsu, 2006a; Lee, 2005; also see section on the Japanese community in Singapore in this chapter). Before the outbreak of the Second World War, the number of Japanese settlers had grown to more than 6,000 (Lee, 2005). During the Second World War, Japan occupied Singapore for a period of three-and-a-half years.

Understanding the history and politics of Japan's 'Moving into the South'

Drawing from post-colonial studies, Qi (2014) notes the importance of paying close attention to particularities and practices that bear on, or are indexical of, the nature of social and political relationships at specific points of contact between actors of different cultural histories. In the context of this present discussion, one would need to understand the significant developments and historical milestones connected to the presence of Japanese institutions in Singapore as part of appreciating the backdrop to subsequent discussion. Apart from the imposing presence of Japanese multinationals, generously funded joint ventures and other small and medium-sized enterprises, businesses catering to the

Japanese community which include department stores and restaurants, there are institutions and agencies in the city state which are unique in their common identification with the 30,000-strong Japanese population (Thang & Gan, 2003; MOFA Japan, 2015). The details of these institutions and their role in the Japanese community are described in Chapter 5.

The evolvement of specific points of contact between Japanese and Singaporean actors can be traced to a mode of discourse that marked the beginnings of Japanese attention towards what lay geographically to the south of the Japanese home islands. In the late nineteenth and early twentieth century, there existed an, albeit early, form of a 'discourse on southward advancement' or *nanshin ron* (Tsu, 2006a, p. 7) where the idea of 'moving into the "South" (the scope of which changed over time)' was recognized as 'the dream of generations of populist politicians, entrepreneurs, business executives, military planners, bureaucrats, and many other types of Japanese since the mid-nineteenth century' (p. 5). The changing scope of this southward attention suggests a range of understandings of what it actually meant to the Japanese for them to be moving or advancing southwards. Such a range of understandings in turn suggests that the Japanese themselves were either unsure or unable to fully explain their own moves (movements) southwards to a distant maritime location like Singapore.

> At times, the dream was nothing more than a fantasy, much grand talking but little action. At other times, it was an inspiration that motivated individuals to make daring career choices and companies to expand strategically overseas. At yet other times, it was a self-delusion that ruined not only lives and fortunes but also, in the form of the Pacific War, the country itself. Most of these permutations of the same dream, from the fantastic and idle to the fanatic and suicidal, had Singapore in them beckoning like a siren.
>
> (Tsu, 2006a, p. 5–6)

The equivocal and at times anomalous nature of Japanese visions of (advancing to) the south can, arguably, be traced to the existence of particularized understandings of the 'south', which Befu (2001) attributes to the influence of Japanese conceptualizations of the wider world outside of Japan. According to Befu (2001), Southeast Asian cultures rank unfavorably in a hierarchy of cultures and polities which accord preeminence to white American or Caucasian cultures (also see Reischauer, 1988). In this steep hierarchy of cultures, the low esteem given to Southeast Asian cultures may be reason for the slightly ambivalent manner in which Singapore's Japanese residents may view Singaporean culture or even Singapore itself, despite the city state's phenomenal economic wealth (see Chapter 5). Indeed, there is ample suggestion that the maintenance of Japanese identity and cultural exclusivity (see example in Toh, 2019) is a matter of priority within a broader range of agendas that attract the presence of the Japanese in the south (see Chapter 5 and 6).

'Moving into the South': narratives, imaginations and mythologies

When Singapore was still a British colony, the southward movement of Japanese people was said to be part of a general 'heeding' of the call to 'advance southward' or *nanshin* (Tsu, 2006a, p. 2). Out of this call, a significant number of Japanese from different walks of life left their homeland to trade, invest and install themselves in Singapore. These were the ones who were able to gather new information and learn about what in the late nineteenth century was still a relatively unknown region and unexplored frontier among the Japanese (Tsu, 2006a). In terms of cultural-political narrative, the south evoked and conjured up for the Japanese certain mythologies which are captured in Tsu's (2006a) description of two Japanese works of political fiction (*seiji shosetsu*). One story tells of how a number of high-minded Japanese sought their fortune in the maritime trade while endeavoring to promote and enforce international justice. Trading with south sea islanders, the heroes capture a British warship which they make their flagship. With their new-found wealth and firepower, they exercise domination over some southern islands, defeat formidable western flotillas and armadas and win the respect of the islanders. Their victories earn them the right to fly the Japanese flag, assert their nationality, and claim a stake in the region for their home country (Tsu, 2006a).

Japanese victories in the Asia-Pacific in 1941 and 1942 meant that Japan had effectively 'usurped the place of the British, French, Dutch, and U.S. colonial powers in Southeast Asia and the Philippines in the name of "coexistence and coprosperity"', thereby 'proclaiming the dawn of a new era' (Dower, 2010, p. 378). In connection with Tsu's (2006a) account of the above 'epic' narrative, Dower's (2010) observations are significant. With Japan's successive and convincing victories in battle, 'Great Nippon' would take the lead as the most powerful nation in Asia, in effect elevating the above narrative to fulfilled dream. According to Dower (2010), natives of the southern regions 'extending across an area of over a million square miles, [albeit] initially embraced these proclaimed anti-imperialist goals', not surprisingly after witnessing 'the rout of the Western colonial powers with astonishment' while in certain instances also 'welcom[ing] the emperor's men as liberators' (p. 378). While those who welcomed the Japanese would eventually realize that they had simply 'traded one set of colonial masters for an even more brutal one', the conquerors on their part legitimized their southward advance by playing the anticolonial card through the propaganda of a 'Greater East Asia Co-prosperity Sphere' and giving (ultimately unfulfilled) promises of independence from colonial rule (Smith, 2006, p. 181).

Not without lofty principle or ideal, narrative envisionings of *nanshin* bore elements of a moralized disaffection or disgust with the perceived injustices of Western colonialism. Tsu (2006a) retells another story, this time of a Japanese hero who meets a Filipino revolutionary who in the plot is relentlessly pursued by the Spanish colonial authorities. After encountering many insurmountable difficulties, the hero manages to help the Filipino fugitive escape to safety.

Readers are told that there is a twist in the plot, in that the Filipino fugitive turns out to be part Japanese, the descendant of a high-ranking samurai exiled to the Philippines (Tsu, 2006a).

Depicting Japanese imaginations of the southern landscape (at least until the end of the Second World War), Tsu (2006a) notes that such imaginations characteristically represent the 'south' to be both 'profitable and gratifying on the one hand and fraught with danger on the other', such dangers being about inevitable '[c]lashes with Western colonial powers' (p. 8). Made justifiable in moral terms, Japanese involvement in the 'south' was envisioned and imagined to be constructive and benign, 'different from Western colonialists', because justice would be upheld and trade with the native peoples would be carried out on a fair and honest basis (Tsu, 2006a). Armed with these lofty ideals of uprightness and propriety, and using Singapore as a forward base, the Japanese 'greatly increased their economic presence in Southeast Asia' in the 1920s and 1930s, as 'blue-chip companies, entrepreneurs, idealist-adventurers pursued a wide range of activities in the region' (Tsu, 2006a, p. 8).

With the war not ending in favor of the Japanese empire, the costly unconditional surrender meant that Japan lost all its wartime acquisitions in entirety. Tsu (2006a) notes in post-war history that the Japanese return to Singapore took place within a relatively short period of time of less than a decade. The speed of the Japanese return 'picked up after Japan regained independence' from Allied occupation (p. 10). The setting up of an embassy as early as 1952 marked the new beginnings of happier cooperation. All-too-apparently, the traumas of a disastrously prosecuted war did not put a stop to Japan's southward advances, managing only to change the mode and tenor of its operations.

Southward inroads of a present kind: Southeast Asia as hinterland

Southeast Asia was apparently 'regarded [by Japan] as the hinterland since before World War II' (Smith, 2006, p. 185), which continues to account for its present-day interest(s) in the region. As noted by Ezrati (1999, p. 141), Japan's international business dealings since the end of the war have been supported by its having 'enjoyed almost an invisible approach to foreign affairs'. Remaining compliantly under 'America's diplomatic and military shadow' for an extended period has meant that Japan has benefited from being 'more flexible than most nations' as regards the making of overseas investment decisions (p. 141).

The benefits once afforded by being in America's shadow may nonetheless have now to give way to the country's 'greater economic and financial integration with Asia' and the consequent need to 'secure her overseas investments' through the influencing of policies in places where Japanese factories and other businesses can be found (Ezrati, 1999, p. 141). With respect to maintaining a Southeast Asian presence, Japan now recognizes in earnest that its commercial linkages and trade partnerships with the ASEAN (Association of Southeast Asian Nations) countries are mutually beneficial, considering its dependence on the resource-rich region for a constant and reliable supply of raw materials (Smith, 2006; also see earlier discussion in Chapter 3). The Malacca Straits constitutes for Japan a 'major trade arterial route' (Smith, 2006, p. 184) where it has strong and vested interests in ensuring that anti-piracy measures are adequately in place to protect the smooth passage of commercial shipping. Moreover, as a necessary aspect of protecting Japanese business interests in Southeast Asia, the government needs to ensure that the welfare and safety of its large number of citizens domiciled in the region continue to be properly looked after, with the 'fast extraction of Japanese nationals' from possible trouble spots being a priority on Japan's security agenda (Smith, 2006, p. 185). With regard to the growing competition between China and Japan for trade and political alliances in Southeast Asia, Japan remains mindful of the need to maintain stability by staying engaged with the region's governments. Not unrelatedly too, history has it that Japan's industrial prowess came about in part because of America's policy of containment, not just of the Soviet Union, but also of China (Ezrati, 1999).

The proliferation of Japanese businesses in Singapore

It was noted in the last chapter that industrial Japan's contribution to economic growth in Singapore was crucial to the newly independent nation's phenomenal claim and climb to prosperity. Corresponding with the period when Japan's economic growth was at its fastest, the coinciding trend in Japan was for Japanese to increasingly go abroad 'with renewed confidence as businessmen, tourists and residents' (Mouer, 2009, p. 118). Tsu (2006a) notes that this new cooperation was not going to be a 'unilateral "southward advancement"', as the Singapore government would on this occasion 'actively seek and direct the transfer of Japanese capital, technology, and personnel' to grow the fledgling newly independent economy (p. 10).

The formation of Singapore's first internal government meant that decisions concerning the growing of the economy would be jointly taken by the new government in consultation with the outgoing colonial government, with both at that point in history sharing a common objective of combating the sometimes-violent communist activities. In the urgency of its plans for Singapore to become industrialized, the newly installed government looked to industrialized Japan both for investment and the provision and transfer of technical knowhow (Shimizu, 2008). Japan, in this respect, became one of the two largest investors in Singapore (the United States being the other), and provided Singapore with the much required technical assistance and financial backing while Japanese companies carried out their business activities in and out of Singapore as part of their business endeavors in the entire region (see Shimizu, 2006). As previously noted, Singapore's largest industrial area in the west of the island was planned and built with the assistance of the Japanese.

Notable instances of successful direct foreign investment in Singapore by Japanese multinational corporations include the Pokka Corporation, a general beverage manufacturer and Kikkoman Corporation, a large soy sauce manufacturer (Shimizu, 2006). For Pokka, the decision to invest in Singapore was based on reasons which included Singapore's ideal position as an international free port and its good physical infrastructure. This initial venture into Singapore was followed by the setting up of a wholly-owned subsidiary, Pokka Food Singapore Pte. Ltd. which became listed on the Singapore Stock Exchange (Shimizu, 2006). As for Kikkoman, it was not the first time it set up operations in Singapore, having been involved in making soy sauce and bean paste for Japanese personnel stationed on the occupied island during the war. Returning after a hiatus of several decades, Kikkoman saw in Singapore benefits to be gained from the availability of high-quality workers, political stability, ease of access to funds as a leading financial center in Asia, among other advantages (Shimizu, 2006).

Shimizu (2006) notes that both Pokka and Kikkoman have made significant contributions to the Singaporean economy in terms of job creation and GDP growth. With regard to corporate social responsibility, moreover, their production and promotion of healthy products have proved popular with the generally health conscious Singaporeans, setting the standards for local producers to follow likewise. For his contributions to public service, Tanida Toshikage, the founder of Pokka Corporation and Singapore's Honorary Consul in Nagoya, was awarded a Singapore Public Service Star medal, an award given in recognition of public spiritedness to people who have contributed significantly either in business or in the arts, culture and sports.

Rather less successful despite its early entry into Singapore in the mid-1950s was Bridgestone Tire Company Limited. Initially, the company served the needs of rickshaw and bicycle owners for tires before diversifying to cars and motorcycles (Shimizu & Hirakawa, 1999). Subsequently, in the 1960s, Bridgestone rented space from the Singapore government to set up its tire factory, which was run by engineers and supervisors sent from Japan and local staff members. The company was given pioneer industry status by the Singapore government, which meant that it was offered tax breaks and other privileges. However, affected by the political crisis which led to Singapore's separation from its two-year union with Malaysia, the company was faced with adverse effects that came with the loss of the Malaysian-Singaporean common market (Shimizu & Hirakawa, 1999). The company then ran into further difficulties not long after the expiry of its pioneer status, which was also when the Singapore government removed a 40 percent customs duty on imported tires. The removal of this duty resulted in the company's loss of its competitive edge as a local tire producer, leading to its cessation of operations in 1980 (Shimizu & Hirakawa, 1999).

Japanese investments into Singapore came in two notable waves, the first in the 1960s and the second in the 1970s, the latter giving rise 'to a second Japanese investment boom' (Shimizu & Hirakawa, 1999, p. 205). Large numbers of manufacturing companies, especially those in the electrical and electronics sector, chose

Singapore as a production base for goods manufactured for the European and American markets. Shimizu and Hirakawa (1999) note the contribution of Japanese firms in the success of Singapore's industrialization efforts. Together with MNCs from European countries and America, Japanese firms came to play a key role in Singapore's transition and transformation from a colony into a newly industrialized country, particularly one that would be successful in making a name for itself in export-oriented industrialization (Shimizu & Hirakawa, 1999).

Involvement in a wider range of businesses

A survey of Japanese businesses establishments in Singapore soon after the turn of the millennium quickly reveals that Japanese companies were already engaged in an impressive range of business and industrial activities ramifying different sectors of the economy (Kompass, 2004). In terms of their impact in commerce, Japanese companies were engaged in the trading of chemicals, plastic resins, rubber linings, glass flake linings, float glass, reflective glass, automotive parts, car electronics devices as well as heavy equipment and machinery. In the manufacturing sector, Japanese companies were involved in the manufacturing of sophisticated ware such as measuring instruments in cellular and optical communications, injection molding products, flame retardant compounds for plastics besides high quality machinery including sheet metal working machines and punching and bending machines. While Japanese contractors were building important infrastructure as part of facilitating economic growth, Japanese service providers were engaged in providing efficient services in freight forwarding, warehousing, software enhancement and network maintenance. In distribution, wholesaling and marketing, Japanese companies dealt with a range of products such as cosmetics, pharmaceuticals, electronic components and electro-chemicals. Meanwhile, Japanese consultancies were set up to provide geological, geotechnical and geophysical consulting services to clients both in Singapore and in the surrounding regions (Kompass, 2004).

Adding to the range of businesses, Japanese companies have also been part of creative ventures as part of plans to expand outside Japan. One notable example was the way in which one of Japan's largest passenger railway companies, East Japan Railway, opened a co-working space in the heart of Singapore's financial district. In its opening of this co-working space, East Japan Railway's Singapore branch (JR East Singapore) sought to create a platform for Japanese and Singapore companies to connect with each other. To achieve this, the company rented a 13,000 square foot area which could accommodate almost 300 people across private offices, desks, workstations and meeting rooms. JR East Singapore saw this eclectic space as a platform for established companies as well as startups from both countries to exchange ideas and technologies, lower barriers and forge connections as companies expanded into each other's markets (Choo, 2019).

In the area of contribution to research and development, Japanese companies have responded positively to the Singapore government's call for more R and D activities in high-technology companies. According to Shimizu and Hirakawa (1999) well-established companies engaging in high-technology operations like Hitachi, Sony International Singapore Pte. Ltd., Yokogawa electric and Aiwa were readily responsive to calls for R and D. At about the same time, overseas or operational headquarters (OHQ) status was granted to companies like Sony International Singapore Pte. Ltd., Fujikura International Management Pte. Ltd., Omron Management Centre of Asia Pacific Pte. Ltd. (Shimizu & Hirakawa, 1999). This latter development, as Shimizu and Hirakawa (1999) note, came about as Japanese companies sought increasingly to carry out their manufacturing operations in China and the rest of Southeast Asia, while exercising general corporate control from Singapore.

The Japanese business community in Singapore

The success of post-war Japan and its economic influence, according to Dower (2012), is a result of close synergies among 'the conservative tripod of ruling party, bureaucracy, and big business' (p. 134), such conservatism being one result of America's deliberate hand in shielding Japan from (or using it as a shield against) communist influence or infiltration (see discussion in Chapter 2). Japan's post-war government by way of a policy that emphasized exports and partnership with America, successfully 'cemented an alliance of big businessmen and government bureaucrats that even today is still powerful' (Weston, 1999, p. 207). With regard to entering into big business ventures, Singapore continues to be an important base for the international activities of Japanese companies, and as has been noted, the Japanese business community both asserts and enjoys a sizable presence (Shimizu & Hirakawa, 1999; Shimizu, 2008). To make possible these activities, the vast majority of Singapore's Japanese residents are company employees and their dependents, a trend or pattern which dates back to the post-war period when the colonial authorities permitted economic activities among Japanese only if they were employed by a Japanese company. This meant that shopkeepers, retailers and other individual Japanese were not permitted to enter Singapore (Shimizu & Hirakawa, 1999), quite unlike what was the case in the pre-war period.

In the years before the war, the Japanese community was comprised of two largely separate groups, the *gudang-zoku* which made up the elite class and the *shitamachi-zoku* or downtown people. The former group comprised employees of trading and shipping companies, banks, and other large companies located centrally in the business district whose stay in Singapore was typically for several years only, while the latter group were generally long-term settlers who worked as traders, shopkeepers, retailers, sundry goods sellers, drapers, hairdressers and also prostitutes (Shimizu & Hirakawa, 1999). When hostilities broke out between the British and the Japanese, many of the long-term settlers were interned by the British in India, while others returned to Japan to take refuge. Consequently, the wartime Japanese community comprised predominantly military and para-military personnel, company employees, Japanese municipal officials and other civilians. The brevity of the wartime occupation meant that change would once again take place after their departure.

After the war, Japanese manufacturers and businesses returned to Singapore. According to Shimizu and Hirakawa (1999), their fairly early post-war return to Singapore could be traced back to reasons that prevailed during the wartime occupation. Local Singaporeans would have had some opportunity to observe for themselves the industrial practices and prowess of Japanese companies during the occupation and this would have been regarded as 'useful in some way to the country's industrialization in the post-war period' (Shimizu & Hirakawa, 1999, p. 210). Subsequently, newly independent Singapore turned again to Japan and readily sought to 'attract [the return of] Japanese manufacturing companies' (Shimizu & Hirakawa, 1999, p. 211), this time as investors and benefactors, rather than as overlords.

The men: managers and executives

In terms of image, the Japanese expatriate is a male, typically in his 30s or 40s, who is accompanied by wife as full-time homemaker and their children (Ben-Ari, 2006; Thang et al., 2006). The typicality of this image has come about principally because Japanese companies work on the basis that Japan is regarded as the center (Ben-Ari, 2006; Sedgwick, 2007) where economic and technological power are concentrated and where business strategies are discussed and approved at top level. Expatriates are sent from the center to various stations and outposts in a company's sometimes far-flung peripheries as part of the growing of their careers (Ben-Ari, 2006). According to Ben-Ari (2006), nearly all of these expatriates are white collar managers and executives, meaning that the Japanese expatriate community is not only 'overwhelmingly comprised of … people who [are sent abroad to] manage various firms and companies' (p. 221) but also 'relatively homogeneous in terms of its demographic and social make-up' (p. 222). Paternalistic philosophies of management are naturalized, made apparent in the fact that expatriates on overseas postings are nearly all men who are well-educated, women in this case being a rarity (Thang et al., 2006; Befu, 2003), except to provide support to the husband and 'to bring up the children' (Ben-Ari, 2006, p. 222). Expatriate men, at this particular time of their careers, are invariably expected to be married, marriage being treated 'as a sign of maturity and responsibility' (221–222).

Japanese managers and executives in Singapore and the question of internationalization

With regard to work performance, Japanese companies are generally said to have high expectations of their business executives sent on overseas postings, such expectations extending beyond their corporate lifestyles into aspects of the conduct of their personal activities (Ben-Ari, 2006; Thang et al., 2006).

> [A]n employee stationed abroad ... must subordinate his whole life during this period of his career. This happens in terms of family life (a woman must give up her career in order to become a supportive wife), and in terms of a general willingness to work long hours and accept an indistinct boundary between work and leisure.
>
> (Ben-Ari, 2006, p. 222)

As expatriate managers are also expected to act as cultural mediators between Japanese management and local Singaporean employees and clients, there is often a fear in some Japanese companies that expatriate managers in such a role may become too well-adapted to local culture (turn native), and in the rather unnoticeable process of which, lose some portion of their innate Japaneseness. On account of this fear, there can be 'a very strong and widespread conception among ... expatriates that they must maintain the appearance – the demeanor, language and attire – of Japanese' (Ben-Ari, 2006, p. 229), the point of deep concern being that 'international business is perceived to pose certain threats to one's "Japaneseness"' (p. 230). As a further precaution to this feared loss of Japaneseness, it is not unknown for companies to summon their executives home to Japan for periods of rehabilitation or re-education on the pretext of updating them with the latest developments at home, the assumption for such a practice being that Japan is a 'unique [and] somehow clean society that must be protected from external influences' (p. 230). Ben-Ari argues that one outcome of such a cloistered ethos is that Japanese managers tend, for example, to wine, dine and play golf among a closed group of the same types of people. Realistic opportunity for Japanese expatriates working within such an ethos to be truly internationalized to some (or any) degree is fairly limited. This is not least because 'Japanese individuals in Singapore live in a world populated by other Japanese' (p. 235), while the purported 'wishes of many managers for outside contacts – with locals and other expatriates – stand in tension with their actual behavior' (p. 236). This latter tension may be seen here in the revealing intimations of a Japanese senior manager:

> [Y]ou have this word 'physical constitution,' this kind of food is suitable for us (sic). Our body does not accept oily food like the Chinese food (sic). I also think that the Japanese food is very good because it does not have added elements of oil or chili sauce.... [W]hen you eat Japanese food you can taste the flavor of the food itself. When I go abroad and I find this kind of [Japanese] food ... I eat it. Here in Singapore, you never know how they prepare the food and what kind of oil or other additives they put in it.
>
> (Senior Manager, cited in Ben-Ari, 2006, p. 236)

In sum, and as Ben-Ari (2006) argues, both the workplace and leisure experiences of a good proportion of Singapore's Japanese expatriates appear to allow only limited room for internationalization in the sense of opportunities for interaction with Singaporeans or with expatriates from other countries, or to cultivate an increased awareness of other cultures. For such expatriates, working overseas 'is not so much a process of "going international" as it is one of "going national"' (Ben-Ari, 2006, p. 237). This pressure to 'go national' ultimately deprives them of the opportunity to genuinely experience overseas life, relocation merely being an extension of their work in Japan, not much different from going abroad on an extended business trip. It is little wonder then that aspects of the schooling of their children reflect a similar pattern, which ensures that the children's Japaneseness remains principally unquestioned and untouched (Chapters 5 and 6).

The women: in Singapore on local contracts

The work and leisure experiences of married expatriate males are seen as being very different from those of the Japanese women who leave Japan to find work in Singapore and the surrounding countries. Thang et al. (2006) note that the lives of these (mostly single) women furnish a stark contrast to the lives of their married male counterparts. Unlike the male expatriate managers, Japanese working women arrive in Singapore generally as independent migrants, making up an 'alternate community to the mainstream Japanese expatriate community dominated by Japanese company men, their wives and children' (Thang et al., 2006, p. 194). Finding new work in Singapore, these women are most likely to be 'making lateral career moves' (p. 195), more often than not for lower salaries and fewer benefits, meaning that many have to source for their own shared accommodation in less prestigious (including government-built) housing areas (Thang et al., 2006). While these women are disadvantaged in terms of the employment benefits enjoyed by the male expatriates and their families, many feel that they are compensated by their not being 'bound to their companies', which allows them the freedom to make career moves of their own choice, including moving on to other locations like Hong Kong or even back home to Japan (p. 197). Thang et al. observe that having a recognizably 'different social position' from the wives of expatriate managers may cause these working women to feel envious of their married counterparts, but others 'express pity for the housewives whom they feel are constrained through their status as non-working women' (p. 195).

Often employed by Japanese companies to do administrative work in the office, their duties may include interpreting for their non-English speaking Japanese bosses, giving rise to the fact that these women are more likely to be conversant speakers of English, and therefore more likely to have friends and contacts who are Singaporean. Thang et al. (2006) note that this albeit less-known group of Japanese migrants is quite 'unlike the mainstream Japanese community which is known for its closed nature' (p. 206). They are more likely to have established local friendships and contacts with local culture by virtue of the 'overlapping [of] their own enclaves with those of the host culture' and in being noticeably more 'fluid in their interactions' (p. 206).

What the experiences and life choices of these working women reveal is that a closed and ghettoed expatriate lifestyle is one that is enforced (or actually self-enforced) by the circumscribing strictures of beliefs about how Japanese expatriates should conduct themselves and live their lives during an overseas posting. The particularity of such beliefs leads to other particularities, foreshadowed in the next section.

Foreshadowing other particularities: the schooling of Japanese children

While Japanese commercial ventures will continue to contribute to the health and growth of the Singaporean economy, it will be seen in later discussion that it is this same venturesome expansion of Japan, Inc. into Singapore (see Reischauer, 1988, p. 334, for a history of the term 'Japan, Inc.') that makes possible the particular type of Japanese school education that will be described. It will also become clear that it is not just Singapore in its physical and geographical context, but more so, the way that life in Singapore is imagined by Japanese domiciled on its shores, which makes possible the type of schooling offered to children of Japanese expatriates. This privileged type of schooling is not normally as visible back in Japan as it is in Singapore. Neither would the elitist aspects of its nature be possible without the contextual and ecological realities that only an overseas cosmopolitan situation like Singapore can uniquely furnish. It will also become apparent that this type of schooling is situated very much within (in fact sustained and feted by) certain ideological, mythological and perspectival influences which bear heavily on the school's beliefs and practices that so typically characterize the type of education it metes and measures out to its students.

In the next chapter, I will describe several important Japanese and also Singaporean institutions and the roles they play with regard to the lives of Singapore's Japanese residents. The former, in particular, are representations of artefacts or enactments of the ongoing Japanese presence in the city state. It will become apparent in light of what has been discussed in this chapter that these institutions represent what Duchene et al., (2013) identify as ideological sites or 'sites of control' (p. 9), where key discourses, resources and frameworks of regulation are legitimated precisely as such. As guardians and bastions of ideological and regulatory frameworks and custodians of cultural and educational resources, these institutions make up an invariable part of what Darvin and Norton (2015) term 'systemic patterns of control' (p. 36) which, while acting invisibly, exert a powerful influence over widely held myths, subscribed to in this case, by the Japanese residing in Singapore.

References

Befu, H. (2001). *Hegemony of homogeneity*. Melbourne: Transpacific Press.

Befu, H. (2003). The global context of Japan outside Japan. In H. Befu & S. Guichard-Anguis (Eds.), *Globalizing Japan: ethnography of the Japanese presence in Asia, Europe and America* (pp. 3–22). London: Routledge.

Ben-Ari, E. (2006). The culture of Japanese business in Singapore. In Y. H. Tsu (Ed.), *Japan and Singapore: a multidisciplinary approach* (pp. 219–239). Singapore: McGraw Hill Education.

Choo, Y. T. (2019). Japanese rail giant East Japan Railway Company opens co-working space in Singapore. *The Straits Times*, 26 August, 2019, C1.
Darvin, R., & Norton, B. (2015). Identity and a model of investment in applied linguistics. *Annual Review of Applied Linguistics*, 35, 35–56. https://doi.org/10.1017/S0267190514000191
Dower, J. W. (2010). *Cultures of war: Pearl Harbor, Hiroshima, 9–11, Iraq*. New York: W. W. Norton.
Dower, J. W. (2012). *Ways of forgetting, ways of remembering: Japan in the modern world*. New York: The New Press.
Duchene, A., Moyer, M., & Roberts, C. (2013). Introduction: recasting institutions and work in multilingual and transnational spaces. In A. Duchene, M. Moyer & C. Roberts (Eds.), *Language, migration and social inequalities: a critical sociolinguistic perspective on institutions and work* (pp. 1–21). Bristol: Multilingual Matters.
Ezrati, M. (1999). *Kawari: How Japan's economic and cultural transformation will alter the balance of power among nations*. Reading, MA: Perseus.
Lee, G. B. (2005). *The Syonan years: Singapore under Japanese rule, 1942–1945*. Singapore: Nation Archives.
Kompass (2004). *Directory of Japanese business in Singapore 2004*. Singapore: Kompass Southeast Asia.
Ministry of Foreign Affairs (MOFA) Japan (2015). *Japan-Singapore relations basic data*. Retrieved from www.mofa.go.jp/region/asia-paci/singapore/data.html on 8 July 2017.
Mouer, R. (2009). Work culture. In Y. Sugimoto (Ed.), *The Cambridge companion to modern Japanese culture* (pp. 113–129). Cambridge: Cambridge University Press.
Qi, J. (2014). Surveillance and normalization: policies and pedagogies of Japanese language education for immigrant children. In M. A. Pereyra & B. M. Franklin, (Eds.), *Systems of reasoning and the politics of schooling: school reform and sciences of education in the tradition of Thomas S. Popkewitz* (pp. 235–247). New York: Routledge.
Reischauer, E. (1988). *The Japanese today: change and continuity*. Cambridge, Massachusetts: Harvard University Press.
Sedgwick, M. (2007). *Globalization and Japanese organization culture: an ethnography of a Japanese corporation in France*. Abingdon, Oxon: Routledge.
Shimizu, H. (2006). Japanese direct investment: Pokka and Kikkoman. In Y. H. Tsu (Ed.), *Japan and Singapore: a multidisciplinary approach* (pp. 115–148). Singapore: McGraw Hill Education.
Shimizu, H. (2008). *Japanese firms in contemporary Singapore*. Singapore: National University of Singapore Press.
Shimizu, H., & Hirakawa, H. (1999). *Japan and Singapore in the world economy: Japan's economic advance into Singapore 1870–1965*. London: Routledge.
Smith, A. L. (2006). Japan's relations with Southeast Asia: the strong silent type. In Y. Sato & S. Limaye (Eds.), *Japan in a dynamic Asia: coping with the new security challenges* (pp. 179–198). Lanham: Lexington.
Thang, L. L., & Gan, S. K. (2003). Deconstructing 'Japanisation': reflections from the 'Learn from Japan' campaign in Singapore. *New Zealand Journal of Asian Studies*, 5(1), 91–106.
Thang, L. L., MacLachlan, E., & Goda, M. (2006). Japanese women working in Singapore. In Y. H. Tsu (Ed.), *Japan and Singapore: a multidisciplinary approach* (pp. 186–218). Singapore: McGraw Hill Education.

Toh, G. (2019). *Effecting change in English teaching: exposing collaborators and culprits in Japan*. London: Palgrave Macmillan.

Tsu, Y. H. (2006a). When 'advancing south' meets 'looking east'. In Y. H. Tsu (Ed.), *Japan and Singapore: a multidisciplinary approach* (pp. 1–19). Singapore: McGraw Hill Education.

Tsu, Y. H. (2006b). A social history of the Japanese in Singapore to 1945. In Y. H. Tsu (Ed.), *Japan and Singapore: a multidisciplinary approach* (pp. 20–52). Singapore: McGraw Hill Education.

Weston, M. (1999). *Giants of Japan: the lives of Japan's greatest men and women*. New York: Kodansha.

5 Japanese schooling in Singapore

Institutions, ideologies and identity investments

Framing the concerns of this book within a problematic that raises questions about the nature, mandate and epistemology of criticality and critical practice as they are borne out in discussions about Japanese education opens up a way of highlighting challenges that are not normally visible in these areas. While more will be said about epistemologies relating to criticality and critical practice in the final chapter, the present concern over this question of lack of visibility is one that needs attention despite the number of critical works that have sought constantly to highlight inequitable practices and power asymmetries stemming from the operations of dissimulated ideologies. Such works, some of which have been examined earlier, have in recent years: (1) highlighted inconsistencies between official and/or purported conceptualizations of internationalization of Japanese education and their actual outcomes and outworkings (Hall, 1997; Hashimoto, 2000; 2007; Kubota, 2002; Yamagami & Tollefson, 2011; Ishikawa, 2011, Hashimoto, 2013; Toh 2016a); (2) questioned the role of English in Japan and the ways in which it is taught, treated and tested, especially vis-à-vis forces which agitate for the preservation of Japaneseness (McVeigh, 2002a; Seargeant, 2009; Rivers, 2013; 2015; 2019; Iino & Murata, 2016; Toh, 2012; 2014a; 2016b; 2019); (3) critiqued the fixedness of identities and subjectivities relating to teachers, learners and speakers of English (Kubota, 2011; Kubota & Fujimoto, 2013; Rudolph, 2016; Rudolph, 2018; Rudolph et al. 2018; Rivers, 2019); (4) exposed contradictory administrative practices regarding the employment and deployment of non-Japanese educators as poor or misleading representations of purported initiatives towards internationalizing Japanese education (McVeigh, 2002a; Rivers, 2010; 2013; 2019; Yamagami & Tollefson, 2011; Breckenridge & Erling, 2011; Toh, 2016a; also see Toh, 2020). In terms of the nature and epistemologies of criticality, I follow famed educator, Paulo Freire, whose compassion for the silenced and marginalized enabled him to look upon criticality as a way of achieving humanization and social justice in education.

I also approach this chapter mindful yet again of the manner in which I am subjectively and yet reflexively positioned as both language educator as well as a parent of school-age children educated entirely in the Japanese system, as I seek to reflexively engage with my experience of the way in which my children have been schooled in the system, alongside different instantiations of Japanese ideology and identity enacted therein. In this endeavor or struggle, the larger problematic of criticality just discussed is once again a potentially enabling factor in the ways in which it features in (and empowers) my praxis. The lived experiences I highlight for review, the stories therein, and the critical insights they yield, make available opportunities for better ways to understand the manner in which Japanese people and institutions come to terms with the challenges of life's realities. In the particular case of my family, these realities have, over the period of more than three years at my time of writing, occurred outside the familiar cultural and linguistic environs of the Japanese home islands, where I had spent close to nine years of my professional life as an educator. The particular point of cross-border contact in this case is my native Singapore, which over the years has been the domicile of a sizable number of Japanese people, mainly Japanese expatriates, but also a minority who have settled in the city state by way of international marriage and/or migration.

I will begin my discussion with a description of several institutions associated with the lives of the Japanese population Singapore, before turning to narrative inquiry to critically analyze an instance of Japanese schooling as it is enacted in a non-Japanese overseas setting, alongside its implications for identity construction as well as ideological deconstruction. As a key approach to identity studies, narrative inquiry has been used to investigate the situated and highly contingent processes of identity construction and negotiation (see e.g. Pierce, 1995; Norton & Early, 2011; Rudolph, 2016; Rudolph et al., 2018). Additionally, as will become apparent later in this chapter, there have also been critical moments in my own lived encounters with different Japanese establishments closely related to Japanese schooling in Singapore which, quite relevantly, have been ones in which my human praxis draws inevitably on my subjectivities as language educator of Singaporean-Chinese extract, married to a Japanese spouse. In my time spent in Japan before returning to Singapore with wife and two children, I taught English for Academic Purposes (EAP) and English as a Lingua Franca (ELF) at two Japanese universities. Before Japan, my work as an English teacher took me to different parts of the Asia-Pacific including Australia, New Zealand, Hong Kong, Thailand and Laos. My time in Japan exposed me to a variety of grounded experiences of institutional processes and practices with regard to ideology and English teaching in general (Toh, 2013a; 2013c; 2014b; 2015a; 2015b; 2015d; 2016b; 2019; 2020) as well as English Medium Instruction or EMI (Toh, 2014a; 2016a) and EAP (Toh, 2013b; 2015c) in particular, which I have taken pains to document. Alongside scholarly studies in language, ideology, conceptualizations of Japaneseness and the cultural politics of language and language teaching in Japan, I now critically assay more recent encounters with Japanese institutions relating directly and principally to the provision of a Japanese education in Singapore. The purpose of my so doing is to extrapolate reflexively clearer understandings of the way the cultural politics, particularly, of language education and ideology, may be symptomatic and/or indexical of the manner in which Japanese institutions and Japanese people approach, imagine, apprehend or otherwise adjust to circumstances outside of the home country, with implications for: (1) what Japanese understandings of internationalization and multiculturalism could mean in terms of cross-border interactions in non-Japanese domains; and (2) enactments of Japanese understandings of language, identity and multicultural education in overseas settings and conceptualizations of the (putative) role of English within such enactments (see Chapter 6).

In giving attention to these concerns, I am yet again reminded of a piece of early wisdom in Appadurai (1990a, p. 297), when he notes the following about challenges to the imagination: 'as international capital shifts its needs, as production and technology generate different needs … moving groups [in the present case, Japanese domiciled in an overseas location] can never afford to let their imaginations rest too long, [not] even if they wished to', as might (possibly or variously) be the case with *nihonjinron*-adherent or *nihonjinron*-enamored Japanese. By the same token, with accelerations in the flow of people, resources and ideas (Appadurai, 1990a), learners (in this case, Japanese children residing overseas with their expatriate parents) are not to be spared the necessary adjustments. Their lived realities have become notably 'more complex and fraught with contradictions' (Darvin & Norton, 2015, p. 42), if only asking to be recognized by those parenting and educating them.

What follows in this chapter is a description of four institutions (Institutions A, B, C and D) associated with the Japanese presence in Singapore, after which will be a series of critical reflections facilitated and set in motion by way of narrative inquiry.

Institution A (IA): a social body for Japanese residents

Institution A or IA is a social body set up in Singapore that brings together the Japanese community and is registered with the registry of societies. IA's presence in Singapore dates back more than a hundred years to a time when Singapore was still a British colony. Japanese schooling in Singapore comes under the venerably and watchfully benign auspices of IA. IA's role in overseeing Japanese education in Singapore means that important occasions, administrative matters relating to the schools that it oversees, are reported in its regular media releases. Apart from its role in superintending and overseeing the education of the children of Japanese expatriates, IA also sees its role in promoting friendly ties and goodwill between Singapore and Japan, which it does through supporting and/or organizing activities for cultural and communal exchanges between Singaporeans and Japanese, as well as through its active engagement with established local charities including, for example, homes for sheltering children or senior citizens in need. Events and joint meetings which promote the exchange of views between Singapore and Japan in areas like trade and education are likely to be hosted in IA's function rooms. IA's premises are located in an area of Singapore bordered by high-end residences and recreational amenities, including colonial clubs and golf courses. The design of the building itself is evocative of what Clammer (2000) would describe as the aesthetics of Japanese capitalism, made to blend very well with Singapore's lush tropical greenery. The building's unique architecture merges tastefully with surrounding foliage especially through the choice of colors and interior décor.

Institution B (IB): a Japanese 'international' elementary school

Institution B (or IB) is an 'international' elementary school. Registered as a private educational institution, it is one of the several schools operating under the auspices and oversight of IA that teaches a curriculum similar to that taught in Japanese state schools. In Japan, IB would be comparable to a Japanese elementary state or municipal school. In Singapore, however, one needs to consider the fact that the cosmopolitan city state is host and home to Australian, American and other international schools for expatriates (see Chapter 3), many of which deliver the education curricula of the countries they represent. It stands to reason therefore that IB would likewise be viewed by locals and expatriates alike as a private 'international' school, as opposed to a local Singaporean or 'neighborhood' school that operates under the superintendence of Singapore's education ministry. Like the Australian and American schools just mentioned, IB is registered with the Committee of Private Education (CPE) in Singapore which is part of a larger statutory board called SkillsFuture Singapore established under Singapore's Ministry of Education (SkillsFutures Singapore, n.d.). The CPE's stated role is to ensure that private education in Singapore is delivered to a high standard of quality and that the operations of private education institutions are compliant with Singapore's Private Education Act. As part of regulating the private education sector, the CPE provides student services, consumer education and facilitates the maintenance of high standards in Singapore's private education industry (Skillfutures, Singapore n.d.; also see Chapter 3).

The closeness of IB's ties with corporate Japan is observable in the following way. Japanese corporations are obliged to make donations to IB if any of their employees have children studying in the school. The actual quantum of the donations varies according to company size, measured by the size of the headquarters in Japan and the number of Japanese employees posted to its Singapore branch or branches. School excursions are organized for IB's students to visit the facilities of premium Japanese companies (airline servicing facilities including hangers; famous food processing ventures) to allow students to witness the scale of Japanese big business in Singapore while skilled professionals from these companies are allowed to visit the school to speak to students about their work. In Japan, it is uncommon for students from elementary schools to be thus favorably exposed, or for that matter, to be taken on board Japanese naval vessels on goodwill visits to Singapore, which speaks clearly of the privilege of having access to such exposure from such an early age. Okano's (2009, p. 106) observation of there being 'significant differences between school and corporate culture' in her discussion on school culture in Japan does not seem to be borne out in this case, where school and corporate culture appear to be operating in symbiosis. IB's teachers and senior administrators are qualified professional educators sent from Japan. IB also employs a small minority of non-Japanese teaching staff, mainly sports instructors and English teachers who are either Singaporeans or overseas hires. The school terms shadow closely those of IB's counterparts in Japan with slight differences in the length of stand-down or vacation periods, to enable families to return to Japan for their breaks. Apart from observing Singaporean public holidays, the school continues to observe several major Japanese public holidays, while the annual sports day (*undokai*) is held at around the same time of the year as schools back in Japan.

Institution C (IC): a registered cooperative society

Readers may wonder why a cooperative society would be included as part of an academic discussion on education. Readers may also ask why such a cooperative society registered with the Singapore authorities would have to be specially set up as a necessary part of facilitating the schooling of the children of Singapore's Japanese residents. This particular cooperative society (henceforth cooperative for short) is given the charge of running the school's commuter bus service, which, as will be seen in ensuing discussion, is an organic and integral aspect of the children's education experience at IB.

Statements from the school, here carefully paraphrased to avoid repeating the exact words, note that the elaborate school bus system operated by the cooperative is a unique (here again, one finds the idea of uniqueness being articulated) aspect of Japanese schooling (in Singapore). Like other Japanese schools operating in the country, IB's youthful charges travel to and return home from school in catered school buses (air-conditioned coaches) that are specially arranged for this purpose. Statements from the school pay tribute to the teachers who routinely make sure that students board their allocated buses in a safe and timely manner. To ferry IB's students to and from school every day during term time, a fleet of some 20 to 30 buses is mobilized, the running of which is outsourced to a local Singaporean bus contractor. For children to be allowed to go to school on the buses, the parents of each family with children commuting on a bus have to become subscribing members of IC, depositing a sum of money with the cooperative in order to qualify for a 'share' in the entity. Parents then pay the children's school bus fares directly to the cooperative inclusive of a goods and services tax imposed by the local government. Bus fares are deducted on a regular basis from parents' bank accounts. The cooperative, which is staffed by a small number of employees as well as parent volunteers, lays down an elaborate network of bus routes complete with designated pick-up and drop-off points. These bus routes typically wind through zones and districts in Singapore where there are concentrated clusters of high-end condominiums housing Japanese residents (see Ben-Ari, 2006), other expatriate foreign nationals as well as well-to-do Singaporeans; (as ordinary Singaporeans set up their homes in government-built flatted tenements).

Apart from planning the bus routes, the cooperative publishes and regularly updates a users' guidebook which provides instructions on the rules and manners to be observed by both parents and children in relation to the daily commute on the buses. The handbook includes pick-up and drop-off routines which parents as members of the cooperative are obliged to strictly adhere to at each designated pick-up and drop-off point, to ensure the safe and smooth running of the system. Monthly circulars are, in addition, issued to parents with reminders concerning observance of certain safety measures and procedures. Each of the bus routes is headed by a parent volunteer who functions as a route marshal. When parents have questions, problems or enquires about their children's bus commute, it is the responsibility of a route marshal to ensure that parents' questions are promptly and properly answered.

As with other cooperative societies registered locally, IC is under obligation to abide by the rules and bye-laws governing its running, as well as guidelines laid down by the host government's registry of cooperative societies. Compliance matters include the need to ensure that the outsourcing of the bus service to a local contractor is done according to set procedures, that the bus drivers drive carefully on the roads in compliance with Singapore's traffic code and that audited accounts are maintained. Together with individual route marshals (normally a wife or spouse with a child on the school bus), the elaborate system that is set up ensures that each child is received by a parent at a designated drop-off point at the end of every school day. Minor behavioral infractions or disagreements among the children during the daily commute are duly and efficiently attended to, as are queries by parents. Such queries may be over any problematic aspect of the bus service, for example, buses failing to enter the condominium to pick up children at a designated point, occasional lateness, public road works around the pickup points, poorly behaved children leading to instances of bullying, or in one rare case, the sudden appearance of a beehive near a pickup point which had the parents around extremely worried. Further details concerning IC will be examined in the reflection and critique section coming later in this chapter.

Institution D (ID): a supplementary weekend language school

Institution D is a supplementary language school that teaches Japanese to children of Japanese parents. These are children, who, on account of their parents' postings to places where Japanese-medium education remains unavailable, would have had to be schooled in English (this is mainly the case) or in another language medium. Having its premises within the same campus as one of the established Japanese-medium schools in Singapore, ID conducts its classes in Japanese language and culture over the afternoons of weekends. ID is regarded as an important institution both to the conservative establishment of Japanese business whose continued prosperity depends heavily on a next generation of Japanese entrepreneurs who would not only need to be fluent in Japanese but at the same time be sympathetic and loyal to the cultural ethos of the establishment. The inclusion of ID in the present discussion provides readers with an understanding of the way proficiency in the Japanese language and knowledge of Japanese culture are regarded as being paramount for children of the Japanese elite even though they would already be attending school and educated comprehensively (albeit) in another system and in another language-medium.

As for the sourcing of teachers, ID has to find its teachers from a limited pool of qualified teachers in Singapore who are able to teach the Japanese language. As classes are conducted in Japanese, English is not used, except for communication with the occasional non-Japanese speaking parent. While a teacher's qualification is stated as a requirement in ID's advertisements for its teachers, ID is not particularly strict about whether applicants are in possession of relevant classroom experience. As a weekend school, ID is also not in a position to sponsor teachers for long-staying or employment permits which means that its teachers will need to be people who would already be in possession of their own permits to live and work in Singapore.

Storytelling

In seeking to carry out my critical analysis and discussion, I am helped by the enabling and empowering facilitations of storytelling, which are in turn energized by equally motivating and transforming possibilities commonly attributed to narrative inquiry (see Connelly & Clandinin, 1990; Bamberg, 2005; Flory & Iglesias, 2010; Barkhuizen, 2011; Goosseff, 2014). The reflexive and interpretative nature of the issues I highlight places clear demands on me to recognize a dynamic understanding of narrative storytelling, in this case, one where stories are seen as 'rhetorical tools for point or claim making', while knowledge, knowing and cognition are seen to 'emerge out of discourse' as 'product[s] of discursive, storytelling practices' (Bamberg, 2005, pp. 215, 223).

Such a dynamic understanding of stories and storytelling is helpful in drawing attention to the way people construct (and contend over) meaning and identity when they relate (to) their stories (Bamberg, 2005), even while the meaning given to stories is 'generated in the interaction between the storyteller and the listener' (Flory & Iglesias, 2010, p. 232). The 'one active teller' can therefore be thought of as co-constructing a story with 'multiple active co-tellers' (Bamberg, 2005, p. 220). In this way, the stories I have to tell are ones that emerge and unfold with respect to: (1) the richly grounded contextual circumstances surrounding my acts of (re)telling; (2) 'character constellations' in the stories and the subjectivities and histories bearing on individual characters' situated positionings (Bamberg, 2005, p. 223); as well as (3) the audiences' meaningful reconstructions and appropriations of what is being related.

In all of these fluidities, I acknowledge that narratives are commonly 'built online', meaning that they are 'fashioned in order to build and work one's way through challenging circumstances … inconsistencies, contradictions, and ambiguities' where pathways are needed for the mitigation of 'interactive trouble[s]'

(Bamberg, 2005, pp. 221–222). Accordingly, I am able to understand narratives as useful means by which storytellers negotiate both ideological and subject(ive) positions from which they engage with prevailing rhetoric or dominant discourses, focalizing 'the momentary history of human sense-making in the form of emergent processes' (Bamberg, 2005, p. 225). In this regard, Goosseff (2014, p. 708) is helpful as he draws attention to the 'experience in language' that narratives offer a participating audience while instantiating meaning towards change and action by way of a narrator's direct experience. Gray (2002) furthermore regards experiential meaning as a means of knowing, realized typically as a 'double move between an ontological register, a way of being in the world based on experience, and an epistemological register through which that being/experience can become a way of knowing' (p. 114). This cognitive dimension of storytelling is also captured in what Barkhuizen (2011) calls 'narrative knowledging' (p. 396), which draws attention to the necessarily cognitive nature of the understanding of experience towards the recognition of new ways of configuring knowledge.

Thus, in my acts of relating the stories I have to tell, I value: (1) the opportunity for the negotiation of fresh meanings made possible by an audience's reading, watching, listening and interaction with a story (Connelly & Clandinin, 1990; Bamberg, 2005; Flory & Iglesias, 2010; Barkhuizen, 2011); (2) the recognition given to 'interactive subtleties and rhetorical finessing' that narratives allow as part of 'daily expressions[s] of attitudes, evaluations … assessments … inconsistencies and equivocations' (Bamberg, 2005, pp. 221–222); and ultimately (3) the opportunity for promoting more humanizing relationships by way of tellers' attempts at seeking a way of explaining themselves to others and the audience's 'understanding [of] an actual life or community as lived' (Connelly & Clandinin, 1990, p. 8). As the stories I tell unfold, it will become clearer that the interpretative, dynamic, contextually borne (and spatially significant) understanding of narrative storytelling I embrace is highly necessary. This is in order to facilitate the praxis of my engagement with the outworkings of identity and ideological positions emerging from *nihonjinron*'s primordialities. To these three aspects of storytelling can be added a fourth which relates to the matter of perspectival viewpoints and their bearings on experience and perceptions of order and boundaries evocatively described in the work of philosopher, psychoanalyst and keen social observer, Michel de Certeau, in Crang (2000) and Thrift (2007). Drawing from de Certeau's different works but especially 'Walking in the City' (in de Certeau, 1984), Crang (2000) and Thrift (2007) are able to call to attention the way in which the apportionment, evocation, enactment, perception and appropriation of space and place are matters to do with both positioning and perspective. In my so relating the stories I tell, I remain ever conscious of the ways in which these various operations of (and on) space and place can be indications or expressions of what Crang (2000) refers to as 'unwritten geographies' (p. 136), which are transformable into experiences either of visibility or invisibility, inclusion or exclusion, placement or displacement, power or disempowerment, strength or helplessness, confidence or diffidence, security or insecurity.

Finally, in threading my story, I am helped, too, by: (1) stories related to me by other storytellers, who by happenstance and grounded life experience have turned out to be uniquely placed individuals in relation to the stories they too have to tell; and as will be seen, their unique trajectories enable fresh viewpoints to come across in the storied reflections and critiques they are nicely positioned to offer; and (2) an observation by Flory and Iglesias (2010, p. 232) that the 'openness of stories enables narrators and listeners to retell [them]' and to furthermore derive meanings from them 'that are relevant to their own social context[s]'. Parent P is a professional in the Japanese culinary industry, who, unlike the vast majority of other professionals, is not employed on expatriate terms by his Japanese employer. Parent P has two children, one enrolled in a kindergarten that operates in the Japanese medium and another older child who is enrolled in IB. As will be seen, the lack of expatriate privileges in the terms of Parent P's employment conditions affects the way in which both he and his wife perceive life in Singapore and schooling at IB. Parent Q is the wife of a professional. She is a homemaker and mother of children studying in IB. Having lived in a Western English-speaking country since going overseas for her high school and university studies, Parent Q is not unfamiliar with life as it is lived outside of Japan and is a confident and opinionated user of English. As a non-working spouse, Parent Q has been coopted, albeit with a degree of reluctance, into various 'volunteer' activities in IB and IC. Parent R and Parent S are a married couple. Parent R is a professional in engineering design who came to Singapore on his own after learning of the opportunities available for people of his expertise. He met his wife, Parent S, in the United States when both were at university. Parent S is not Japanese but is a homemaker who comes from one of the neighboring Southeast Asian countries. They have one child studying in IB. Parent S is unable to communicate in Japanese and is therefore not required to be part of the 'volunteer' roster required of non-working Japanese mothers.

Deconstructing the workings of ideology: a critical analysis of ideological enactments involving Institutions A to D

In terms of the legitimation of ideological agendas and the naturalization of embedded ideologies, there is evidently some degree of awareness among the institutional stakeholders highlighted here that ideology and power must be put into effect with the sort of subtlety in which the 'pushing [of] power … down to the people' is carefully circumvented (Duchene et al., 2013, p. 10). Instead, power is exerted and exercised through 'local systems' that have been put in place with some degree of strategy or foresight, where 'the centralizing power either of the state or the organs of globalised capital' are respectively 'masked and enhanced' (p. 10). Such is the way in which 'soft power' (p. 10) is set to operate, in part enabling Okano (2009) to make the point that 'schools are oppressive to students in some way, and simultaneously nurturing in other ways' (p. 95).

In the present instance, the local systems and their technologies which are ostensibly the conduits of this power are those of a cultural community fronted by the prime movers of big business (IA), a school mirroring (magnifying) and reifying a particularized system of education (IB), a cooperative society which affirms and administers the technologies, paraphernalia and pararealities of structural and social regulation (IC), and last but not least, a school for language, cultural maintenance and purification and 'de-Othering' (ID) as individual cases would require. Duchene et al. (2013) are acutely observant when they note that 'the capillary effects of power deeply embedded in the [seemingly] ordinary and the banal' can in reality 'only be identified through long periods of fieldwork' (pp. 10–11), which I was positioned to do by virtue of my acquaintances with Parents P, Q, R and S, as well as my (ordinary and banal, yet faithful and regular) attendances at IA's member events and IB's open events, which also enabled me to come into fascinating storied information regarding IC and ID. Thus enabled, I am able to resonate with Okano's (2009) observation that it is only through the understanding of 'diverse, inconsistent and contradictory incidents and messages' that the complexities and particularities of a school's culture can be understood (p. 95). The evolving nature of these complexities make it in turn necessary for an understanding of school culture that is contingent and dynamic and as a matter which has to be 'experienced by participants and understood by observers' (Okano, 2009, p. 93). As will be seen in subsequent critique of schooling in IB, 'covert messages through school routines' (p. 96), 'interactions amongst participants, institutions and external conditions … family backgrounds of students (social class) … composition of teachers, school missions and the nature local communities' are factors which affect the nature and quality of the type of schooling a school provides (p. 93).

Furthermore, in my critique of matters relating to schooling in IB and in particular, epistemological and ontological aspects of teaching and learning, it is important that my own sympathies with beliefs that support the humanizing attributes and potential of education (Freire, 1985; 2000) be clearly stated. Learning, for me, takes place meaningfully in contextually and ecologically constituted and situated environments which are recognized to be in continual flux (Dale & Hyslop-Margison, 2010). Learner identities, as much as the nature of learning itself, are both situated and dynamic (Darvin & Norton, 2015), forged and negotiated in full recognition of what Atkinson et al. (2007) see as 'ever-changing mind-body-world environments' inherent of and inhering 'integrated mind-body-world ecologies' (p. 171). Moreover, true and meaningful learning is socio-cognitive, a 'default process by which humans survive in an unpredictable environment', entailing and demanding continuous learner engagement in 'a permanent process of dynamic adaptivity' (Atkinson, et al., 2007, p. 171). Such demand and entailment of learner engagement is, rather unfortunately, not apart from another stark reality taking the form of the power-infused relationship between social practices and dominant discourses. To recall earlier concerns (Chapter 1) about the fact that social practices are 'elaborated in and through discourse', while 'discourses [in their turn] play a role in constructing subjects' (Williams, 2010, p. 145), these concerns suggest also that the continuous learner engagement referred to in Atkinson et al. (2007) must assume a form of dynamic adaptivity on the part of the learners. This dynamic adaptivity is, of necessity, to be placed within an ecology of social practices and dominant discourses. It is not without a tinge of irony that such social practices and dominant discourses may, in the meantime, be seeking to curtail this very adaptivity.

Ritual and ceremony versus day-to-day reality

School assemblies are conducted in IB's school auditorium on important occasions. Ceremonies conducted on these occasions can oftentimes be graced by the presence of members of the ambassadorial corps. The arrival and entrance of important guests is considered to be as a solemn affair. Appropriately dressed students are properly rehearsed by their teachers to adhere to a certain welcome routine that requires them to stand up smartly in split-second unison upon being so precisely cued. In the presence of distinguished guests, boys are told to sit upright (slouching is seriously frowned upon as it indicates listlessness or a lack of self-discipline) with both of their fists clenched earnestly in tightness. Girls on their part are told to sit with their palms faced down, one palm over the other in the daintiest or demurest of fashions. Self-regulation and visible renditions of disciplined behavior serve as clear indications that the self is regarded as a project for discipline in temperance, loyalty and conformity, all toward the production (and more importantly, a *re*production) of solidarity in identity. Furthermore, the promotion of such organized somatized behavior or 'body practices' (see Clammer, 2000, p. 216) in the presence of important people gracing a grand occasion serves not only as a mark of discipline and reverence for propriety and fortitude, but also evokes a warm intimacy of ties between education as it is wholesomely embodied in IB and the superintendent authorities overseeing its functions in didacticism. While these authorities are personified in and symbolized by the presence of esteemed members of the community, their ostensibly statist and capitalistic nature (see below) is evinced and reinforced by the organized presence of 'docile, disciplined bodies occupying their allotted places in social space' (Clammer, 2000, p. 216).

It can also be argued that Japanese schooling, as laid out and affirmed in such a fashion, is likely to function as 'an arm of the state' itself, exerting a dissimulated form of (albeit soft) 'power [that] is normalized so that it does not look [that much] like power' nor even hint of 'moral regimentation' (Duchene et al., 2013, pp. 10–11). Using the body as 'site of intervention' (Clammer, 2000, p. 217), performance of choreographed behaviors proves to be a form of instantiation of social space. And both, as can be seen in Gulson (2007), are a reflection not only of the workings of power but also policies that legitimate, and are in turn legitimations of, such power. If these latter observations are indeed valid, then one other useful connection may well be made in light of an interesting point made by McVeigh (2002b) that politeness and well-constituted form(ality) have an integral role to play as performable lubricants (or lubricating technologies) of undertakings and projects of statism, nationalism and also capitalism. Promoted in diverse social arenas including business, bureaucracy, education, acquaintanceships and friendships, and even family relationships, the emphasis on politeness, according to McVeigh (2002b), may not be so importantly about internalized character but more about the projecting or displaying of an externalized form of civility and acceptable social behavior (see Chapter 2). Such acceptability or amenability promotes a favorable face or insignia which is thought fittingly to complement the country's 'grand projects of modernity' (McVeigh, 2002b, p. 121). Politeness and good form are considered thereafter to be part of a larger nation-statist project, not just for the forging of a common identity and the protection of sociality (Clammer, 2000) as such, but also as part of the property and prosperity of the nation state, since both are ostensibly rooted in 'politico-economic motivations' as well (McVeigh, 2002b, p. 122).

Day-to-day concerns

While politeness and propriety in form constitute one fine area of education that IB excels in, some parents like Parent P find it still more of a priority to direct their immediate concerns toward earning enough money to pay for their children's school fees. This is an area of concern where Flory and Iglesias' (2010) understanding of the interpretative nature of narratives comes in very usefully in its given opportunities to explore 'details about feelings, emotions and processes' relating to different actors, with the expressed hope and aim of obtaining a 'much more comprehensive understanding [of different] phenomena', including lived experiences (p. 115).

As a school that mainly takes in children of parents who are in Singapore on expatriate contracts, Parent P finds himself among a tiny minority of IB fathers who are not in the same league. As such, the fees he needs to pay for his child's education comes only from his monthly take-home wage. Parent P's situation, while atypical, sheds light on the fact that an education in IB, costly for an ordinary wage earner as it is, is an avenue of schooling that someone like Parent P would not quickly be taking for granted. This man hopes to return to Japan in the near future to set up his own business in the culinary industry and both of his children will eventually return to the Japanese state system of education where school fees are not charged and where parents only have to pay for the children's daily serving of lunch, known as *kyushoku*. As for the present, for Parent P's child to be schooled in IB which seems to be the only logical choice in order for the child to eventually be seamlessly reintegrated into the Japanese system, Parent P has to set aside close to one-tenth his monthly take-home salary for this purpose. Difficult though it is to have one child in IB and another in a Japanese-medium kindergarten which is also expensive, Parent P is not unappreciative of the fact that IB's fees also pay for his child's swimming lessons in the school's very decent sized swimming pool and the enjoyment of other facilities and privileges not on offer in state or municipal school campuses back home.

As for Parent R and Parent S, the school fees for their child is also paid out of the father's monthly wage. Unlike Parent P, Parent R's income allows him not only to manage to pay the school fees comfortably, but also to afford the high rental cost in a fairly new condominium development. Having decided to move his family to Singapore from one of the neighboring Southeast Asian countries where his wife, Parent S, comes from, Parent R welcomes the idea of the Japanese-medium education that an established school of IB's size is able to provide, more so as his child's previous Japanese-medium school was located in a much smaller city. With only a small enrolment of less than a hundred, his child's previous school, in his opinion, did not have the atmosphere of a full-sized urban Japanese elementary school like IB. Parent R and Parent S's intention is to have their child remain in IB and on his reaching high-school age, will enroll him in a Japanese-medium high school. Both parents are grateful for the fact that their child is a proficient speaker of English and his mother tongue (Parent S's language), and that he now has the chance to improve more quickly in his Japanese language, given IB's strongly Japanese-medium and cultural environment.

The structuring of work and work-related structures

The nature of IC's activities brings together parent appointees and other volunteers. The copious amounts of paperwork that is generated through their meetings includes the ubiquitous route maps, year-to-year modifications of bus routes, lists of names of condominiums along designated routes and the location of specific pick-up (and drop-off) points. The necessity for designated pick-up points to be pinpointed is due to the fact that high-end condominiums can be erected within big compounds with different entrance and exit gates, each guarded by attendants employed by the condominium management. These pick-up points can be near the condominium guardhouse or typically, in a sheltered area near the main entrance, main lobby or portico. Circulars and reminders are sent out to parents concerning pick-up and drop-off routines, safety matters and dealings with the local Singaporean bus contractors to whom the bus service is outsourced. Such amounts of paperwork also mean that the cooperative's volunteers have to come together regularly for meetings. These meetings may be held on the school campus but more important ones are convened in one of IA's nicely furnished conference rooms.

IC meetings that instantiate Japaneseness

Through its regular meetings conducted in a style befitting and observant of Japanese social formalities, IC's existence becomes a good opportunity for volunteers and appointees from this community of school parents to meet and use the Japanese language, and for various enactments of Japaneseness to be realized or otherwise rehearsed and maintained in a location outside of Japan (see Chapter 6 for related narrative on bus routes). The operations of IC and the ancillary activities accompanying these operations can be regarded as being part of practical acts of performing (and thereby verifying and reifying) Japaneseness. Such performances of Japaneseness are not apart from the role participants play in parallel efforts to instantiate (thereby to demarcate and delineate) the Japaneseness of the very spaces in which these performances are made to take place (see Gulson, 2007). To be clear, the activities that these appointees and volunteers are involved in are in large part necessary bona fide work, if perhaps some aspects of it, if Parent Q is right, may appear to be work for work's sake. More immediately, the meeting, eating and tweeting entail acts that are played out to rehearse particular enactments of Japanese identity, unity and solidarity, while also instantiating Japanese space.

As would be inferable, regular meetings and obligatory gatherings can be harnessed to serve as one way of ensuring that the Japanese involved in the running of activities like those of IC's are never kept too far away from other Japanese, people of their own kind, almost as a protection against having too much access or exposure to non-Japanese influences or elements, besides perhaps being a form of insurance that guarantees that one gets to meet and speak in Japanese with other Japanese on a regular(ized) basis. The scheduling of regular meetings may, moreover, serve conceivably as a sort of vaccine against anyone becoming too comfortable or confident in English. In this connection, while spouses (practically all of these spouses are wives – see Ben-Ari, 2006; Thang et al., 2006) who are not engaged in full-time employment are generally required, over the course of their children's time in the school, to participate in some volunteer parent-school activity, it is a notable point that non-Japanese speaking spouses will find it difficult if not impossible to have a sensible role in these activities as they are conducted solely in Japanese. This was the case with Parent R, whose wife Parent S, from a neighboring Southeast Asian country, could not be part of these volunteer activities for her lack of felicity in Japanese. Parent R and Parent S have also come resignedly to accept the fact that there can be other aspects (besides her non-proficiency in Japanese) where Parent S could be seen to stand out differently simply because of her non-Japaneseness (see Befu, 2009, for essentialized perceptions of Japaneseness). Parent S acknowledges the fact that the lunch boxes she prepares for her child do not look typically like the nicely (pro)portioned bento boxes made by Japanese mothers, a matter that is vulnerably subject to uncomplimentary remarks from people around.

Another matter that may be highlighted about the fact that the bespoken spouses of Japanese expatriates are in practical reality the *wives* is one that resonates with a fairly sharp observation by Reischauer (1988) about married women in Japan. This observation in part accounts for the regulated and group-oriented (if also groupish) nature of the manner in which organizations like the IC are liable to be managed. The following writing in Reischauer (1988) could just as well be one about the lives of Japanese expatriate wives in contemporary Singapore:

> [m]arried women … have virtually no social life outside the family. Except for a very few at the top of society, who may participate stiffly and unhappily in formal banquets, usually those that include foreigners, married women rarely go out with their husbands to dinners and parties or entertain outsiders in their homes … Their life is likely to be limited to husband, children, a few close relatives, some old school-day girlfriends, and possibly the activities of the PTA. (p. 179)

The mirror-image similarities in the lives of Japanese women in Singapore and Japan hint uncannily at how successful aspects of Japanese society and Japaneseness are made to be replicable (and actually replicated) in an overseas location, given the presence and willing conformity of sufficient numbers.

IC meetings that become part of an 'educatio-bureaucracy'

Regarding the involvedness of meetings such as those of the IC's, one is obliged to consider whether the schooling or education that organizations such as the IC are thought to support is conceived of principally as a pedagogical, didactic and humanizing undertaking, or rather more executively, as one that needs to be managed around administrative structures (see McVeigh, 2006). McVeigh (2006) draws attention to the existence of a form of 'educatio-bureaucracy' among Japanese managers of education (p. 137) which he argues is liable to become the very purpose for which other supposedly educational activities or paraphernalia (for example, bus committee meetings, in this case) are caused to exist.

McVeigh (2006) argues that in such a kind of situation, education itself is reified for purposes of feeding, serving, and supporting a larger monolith of bureaucracy, or rather the felt need to create one (p. 137). Viewed in this way, 'Japan's educational bureaucratism' (p. 130) is said to be able to command immense staying power, not least because the subtle workings of this familial 'educatio-bureaucracy' (p. 137) can prove to be very hard to understand, fathom or even detect. McVeigh further reveals that '[p]art of the staying power of Japan's educational bureaucracy is not only its ability to substitute *real* with *parareal* practices, but how it ensures that individuals have a difficult time evaluating the difference' (p. 130). In addition, what might be called 'structure-to-structure behavior' (p. 138), where the activities of 'parareal' structures are mapped onto other 'parareal' structures, highlights the problem of how moral selves and reflexive practice are at risk of being given less priority when the system becomes more fixated or transfixed on structural and form-focused concerns. Fixations on such concerns have their away of drawing attention away from pedagogical ones (Toh, 2013c provides examples of other structure-to-structure behaviors).

Structure-to-structure behavior can be both depersonalizing and contradictory, possibly bordering even on the ludicrous, as can be seen in a storied account of such behavior. This account by Parent Q demonstrates what can happen when lengthy discussions among appointees and volunteers have to take place once every so often. In this particular instance, the attendees concerned had to make a decision on when their next meeting would be. The difficulties over arranging for their next meeting arose because the meeting in question had been scheduled to take place on a day when the children would be let off early from school. The children's early dismissal time meant that mothers would have had to be back home early enough to meet their children as they got off their buses (which has been one of IC's guidelines that parents must follow).

The irony here was that if structure-to-structure behavior prevailed, the meeting itself would have had to take priority over the picking up of the children whose schooling and commuting were the very reasons for the same meeting to have to be taking place. On this occasion, this particular group of attendees were faced with the quandary of having to become contraveners of the group's very own (well-meaning) rules, which would surely have been quite ironic as it came down to choosing between holding their meeting as scheduled or picking up their children. With regard to what may seem here to be a trivial matter treated needlessly as if it was some colossal dilemma, Clammer (2000) is helpful in noticing that within 'a culture which valorizes conformity' (p. 215), suitable reference points on which to base even simple decisions are in reality '*very difficult* to find' (p. 215, italics added). According to Clammer (2000), such cultures betray in-group tendencies toward being engaged circuitously in 'creating and then 'solving' problems and doubts' (pp. 214–215), but all the time with the same few reference points to rely on, making decision making a laboriously long-drawn exercise.

In a bid to shorten this exercise, Parent Q reported that she tried to draw attention to the fact that the safety and well-being of the children were precisely the reason why the meeting had to be convened. It would therefore have been somewhat of a paradox if the actual purpose of the meeting (the children's safe bus commute) was in some unthinking way overshadowed by the mere need to adhere inflexibly to an original schedule. Someone had said that if the scheduled meeting could not be changed to accommodate the children's early dismissal, then another possibility would be for the meeting to be conducted in the school itself, instead of in a meeting room in IA (where lunch would normally be served to all present). Simply changing the venue of the meeting would allow mothers to be on hand to pick up their children whose safety must presumably (or surely) be a priority. Parent Q then volunteered to relate how another attendee then suggested that the mothers could first make their way to the school at dismissal time, meet their children, and then have them brought along to the meeting at IA (which was a good ten kilometers away). This suggestion gave rise to the question of what the children would be doing to amuse themselves while the meeting was in progress. As an aside to this latter suggestion, Parent Q commented on a matter related to the use of the Japanese language at these meetings. Noting that the presence of *kuki yomanai hito* [people who speak insensitively or are unable to read into what should already be very obvious] can impede the smooth running of the meetings, this parent not only expressed her objection to what she thought was an inconvenient suggestion that the mothers should first pick up their children before having them brought along to the meeting at IA. She was also remarking the fact that insensitivity could occur even among Japanese speakers, hence tacitly equating or conflating Japanese speakers and their Japaneseness with sensitivity (*kuki ou yomu*) and the knack for making good practical suggestions (see discussion on *sasshi no bunka* in Chapter 2).

Also, in effect calling out an instance of structure-to-structure behavior, Parent Q added that someone had made a note of the fact that meeting dates could not normally be changed. The reason given was that the meeting room in IA had already been booked a year in advance for the purpose of this very meeting, and holding the meeting at the scheduled time and venue would be important to honor this booking, which was indeed made a full year ahead. Here, structure-to-structure behavior is seen in the attention given to the booking schedule itself, rather on the actual reasons of the meeting for which the booking had been made. Structure-to-structure behavior is liable to end up being an inexorably illogical exercise of administrative and/or managerial tail-chasing.

Evidence and ramifications of structure-to-structure behavior

While it should be noted that McVeigh's (2006) engaging description of structure-to-structure behavior is in the context of Japanese higher education, the above accounts show clearly that structure-to-structure behaviors and relationships are not unique or restricted to the loftiness of university sites alone. The reason given for the 'impossibility' of adjusting a previously arranged meeting time was that the venue had already been booked. This tends to confirm McVeigh's (2006) point that structure-to-structure behavior is fundamentally about safeguarding managerial practices protective of the status quo and that such behavior is characteristically not malleable or amenable to change. As McVeigh (2006) would readily resonate with, once a parallel reality is allowed to take root, the enamoring paper work and even the defining characteristics of power lunches or luncheons (see below) not excluded, what McVeigh (2006) calls the parareal takes on a life and id of its own, possibly blindsiding those involved from further recognizing the original purpose of the meetings. McVeigh's (2006) observations seem therefore to be generalizable to other situations relating to Japanese education projects and technologies, perhaps much more generalizable than McVeigh himself might have imagined when he provided his own account of group-think, depersonalization and para-reality within institutionalized behaviors.

Amidst the commanding influence of group-think and concomitant predispositions toward the inflexibilities of structure-to-structure behavior, Clammer (2000, p. 218) helpfully raises an interesting point about the fact that quasi-groups like these are in reality 'constituted of strangers' (albeit strangers who are identifiably all Japanese). The temporary semblance of unity among these strangers is one that dissolves as soon as they are sent home to Japan with their families or as soon as a new committee is formed at the start of a school year.

The delicious lunches they consume, the bus route maps they pore over, the petty or colossal issues they bicker over, characterize the particular nature of the materiality or circumstantiality that happen to be the reason for these people to converge in such a flimsy 'materiality of social bonds' (Clammer, 2000, p. 218), however superficial such 'bonds' would be. In such an airy and temporal light of things, the persistence of certain patrolling structure-to-structure behaviors seems all the more remarkable, especially if while people come and people go, the same structure-to-structure behaviors carry on ad nauseam.

As a final comment for this section on the culture of educatio-bureaucracy and as a preamble to the next section on ideological instantiations of space, some remaining observations on IA being the venue for some of IC's meetings are in order. These meetings are understood to be held in one of IA's several well-furnished meeting rooms. Typical of such rooms are their formal décor and furnishings, complete with big round meeting table and leather seats, which would be just as suitable for hosting more important dignitaries. A waiter from one of IA's restaurants is charged with serving the exquisite lunches and replenishing servings of tea and coffee for the meeting's attendees. Given the exclusivities of such a space, it is possible to surmise that the matter of choice of venue is influenced by the degree of formal importance that a room in IA is able to provide. Perhaps more than being a simple matter of needing a clean and quiet place for a meeting, the choice of a fine venue in IA may in fact be a case of having this type of activity related to IB schooling augmented by the excellent service and fine repute widely associated with IA.

Bus routes as inventions of borders and as operations over (on) space and place

In their deliberations on space and place as represented (more accurately, evoked) in the work of de Certeau, especially 'Walking in the City', Crang (2000) and Thrift (2007) sought to provide understandings of ways in which the dimensions of space, place, and also placement and displacement, can be implicated in various renditions of human practice. As noted earlier, operations of (and on) space and place are liable to be indicative or symptomatic of what Crang (2000) refers to as 'unwritten geographies' (p. 136). The workings of these 'unwritten geographies' are in turn transformable or translatable into, and interpretable as, experiences of visibility or invisibility, inclusion or exclusion, placement or displacement, power or disempowerment, security or insecurity, confidence or diffidence, magnanimity or pettiness.

The ubiquitous maps that the IC works with, if one follows de Certeau's rendition of Manhattan, New York, from the top of the World Trade Center, are also beheld from a top-down perspective (see Crang, 2000; Thrift, 2007). Looking down at maps as a team of appointees and volunteers from such a positioning (both literally and figuratively) might well be by force of perspectival circumstance, but could also represent or give rise to an assumption of power and privilege, and therefore a reassuring experience of inclusion.

Given that *nihonjinron* places high value on group loyalty and inclusion (Ezrati, 1999), one may conclude that the bespoken maps serve imperatively as a focal artefact around which people can gather for discussion (and a sense of importance or inclusiveness). One bears in mind that de Certeau (cited in Crang, 2000, p. 137) writes insightfully about 'the city as a metaphor for modern life' (Singapore too is a big modern city) evoking the insecurities that come with people having to make do in circumstances where they (like the Japanese living away from Japan) are '[c]ut loose from the traditional communities that [have] circumscribed their functioning' (de Certeau, cited in Crang 2000, p. 137). According to de Certeau (cited in Crang, 2000), such people who are disoriented and cut loose from the delineating or mollycoddling aspects of community may feel like they have:

> begun to wander everywhere in a space which is becoming at once more homogeneous and more extensive.... The system in which they move is *too vast* to be able to fix them in one place, but *too constraining* for them to ever be able to escape from it or go into exile elsewhere. There is [indeed] no longer an elsewhere (de Certeau, cited in Crang, 2000, p. 137, italics added)

except perhaps to seek inclusion and new-found confidence in places (social buttresses) like the IC and the (beloved) maps IC members get to behold from above.

In this way, the appropriation of these maps of bus routes winding through luxurious condominium after luxurious condominium qualifies and encapsulates the powerful 'viewpoint of planners', the 'panoptic disciplining of space' (Crang, 2000, p. 136) as well as the invention of borders and maintenance of the same (Rudolph, 2018). Space is disciplined in that what is reified, stop-by-stop, point-by-point, junction-by-junction on these maps are ultimately those middle to high-end condominiums which serve to regulate or regularize a particularized 'practice of traveling' (Crang, 2000, 138). This is not to go as far as de Certeau's (cited in Thrift, 2007, p. 78) rendition of bus (or train) travel where 'human bodies are able to be ordered' as 'the passengers are [held] immobile' while the vehicle is set in motion, in this case, along a predetermined and pre-imagined routing.

> Only a rationalized cell travels. A bubble of *panoptic* and *classifying* power, a module of imprisonment that makes possible *the production of an order*, a *closed and autonomous insularity* – that is what can traverse space and make itself *independent* of local roots. (de Certeau, 1984, p. 111, cited in Thrift, 2007, p. 78, italics added)

While de Certeau's description of bus travel is uncannily reminiscent of a particularized form of insularity, protectiveness, encapsulation or standoffishness (as the case may be) that evokes or invokes certain more selfish or claustrophobic aspects of *nihonjinron*'s strictures, bus travel itself, as will be seen, is allowed to be synecdochical of larger metaphorical orders of discipline. These orders of discipline are to be found within schooling and its associated forms of social regularization, including border and identity patrolling (see Rudolph, 2018).

As should be pointed out, the disciplining of space as is made possible through the strictly regulated point-to-point navigation of the bus from one condominium to another, becomes very real for the young commuters who have to be sitting inside the buses for a good 30 or 40 minutes, each way, daily. Space is disciplined in the interests of upholding preference and exclusivism despite the fact that a typical bus route would sometimes have to wind nonchalantly through blocks and blocks of those ubiquitous if sometimes dull-looking government-built tenements that line the streets of suburban Singapore. Yet expatriates, generally or as a rule, are not accommodated by their companies in such forms of tenement housing (see Ben-Ari, 2006) which are usually the preserve of their mostly working-class dwellers. Clammer's (2000) reference to 'hierarchical standards of social ranking' is very much part of Japanese 'bourgeois capitalism' and the 'conservative mercantile class' it supports (p. 216). The maintenance of social ranking suggests the need for particularized spatial practices aimed at making sure that much-valued expatriate employees are socially distinguished and spatially distanced from the throngs of Singaporean humanity (see Thang et al., 2006). Indeed, if new or potential students of IB need to utilize the school bus service, their parents must sign and ink rental contracts that give them residential status in one of these well-placed condominiums or at least (or worst) be within walking distance of one of the condominium pickup points. These habituated practices of space help to reify a particularized form of schooling almost inseparably associated with being afforded a condominium lifestyle.

Recalling earlier discussion on parents working in Singapore on non-expatriate contracts, parents like Parent P and Parent R, too, are obliged to factor in the cost of rental in a suitably located condominium development for reasons to do with accessibility to a bus pick-up point. In Parent R's case, the location of the nearest pick-up point happened to be some 800 meters away. In such instances, both child and accompanying parent would have to plan carefully for the time it takes to walk to and from the pick-up points. One outcome of the proximity of different favored condominium clusters is that the children going to school in the same buses get to learn alongside friends in the same or neighboring classrooms. The same children also interact, swim and play in the same swimming pools, train with the same (usually Japanese) swim or tennis coaches, and attend the same birthday parties. Near enough to these condominium clusters too are businesses and services catered to the preferences of the Japanese community – specialist supermarkets, butchers, hairstylists, spas, cinemas, coffee joints, ballet, music and cram schools, helping to verify Clammer's (2000) observation that in capitalist societies, 'what is fashionable, consumable, healthy, and appropriate is largely constructed by the capitalist system itself and changes as that system itself evolves and expands' (p. 213). Such can be the socially and culturally situated ramifications of the disciplining and the performing of space (Crang, 2000; Thrift, 2007; Gulson, 2007), while particularized (bourgeois) subjectivities and identities are similarly instilled and reinforced: 'Japanese capitalism itself has its own distinctive features [and] so do the subjectivities it shapes' (Clammer, 2000, p. 215).

To be sure, the disciplining of space in such a patterned and habituating manner is an outcome of larger tendencies to form and congregate in enclaves when faced with the challenge of having to adapt in unfamiliar territory (Ben-Ari, 2006). Congregating in such enclaves would be one way of leaving Japan without actually leaving its centripetalizing spheres of social and emotional influence (apron strings). Ben-Ari (2006) notes that Japanese families tend to be concentrated in 'three or four particular residential areas around the island which tend to be the more well-to-do areas of Singapore (usually upper-middle class precincts)' (p. 231). While it is recognized that 'proximity to the Japanese educational establishments' is an important factor in the choice of a suitable condominium for Japanese families, it seems relevant to the above discussion that 'the network of routes of school buses further contributes to the reproduction of the system', one in which space is marked out for purposes of differential exclusivity (p. 231). Not unexpectedly, among expatriates in Singapore, it is the Japanese who 'tend to be the most segregated high-skill group' (p. 231). Schooling, as can be seen, is one complicit factor in such segregatory delineations and designations of space.

Preparing students for the homeland: the question of (in)tolerance of diversity

ID's existence and the activities it organizes are a reminder of the way in which erstwhile unchallenged forms of 'regimentation and control of dominant national languages', in this case, Japanese, as well as the rigidities and hegemonies thereof (Duchene, et al., 2013, p. 8), can be destabilized by situations in which a wider world of multilingual possibilities would influence the languaging habits of a younger or more mobile generation. In multilingual and multicultural Singapore, ID's curriculum and its rationale function as a means or tool for the promotion of ties with the homeland culture, ostensibly as a project of Japan, Inc. (see Reischauer, 1988). In so fulfilling the rationale for its existence, ID and its overseers are in full awareness of the fact that geographical relocation has its own way of 'insert[ing] individuals into particular symbolic spaces which reinforce and give legitimacy, or the opposite, to both forms of language and those who speak them' (Duchene et al., 2013, p. 11), thereby justifying the need for intervention where matters to do with the maintenance of the Japanese language, among the young, are concerned.

In a certain sense, ID would not be unlike the ubiquitous 'Chung Wah' societies which teach Cantonese, Mandarin, Kung Fu or lion dance to children of Chinese descent (and other interested comers) in big and small cities in Britain, the United States, Canada or Australia. Cultural activities including training in calligraphy are provided as part of inculcating children with an understanding of desirable qualities like patience, temperance, obedience and coordination. However, the Japanese case as played out in ID may be somewhat more ideological. Considering an observation in Hashimoto (2013) regarding the felt need for Japanese children who have grown up in foreign locations and schooled in foreign systems to be reacquainted with Japanese culture, such a process stems from the feeling that such children are likely to be 'treated as Others' if they are not so reacquainted (p. 29; see further discussion in Chapter 7). Arguably then, an ostensible reason for ID's existence is for it to spearhead 'attempts … to "de-Other" them' through transitioning experiences in classes and programs provided by organizations such as itself.

Commenting on changes in Japanese school culture, Okano (2009) notes that there has been what she describes as 'an increasing *tolerance* towards the *diverse backgrounds* that students bring to school' (p. 106, italics added). In relation to the call for this sort of 'tolerance', Okano (2009) discusses the matter of 'Japanese families returning from lengthy postings overseas' as an issue which calls to mind the question of diversity (p. 106). Returning Japanese families are treated or regarded as the cause for the creation of 'special transition classes catering for their [children's] Japanese language needs and "cultural adaptation"' (p. 106). What is considered '[a]ccommodation of diversity' in Okano (2009, p. 106) seems extremely ironic in that such so-called 'accommodation' is collocated with the notion of tolerance, as if both of these ideas might perforce be collocated vis-à-vis Japanese returnees. Paradoxically, the need for the special transition classes that Okano (2009) refers to is perhaps more suggestive of a lack of tolerance for diversity, than a big-hearted way of accepting its growing presence. These transition classes, or in the present case, the work of institutions like ID, may ultimately be more of a homage or deference to conformity. In discussions of accommodation and diversity, the assumption that in Japanese schools, 'all students are "Japanese", speak Japanese as their mother tongue, and have been socialized in mainstream Japanese lifestyles' (Okano, 2009, p. 106) while remaining difficult to change or dislodge, speaks ironically of the persistence of underlying forms of intolerance. The very attempt to compensate for diversity among students who may not be proficient in Japanese, betrays an underlying general intolerance for precisely the same. Thus, insofar as institutions like ID exist as halfway houses to ameliorate an unacceptable or intolerable situation, their very existence attests to the possible exclusion of Japanese young people who have spent the best or the happiest of their growing years elsewhere.

IA, IB, IC and ID: producing subjective identities of privilege and exclusivism

Singapore may prove veritably and verifiably to be an offshore base for the nurture and engenderment of a future generation of well-schooled Japanese elites. IB and its sister institutions are the command centers where the offspring of the best and cleverest of parents are gathered for the discernable or evident purpose of having them educated in the *Japanese* way, in an overseas cosmopolitan location. Where IA, IB, IC and ID are concerned, their presence makes possible the sort of performativity which lends itself readily to the enactment, rehearsal, sedimentation and maintenance of Japaneseness, in a faraway location. It may be fairly said, too, that all four institutions are involved and therefore agentive not only in the production and perpetuation of privileged identities among Japanese expatriates and their offspring, complete with the 'cans', 'shoulds' and 'ares' of such coveted identities (Rudolph, 2018; Rudolph et al., 2018), but also in the projection and representation of Japan itself as a successful and benignly powerful benefactor nation. For this to happen, power as it only can be cultivated through an essentialization of discourses must take effect alongside the invention and perpetuation of essentialized borders of place, identity and understanding (Rudolph, 2018). Such forms of essentialization, as noted by Rudolph (2018), are revealed in constructions of binaries that reductively typify inside-outside, us-them, pure-impure, relations.

In any of such instances too, one must not fail to consider an observation made in McVeigh (2006) which draws attention to the fact that Japanese institutions have to be recognized not only for their external face (or façade) but also for their (less obvious) internal face. According to McVeigh (2006), the upkeep and (high) maintenance of an external face calls for tremendous amounts of labor or internal arrangements behind the scenes. The laboriousness of maintaining an outward façade may be one reason why a Japanese institution might come across as being impermeable, resistant or slow to change: '[i]n order to generate fronts, a tremendous amount of informal labor is required within an institution' (McVeigh, 2006, p. 111). Apart from repeated attendance at meetings, these forms of labor 'may involve keeping secrets, maintaining confidentiality, guarding restricted areas, and in general controlling what is usually not displayed to outsiders' (p. 111). Anything which may be regarded as an external perturbation or disturbance to any of these controls may be reacted to as a threat – against the very façades themselves (see Goosseff, 2010). What Orientalists of yesteryear (see Said, 1978), might have wanted to describe as inscrutability on the part of Japanese individual or institutional behaviors might now be understood in a plainer way, as a matter of the need to be adequately (window-)dressed for non-Japanese eyes.

Notwithstanding the involvedness of such efforts at window-dressing, the investments of energies necessary for such laborious activity would be highly superfluous without the co-operation (or co-optation) of Singapore's part as the real-life location for such depictions of Japaneseness to be so realistically enacted. If not for Singapore and the way it is autopoietically but yet fertilely mapped out in the Japanese imagination, the particularized realizations of the types of schooling described in this chapter would be all but impossible to achieve. Neither would have been the writing of this chapter.

References

Appadurai, A. (1990a). Disjuncture and difference in the global cultural economy. *Theory, Culture and Society*, 7, 295–310. https://doi.org/10.1177%2F026327690007002017

Atkinson, D., Churchill, E., Nishino, T., & Okada, H. (2007). Alignment and interaction in a sociocognitive approach to second language acquisition. *The Modern Language Journal*, 91(2), 169–188. https://doi.org/10.1111/j.1540-4781.2007.00539.x

Bamberg, M. (2005). Narrative discourse and identities. In J. C. Meisters, T. Kindt, W. Schernus, & M. Stein (Eds.), *Narratology beyond literary criticism: mediality, disciplinarity* (pp. 213–237). Berlin: Walter de Gruyter.

Barkhuizen, G. (2011). Narrative knowledging in TESOL. *TESOL Quarterly*, 45(3), 391–414. https://doi.org/10.5054/tq.2011.261888

Befu, H. (2009). Concepts of Japan, Japanese culture and the Japanese. In Y. Sugimoto (Ed.), *The Cambridge companion to modern Japanese culture* (pp. 21–37). Cambridge: Cambridge University Press.

Ben-Ari, E. (2006). The culture of Japanese business in Singapore. In Y. H. Tsu (Ed.), *Japan and Singapore: a multidisciplinary approach* (pp. 219–239). Singapore: McGraw Hill Education.

Breckenridge, Y., & Erling, E. (2011). The native speaker English teacher and the politics of globalization in Japan. In P. Seargeant (Ed.), *English in Japan in the era of globalization* (pp. 80–100). Houndmills: Palgrave Macmillan.

Clammer, J. (2000). Received dreams: consumer capitalism, social process, and the management of the emotions in contemporary Japan. In J. S. Eases, T. Gill & H. Befu (Ed.), *Globalization and social change in contemporary Japan* (pp. 203–223). Melbourne: Transpacific.

Crang, M (2000). Relics, places and unwritten geographies in the work of Michel de Certeau. In M. Crang & N. Thrift (Eds.), *Thinking space* (pp. 136–153). London: Routledge.

Connelly, F. M., & Clandinin, D. J. (1990). Stories of experience and narrative inquiry. *Educational Researcher*, 19(5), 2–14. https://doi.org/10.3102%2F0013189X019005002

Dale, J., & Hyslop-Margison, E. (2010). *Paulo Freire: teaching for freedom and transformation*. Dordrecht: Springer.

Darvin, R., & Norton, B. (2015). Identity and a model of investment in applied linguistics. *Annual Review of Applied Linguistics*, 35, 35–56. https://doi.org/10.1017/S0267190514000191

De Certeau, M. (1984). *The practice of everyday life* [translated by S. Rendall]. Berkeley: University of California.

Duchene, A., Moyer, M., & Roberts, C. (2013). Introduction: recasting institutions and work in multilingual and transnational spaces. In A. Duchene, M. Moyer & C. Roberts (Eds.), *Language, migration and social inequalities: a critical sociolinguistic perspective on institutions and work* (pp. 1–21). Bristol: Multilingual Matters.

Ezrati, M. (1999). *Kawari: How Japan's economic and cultural transformation will alter the balance of power among nations*. Reading, MA: Perseus.

Flory, M., & Iglesias, O. (2010). Once upon a time: the role of rhetoric and narratives in management research and practice. *Journal of Organization Change Management*, 23(2), 113–119. https://doi.org/10.1108/09534811011031274.

Freire, P. (1985). *The politics of education: culture, power, and liberation*. Westport, CT: Bergin and Garvey.

Freire, P. (2000). *Pedagogy of the oppressed* (30th anniversary edition). New York: Bloomsbury.

Goosseff, K. A. (2010). Autopoiesis and meaning: a biological approach to Bakhtin's superaddressee. *Journal of Organizational Change Management*, 23(2), 145–151. https://doi.org/10.1108/09534811011031319

Goosseff, K. A. (2014). Only narratives can reflect the experience of objectivity: effective persuasion. *Journal of Organisational Change Management*, 27(5), 703–709. https://doi.org/10.1108/JOCM-09-2014-0167

Gray, A. (2002). *Research practice for cultural studies: ethnographic methods and lived cultures*. London: Sage.

Gulson, K. N. (2007). Mobilizing space discourses: politics and educational policy change. In K. N. Gulson & C. Symes (Eds.), *Spatial theories of education: policy and geography matters* (pp. 37–56). New York: Routledge.

Hall, I. (1997). *Cartels of the mind: Japan's intellectual closed shop*. New York: W. W. Norton.

Hashimoto, K. (2000). 'Internationalization is Japanization': Japan's foreign language education and national identity. *Journal of Intercultural Studies*, 21(1), 39–51. https://doi.org/10.1080/07256860050000786

Hashimoto, K. (2007). Japan's language policy and the 'Lost Decade'. In A. B. M. Tsui and J. W. Tollefson (Eds.), *Language policy, culture, and identity in Asian contexts* (pp. 25–36). Mahwah, New Jersey: Lawrence Erlbaum.

Hashimoto, K. (2013). 'English-only', but not a medium-of-instruction policy: the Japanese way of internationalising education for both domestic and overseas students. *Current Issues in Language Planning*, 14(1), 16–33. doi:10.1080/14664208.2013.789956

Iino, M., & Murata, K. (2016). Dynamics of ELF communication in an English-medium academic context in Japan: from EFL learners to ELF users. In K. Murata (Ed.), *Exploring ELF in Japanese academic and business contexts: conceptualization, research and pedagogic implications* (pp. 111–131). London: Routledge.

Ishikawa, M. (2011). Redefining internationalization in higher education: *Global 30* and the making of global universities. In D. B. Willis & J. Rappleye (Eds.), *Reimagining Japanese education: borders, transfers, circulations, and the comparative* (pp. 193–223). Oxford: Symposium.

Kubota, R. (2002). The impact of globalization on language teaching in Japan. In D. Block & D. Cameron (Eds.), *Globalization and language teaching* (pp. 13–28). London: Routledge.

Kubota, R. (2011). Learning a foreign language as leisure and consumption: enjoyment, desire, and the business of eikaiwa . *International Journal of Bilingual Education and Bilingualism*, 14(4), 473–488. https://doi.org/10.1080/13670050.2011.573069

Kubota, R., & Fujimoto, D. (2013). Racialized native speakers: voices of Japanese American English language professionals. In S. A. Houghton & D. J. Rivers (Eds.), *Native speakerism in foreign language education: intergroup dynamics in Japan* (pp. 196–206). Clevedon: Multilingual Matters.

McVeigh, B. (2002a). *Japanese higher education as myth*. New York: M. E. Sharpe.

McVeigh, B. (2002b). *Aisatsu*: ritualized politeness as sociopolitical and economic management in Japan. In R. T. Donahue (Ed.), *Exploring Japaneseness on Japanese enactments of culture and consciousness* (pp. 121–145). Westport, CT: Ablex.

McVeigh, B. (2006). *The state bearing gifts: deception and disaffection in Japanese higher education*. Lanham: Lexington Books.

Norton, B., & Early, M. (2011). Researcher identity, narrative inquiry, and language teaching research. *TESOL Quarterly*, 45(3), 415–439. https://doi.org/10.5054/tq.2011.261161

Okano, K. (2009). School culture. In Y. Sugimoto (Ed.), *The Cambridge companion to modern Japanese culture* (pp. 92–112). Cambridge: Cambridge University Press.
Pierce, B. N. (1995). Social identity, investment, and language learning. *TESOL Quarterly*, 29(1), 9–31. https://doi.org/10.2307/3587803
Reischauer, E. (1988). *The Japanese today: change and continuity*. Cambridge, Massachusetts: Harvard University Press.
Rivers, D. J. (2010). Ideologies of internationalization and the treatment of diversity within Japanese higher education. *Journal of Higher Education Policy and Management*, 32(5), 441–454. https://doi.org/10.1080/1360080X.2010.511117
Rivers, D. J. (2013). Institutionalized native-speakerism: voices of dissent and acts of resistance. In S. A. Houghton & D. J. Rivers (Eds.), *Native-Speakerism in foreign language education: intergroup dynamics in Japan* (pp. 75–91). Clevedon: Multilingual Matters.
Rivers, D. J. (2015). The authorities of autonomy and English-only: serving whose interests? In D. J. Rivers (Ed.), *Resistance to the known: counter-conduct in language education* (pp. 94–118). Houndmills: Palgrave Macmillan.
Rivers, D. J. (2019). Walking on glass: reconciling experience and expectation within Japan. *Journal of Language, Identity and Education*, 18(6), 377–388. https://doi.org/10.1080/15348458.2019.1674149
Rudolph, N. (2016). Negotiating borders of being and becoming in and beyond the English language teaching classroom: two university student narratives from Japan. *Asian Englishes*, 18(1), 2–18. https://doi.org/10.1080/13488678.2015.1132110
Rudolph, N., Yazan, B., & Rudolph, J. (2018). Negotiating 'ares,' 'cans,' and 'shoulds' of being and becoming in English language teaching: two teacher accounts from one Japanese university. *Asian Englishes*, 21(1), 22–37. doi:10.1080/13488678.2018.1471639
Rudolph, N. (2018). Education for glocal interaction beyond essentialization and idealization: classroom explorations and negotiations. In A. F. Selvi & N. Rudolph (Eds.), *Conceptual shifts and contextualized practices in education for glocal interaction: issues and implications* (pp. 147–174). Singapore: Springer.
Said, E. W. (1978). *Orientalism*. New York: Random House.
Seargeant, P. (2009). *The idea of English in Japan: ideology and the evolution of a global language*. Bristol: Multilingual Matters.
SkillsFutures Singapore (n.d.). Information for PEIs and students: private education institutions in Singapore. Retrieved from www.ssg.gov.sg/cpe/peis.html on 10 April, 2017.
Thang, L. L., MacLachlan, E., & Goda, M. (2006). Japanese women working in Singapore. In Y. H. Tsu (Ed.), *Japan and Singapore: a multidisciplinary approach* (pp. 186–218). Singapore: McGraw Hill Education.
Thrift, N. (2007). *Non-representational theory: space, politics, affect*. London: Routledge.
Toh, G. (2012). Having English as a resource for multicultural understanding: exploring possibilities in Japanese ELT. *Journal of Multilingual and Multicultural Development*, 33(3), 301–311. https://doi.org/10.1080/01434632.2012.655248
Toh, G. (2013a). Scrutinizing the native speaker as referent, entity and project. In S. A. Houghton & D. J. Rivers (Eds.), *Native-Speakerism in foreign language education: intergroup dynamics in Japan* (pp. 183–195). Clevedon: Multilingual Matters.
Toh, G. (2013b). Where realities confront ideals: the personal, professional, philosophical and political in the teaching of academic English in a Japanese setting. *Policy Futures in Education*, 11(5), 589–605. https://doi.org/10.2304%2Fpfie.2013.11.5.589
Toh, G. (2013c). Locality, re-localization, structure-to-structure localism and the TOEIC test: Implications for English language education at tertiary level in Japan.

In R. S. Webster & S. A. Stolz (Eds.), *Measuring up in education* (pp. 251–226). Melbourne: Philosophy of Education Society of Australasia.

Toh, G. (2014a). English for content instruction in a Japanese higher education setting: Examining challenges, contradictions and anomalies. *Language and Education*, 28 (4), 299–318. https://doi.org/10.1080/09500782.2013.857348

Toh, G. (2014b). The cosmetics of teaching English as an international language in Japan: critical reflection. In R. Marlina & R. Giri (Eds.), *The pedagogy of English as an international language: perspectives from scholars, teachers, and students* (pp. 175–188). London: Springer International.

Toh, G. (2015a). 'A tale of two programs': interrogating 'open(closed)ness' and 'cultural diversity' through critical observations of two Japanese University English language programs. *Policy Futures in Education*, 13(7), 900–916. https://doi.org/10.1177%2F1478210315578064

Toh, G. (2015b). Exposing and dialogizing racism through counter-storytelling and critical pedagogy in a Japanese EAP situation. *Power and Education*, 7(2), 169–180. https://doi.org/10.1177%2F1757743815586519

Toh, G. (2015c). Teaching English for academic purposes in a Japanese setting: problematizing and dialogizing essentialist constructions of language pedagogy, culture and identity. In M. A. Peters & T. Besley (Eds.), *Paulo Freire: the global legacy* (pp. 335–350). New York: Peter Lang.

Toh, G. (2015d). Dialogizing 'the known': experience of English teaching in Japan through an assay of derivatives as a dominant motif. In D. J. Rivers (Ed.), *Resistance to the known: counter-conduct in language education* (pp. 144–167). Houndmills: Palgrave-Macmillan.

Toh, G. (2016a). *English as medium of instruction in Japanese higher education: Presumption, mirage or bluff?*Houndmills: Palgrave-Macmillan.

Toh, G. (2016b). Doing justice to an English as a lingua franca paradigm. *Journal of English as a Lingua Franca*, 5(2), 355–367. https://doi.org/10.1515/jelf-2016-0024

Toh, G. (2019). *Effecting change in English teaching: exposing collaborators and culprits in Japan*. London: Palgrave Macmillan.

Toh, G. (2020). Foreword. In J. P. N. Bradley & D. Kennedy (Eds.), *Engaged pedagogy in the Japanese university* (pp. ix–xvii). Leiden: Brill Sense.

Williams, G. (2010). *The knowledge economy, language and culture*. Bristol: Multilingual Matters.

Yamagami, M., & Tollefson, J. (2011). Elite discourses of globalization in Japan: the role of English. In P. Seargeant (Ed.), *English in Japan in an era of globalization* (pp. 15–37). Houndmills: Palgrave Macmillan.

6 Japanese engagements with English overseas as a cultural politics of control

Given the influence of institutional forces, which, as has surely been witnessed in the last chapter, bear powerfully upon the lives of Singapore's Japanese residents, the question may be asked about what impact these powerful influences might in turn have on the way in which Japanese students in Singapore would be learning a foreign language like English. This chapter therefore sets out to further examine ideological enactments of Japaneseness in Japanese schooling in Singapore, with particular regard to the treatment, appropriation and teaching of English. On the matter of the way English is appropriated and taught, it will become increasingly apparent as the discussion unfolds that English is treated more as a school subject and not so much as a lingua franca useful for enabling one to make meaningful, as opposed to superficial, connections with Singaporean society. The curriculum itself, as will be seen, is one that is heavily dependent on textbooks produced by publishers in traditional native English-speaking locations, spatially, geographically and culturally remote as they are from present-day Singapore. English, in this sense, is taught very much as a language that allows it to continue to be regarded as foreign (and therefore distant, exogenous, extraneous, alien, non-relevant). Learners are in turn ideologically, subjectively and practically, positioned as speakers of 'other' languages (see Toh, 2019, for a critique of the Japanese practice of teaching English to students positioned as speakers of 'other' languages).

Such a treatment of English and English teaching is to be set against the Singaporean backdrop where English is the principal and dominant language of business, politics and education. Singapore schools, polytechnics, vocational and tertiary institutions teach and operate entirely in the English medium, while Singapore's law courts hear and deliberate their cases in the language of their erstwhile colonial overseers (see Bolton & Botha, 2017). In Japan, English is hardly used as a language of communication except in niche industries such as tourism and hospitality. Apart from people associated with these niche industries, it has been observed that the only other notable beneficiaries of English ability are actually middle- and upper-middle class individuals with work linked to international concerns (see Stewart & Miyahara, 2011, and later section of this chapter on English's elitist associations). In addition, if looked upon as a subject of study (as opposed to being a language or still less a lingua franca) mostly to be associated with assessment for the passing of qualifying tests or examinations (Toh, 2016), one would have little choice but to assent to the fact that 'education becomes a key mediating factor in the [very] existence of the language' in the Japanese psyche, the acquisition of which would 'most usually [be] the product of formal education' (Seargeant, 2009, p. 154). Such a reality with regard to English is a reminder that formal education and its ideological loadings, in the present case vis-à-vis an overseas Japanese community, are 'pre-eminent sites for the regulation of language and linguistic behavior', the outcomes of which invariably 'become disseminated into the social environment' (Seargeant, 2009, p. 155). It is therefore my contention in this chapter and the next that education and its ideological loadings, while commissioning and mediating the teaching and learning of English in the elementary school in question, are crucial factors influencing the form and manner in which the latter is shaped and permitted to take place. If it can be said here, English teaching, idiomatically speaking, is kept on a tight leash.

Explanation of the idiomatically and ideologically short leash

In terms of prevailing discourses and the question of overriding and underlying ideologies, the discussion that follows in this section will focus its attention on *three* ideological strands that are subtly dissimulated within the structures and practices of the operations of IB, the Japanese elementary school where the scene is set. The first strand relates to the fact that the school concerned educates Japanese children of parents (actually mostly fathers – see Ben-Ari, 2006; Thang et al., 2006), the vast majority of whom are employed by Japanese businesses and multinational corporations, attesting to the fact that the operations and ideologies powering Japan, Inc. are a major reason for the school's very (and continued) existence. The Chairperson (Chairman) of the school notes in his message on the school's website that student numbers reflect a natural decrease in times of economic downturn when there is less of a need for Japanese management staff to be stationed in Singapore. The second ideological strand relates to the fact that an education based entirely on the Japanese state curriculum complete with teachers seconded from Japanese state schools (whereas there is no lack of state, private and international schooling in Singapore – see Chapter 3) is suggestive of (or testimony to) the statist nationalistic ideologies that need ostensibly to be reaffirmed among a younger generation. Such reaffirmation is in turn constituted as a way of counteracting the perceived un-Japanese influences of those very forces of globalization and mercantilism that, in the first place, make it necessary for such families to relocate outside of Japan. The third strand relates to the teaching and learning of English and how, alongside the mercantile and mercenary motivations of the first and the nationalistic motivations of the second, the teaching of English is given to particularized ideological outworkings to be seen in: (1) enactments of curricular, pedagogical and administrative practices, and their influence on (2) identity positionings and investments among teachers and learners.

The teaching and learning of English in, IB, the elementary school concerned

The way English teaching is carried out, as mentioned, is reminiscent of its treatment as an undertaking particular to TEFL (Teaching English as a Foreign Language) and TESOL (Teaching English to Speakers of Other Languages) professional conceptualizations (see Toh, 2019, for a detailed critique of both within a Japanese milieu). English lessons are conducted using set texts like the Oxford *Family and Friends* series alongside the ubiquity of their accompanying workbooks. These workbooks are distinguishable by the presence of equally ubiquitous but reductionist grammar and vocabulary exercises. The textbooks, as might be expected of merchandise produced for profit, are not cheap items. While the textbooks for the taught-in-Japanese subjects (mathematics, social studies etc.) do not have to be purchased, English textbooks have to be paid for separately in cash.

In terms of the cultural content that students are exposed to in English class, characterizations ('caricaturizations') of people and places in the chapters of *Family and Friends* repeatedly display culturalist tendencies within 'one culture–one country' (Horii, 2015, p. 155) representations. Whether it is the children or the type of food they are forever supposed to be eating as a matter of invariable 'cultural' habit, the textbook content naturalizes simplistic categorizations reifying 'the ideology of one culture in one country', which Horii (2015, p. 155) finds objectionable in her observations of another textbook, *Eigo Nooto* [*English Notebook*] produced in Japan. A domestically produced textbook used for *gaikokugo katsudou* [foreign language activities], *Eigo Nooto* is used in elementary schools in Japan (see critique in Chapter 7). Further discussion on the nature of the foreign language activities conducted as part of *gaikokugo katsudo* can be found in the commentary in the next section.

Textbooks, cultural content and the workings of ideology

The matter of textbooks and their cultural and ideological content has been studied and critiqued by educators writing in the area of critical literacies and critical pedagogy (Toh, 2001; 2006; Risager, 2011; 2018; Xiong & Qian, 2012; Risager & Chapelle, 2013; Horii, 2015; Davidson & Liu, 2018; also see Freire, 2014). These studies, which contain detailed commentaries on the ways in which people, places and cultures are featured and represented in materials used for classroom teaching, provide a means of understanding the manner in which ideology and power relations are reflected in portrayals of the same. Concerning the matter of imbalanced or stereotyped portrayals of people, places and cultures, such imbalanced cultural representations are noted to have 'negative educational consequences including … missed opportunities to deepen intercultural awareness' apart from risking 'the perpetuation of stereotypes' (Davidson & Liu, 2018, p. 4). If one considers the fact that English is (rightly or wrongly) increasingly discussed in its relations to meanings and responsibilities of global citizenship, as is done in Davidson & Liu (2018), examining ways in which English 'language textbooks encourage values of global citizenship' is one way of seeking to 'confirm the centrality of intercultural awareness to a well-founded education' (p. 3). Examining the cultural content of a series of English elementary school textbooks, *Hi Friends!*, published in Tokyo by Shoseki Publishers, and used mandatorily in elementary schools across the nation, Davidson and Liu (2018) discover 'a substantial imbalance between Japanese and non-Japanese cultural representation' with Japanese culture 'represented more often than any other country' (p. 8). This latter finding is offered as a reason for the fact that the content was 'lack[ing in] cultural diversity and depth', by dint of the 'paucity of non-Japanese items' (p. 12).

For Freire (2014), the inclusion or exclusion of textbook content represents an exercise of choice, which moreover constitutes a 'fundamental problem – a problem of political nature, and colored by ideological hues', implying also that questions of 'who chooses the content and in behalf of which persons' (sic) are both important considerations of a highly curricular nature (p. 100). With regard to evaluations or analyses of textbook content for the teaching of language, an observation highlighted in Risager (2006, p. 1) is relevant in that it problematizes for consideration what she regards as over-simplified connections that are made between language and culture. Risager (2006, p. 1) identifies in her critique the problem of 'an unambiguous focusing on the close relationship between language and culture, one that has a tendency to imply a simple identification of language and culture'. Such simple identification gives rise to the hackneyed use of clichéd mottoes like 'language and culture are inseparable' or 'language is culture and culture is language' (p. 1).

In this vein, *Family and Friends* presents a culturally stilted and stereotyped textbook world that positions learners, in this instance, as outsiders gazing into this world as if they had little or no part in it. Babies, for example, in a textbook of such culturalist nature, are born into the world with blue eyes. In typical one-country one-culture (in this case, one-country one-diet) fashion, a typical white English-speaking child subsists on a diet of fish, peas, fries and cheese, while lemon ice cream is eaten for dessert. Pete from Scotland is portrayed as having a bowl of cereal with milk before eating his toast topped with butter. Pete, moreover, enjoys having many types of cereals at home, but his favorite is corn flakes. Abd Allah from Egypt eats *fuul* and flat bread for breakfast. *Fuul*, which contains mashed beans, is consumed with olive oil and flat bread by all his fellow Egyptians. As for sport, the first world tennis championship was held in 1877 at Wimbledon in the United Kingdom while further back in history, King Henry XIII (complete with portrait captioned), who built an indoor tennis court in one of his favorite palaces, was one of the game's earlier players, alongside a regalia of notable enthusiasts like the many kings of Europe. Nearer the present, Wimbledon tennis was first televised in 1937 (*Family and Friends* 4).

Another series, a later introduction to IB and competitor to the Oxford series, is Cambridge University Press's *Super Minds*, which is retailed at twice the price of the Oxford series. The style of bantering and counter-bantering in the *wishidishing* game (*Super Minds* 5) as with other featured conversations, stilted as they are, comes across as insularly native speakerist in idiom, if or when they make some sense:

> Sue: Do you want to go through the gate too?
> Ben: Let's follow the friends till the story ends!
> (Cambridge *Super Minds* 5, p. 6)

Used for the teaching and learning of English in Singapore, the textbook in use features students doing geography projects in faraway Mexico. The frightening instance of an earthquake is one that shakes equally distant London, where a suburban character by the name of Caroline from Wimbledon (last seen featured for its tennis in *Family and Friends*) is heard exclaiming how terribly scary the experience was for her. In the chapter on the theme of storytelling, students are told that William Shakespeare is considered by a good many to be the greatest writer in the English language whose plays were performed in the renowned Globe Theatre. The vocabulary section of the same unit somewhat anachronistically features words like lute, candles, swords, wigs, costumes, masks, tights. As for music and song, students are told that singers in a romantic ballad are a man and a woman who sing about bygone times good and bad, while sea shanties played on accordions and tin whistles were sung by seafaring sailors bored with hard work and endless days at sea. In the unit on seas and oceans, students are asked to locate the Black Sea, the Aral Sea, the Sea of Azov, the Caspian Sea and the Mediterranean Sea. The nearest to any mention of Japan at all is with reference to the Mariana Trench, the earth's deepest point which lies in an area of deep ocean to the south of Japan and the east of the Philippines.

In another unit discussing the rainforest in *Super Minds* 5, three adventuresome time-travelling children, Alex, Phoebe and Patrick visit the Amazon jungle and encounter a frightening experience when they hear noises from up in the trees. As they start climbing one tree, the terrible noise gets even louder. It turns out that the hairy black arms and tail they see belongs to a howler monkey, the same which was responsible for the frightening din. After this supposedly (or extremely) terrifying experience, the children meet a man with a spear who takes them to a small village complete with huts. Two other men appear who lead them to the village chief. Alex gallantly gives a present to the chief (actually, his pen knife) and the chief becomes ever so pleased that he offers the children delicious food cooked in fire. In similar vein, European travelers to North America in the 15th century mistakenly thought that they were in India and called the first people they met Indians. These seafaring Europeans did not like the many different tribes of Indians 'because they were very different from the Europeans' (*Super Minds* 5, p. 64). In the ensuing fighting, many people lost their lives. These days, as readers are then told, American Indians can still be found living in North America. Some remain in areas of land called reservations, and continue to be proud of their history and traditions (*Super Minds* 5). In one exercise in this unit, the same manner of stereotyping and Othering is duly reinforced. Students are asked to think of examples of different places and how they thought the American Indians would 'describe these places' (p. 65). Offered as examples, London would be a 'place of many people', Paris would be a 'city with big tower' (sic), and Rio de Janeiro would be a 'place of beautiful beaches'.

In relation to the point made in Davidson and Liu (2018) about English being increasingly associated with the meanings and responsibilities of global citizenship, one may need to question the ways in which both of the abovementioned textbook series might qualify as classroom materials which promote values of global citizenship and the 'centrality of intercultural awareness [in] a well-founded education' (p. 3). While Shoseki's *Hi Friends!* may be glaringly lacking in cultural variety, particularly in non-Japanese content, representations of people and places in Oxford's *Family and Friends* and Cambridge's *Super Minds* reveal the sort of stereotyping that suggests a lack of depth (see Davidson & Liu, 2018) in albeit the portrayal of a spread of cultures. Moreover, as 'values indexed with English are closely related to the material in which it is used', or in this case, in the materials used to teach it (Hult, 2017, p. 271), the choice of textbooks in this regard reveals underpinnings that link English to being an extraneous, foreign or even rarified curricular ornamentation, rather than a language that Japanese learners can use uninhibitedly to express or represent themselves wholesomely. The next section elaborates on this fairly concerning matter.

Commentary on the teaching and learning of English in IB

The inclusion of a formal English curriculum from the very first year in elementary school is not common in public schools in Japan (see Horii, 2015). This uncommonness is itself worthy of further examination, alas if only it could be as straightforward (actually, simplistic) as reducing matters to teaching students to utter a few words of English. Such smatterings of English might then be used for talking with the Singaporean bus driver (in Singaporean parlance, the 'bus uncle') they see every school day, or for superficial contact with some fictive or faceless Singaporean or foreigner, of which there are many coming through Singapore's crossroads. But this is truly not the case.

The speakers of English in the abovementioned *wishidishing* game (*Super Minds* 5) are not remotely Singaporean, or even East or Southeast Asian, which is where IB is not incidentally located (but perhaps only physically – see discussion on Singapore as 'theme park'). Singaporeans, East or Southeast Asians are scarcely featured in either of the two textbooks, except for Huong, the lone Vietnamese girl who, like Abd Allah from Egypt, is singled out for the type of food she eats. Breakfast for Huong is typically noodles in soup and rice balls with beans, cooked lovingly by her grandmother (*Family and Friends* 4). Evidently, English teaching as it is carried out in this particular case of Japanese schooling in Singapore may as well be thought of as what Norton and Early

(2011) would call out as an act of doing self and other. This is truly a type of disinformation based on bald stereotypes, or what Blommaert (2003, p. 610) calls the availing of 'semiotic opportunity', which more cynically, is a case of semiotic opportunism. Within this 'semiotic opportunity' or opportunism is a very real element of an 'organizing and reorganizing [of] a sense of who [the learners really] are' (Pierce, 1995, p. 18), bearing in mind their total unlikeness to the English speakers and the other stereotyped characters in the textbooks they are made (or suffered) to learn from.

Hashimoto's (2000) critique of Japanese government policy on internationalization reveals that so-called internationalization may actually be viewed as another form of Japanization and that the learning of English is really part of an agenda towards the cultivation of a stronger national identity, in effect, the Japanization of Japanese English learners. Seargeant's (2009) concurrence with this observation is expressed in the form of 'an interesting paradox whereby promotion of a nationalist sentiment requires the embracing of a foreign language' (p. 79). Thus, the teaching of English to Japanese learners could well be considered as one way to reify and promote Japaneseness through its juxtapositioning with the Otherness represented by English, English speakers, as well as the hackneyed or motley array of stereotyped characters found populating English textbooks. Such forms of Othering may be part of a deliberate if resonantly autopoietic jettisoning of English from the core identity of Japan (Hashimoto, 2000). Such jettisoning is made possible because the foreignness and Otherness of the textbook characters are caused or made to function like a bait for Japanese readers to contemplate how manifestly different they are, thereby to create a measure of disidentification with the content and the language itself. If, according to Donahue (2002b), '[s]harp distinctions are often made between Japanese and foreign things' in order that perceived 'foreign elements can be placed at a psychologically safe distance' (p. 14), it is no wonder then that keeping English at proverbial arm's length (or at a psychologically safe distance) involves the use of hackneyed formulaic workbook exercises as well as wearisome materials that constantly reinforce the foreignness of English (Stewart & Miyahara, 2011; Toh, 2012).

In more amenable or less critically conscious contexts, there might be some chance that these expensively bought textbooks in question may turn out to be a 'suitable' fit for the teaching and learning of English. Yet for their use with young Japanese learners in a situation like the one being discussed, the sort of cultural and ideological content they present could well be a form of disinformation, a way of disinforming students of what globalization or humanization are really about, hence attracting the sort of critical and pedagogical questioning offered here. Risager (2006) is helpful in her observation that the relationship between language and culture may be less essentialist than textbook content students are exposed to seems to suggest. What, to Risager (2006, p. 2), is more truly representative of reality is 'that languages [actually] spread across cultures, and cultures spread across languages'. What could also be a more refined way of looking at the matter is that '[l]inguistic and cultural practices change and spread through [differential] social networks along partially different routes' (p. 2). The differential and partial nature of these routes and networks in turn prevails 'principally on the basis of [complex] transnational patterns of migration and markets' (p. 2). These transnational patterns would be familiar to seasoned and venturesome entrepreneurs like the Japanese discussed here. Regular or periodic movements of Japanese expatriate families are obliged to shadow these same patterns, their deep-rooted Japaneseness notwithstanding. It is therefore a little ironic or surprising that understandings of culture in textbooks used to nurture a next generation of venturesome Japanese entrepreneurs fail so unsubtly to support the same flexibilities, mobilities and open-mindedness.

Nonetheless, and not aside from the matter of content and its cultural and ideological implications, there remains the possibility that both textbook series might have been chosen for reasons to do with their excellent layout, visually engaging illustrations and glossy finishing, or more generally, for reasons best known only to the teachers and curriculum planners whose responsibility it is to adopt them for the students they are entrusted to educate. There are aspects of both series which portray life in all its generic, if mundane, materializations – eating, traveling, schooling, making friends, watching TV, visiting cousins and celebrating birthdays. In a certain wry sense, the truth remains that textbook writers, however they make their choices, invocations, representations or assemblages of content, have little or no influence on who might choose to use their textbooks, on whom, at what time, in what context, for what particular reasons or agendas, and in service (or deference) to what overriding or underlying hegemonies. Publishers' sales teams may have a little more of an influence on this score, even though the final decision to adopt any textbook lies with the very teachers tasked with the big challenge of making decisions on the curriculum. The point here is that textbook adoption is subject to teacher (and sometimes, administrator) decision: 'exercising professional judgment about what content to teach and what materials to use in doing so' do actually fall within the job description of educators (Hult, 2017, p. 271). In instances where, perhaps because of oversight, the decisions taken result in the adoption of textbooks that are contextually ill suited, or culturally, subjectively or ideologically marginalizing of students, the sometime glib attempts at making sweeping claims to 'possibilities for educational intervention' can turn out to be quite ludicrous. It may likely be the case that the very parties responsible for such oversight are the same ones called upon to intervene educationally (Pierce, 1995, p. 16) – which would be too much of an asking. Genuine intervention, if one takes seriously Iino and Murata's (2016) account of the laborious manner in which EFL students had to be retaught to have them thereafter empowered to become effective communicators in English, is one that takes both an enlightened resolve to help students out of their socio-cultural inhibitions and a willingness to think beyond the hackneyed paradigms that TEFL, TESOL (see Toh, 2019) and textbooks written after them, have to offer.

Elitist associations

Almost paradoxically, and despite (or perhaps precisely because of) its ideological associations with non-Japaneseness, the opportunity is made available for English to be used as a signal for a different form or regime of indexicality. Taking advantage of the fact that English is widely spoken in a non-Japanese cosmopolitan situation like Singapore, the new opportunity for semiosis is one which allows the school's English lessons to be used synecdochically as enactments of overseas living: living overseas means learning and speaking a semblance of English. Such a way of representing or instantiating an experience of overseas living is done without so much as having to admit what it could represent in terms of subtle privilege and social differentiation, especially to those who have to remain back home in Japan. As noted by Yamagami and Tollefson (2011), 'the major beneficiaries of English language ability in Japan are a relatively *small* number of middle- and upper-middle class individuals: employees in international companies, international organizations such as the United Nations, and some non-governmental organizations' or in this instance, their offspring (p. 32, italics added). So, while English continues to carry the weight of an alien non-Japanese identity for the Japanese, the elitist or otherwise richly symbolic aspect of having one's offspring learn the language from an early age is, at the same time, not to be missed or taken lightly. Neither should it be past notice that the teaching and learning of English within the walls of a Japanese institution must well be suggestive or indexical of its very claims to superior status, representing social meanings of privilege and differentiation.

Containment of diversity

Continuing from earlier discussion, Horii (2015) makes known an observation about the manner in which *gaikokugo katsudou* remains focused almost exclusively on English, while the more generalized meaning of foreign language activities as being rightly inclusive of other languages besides English seems to be conveniently overlooked. This type of oversight is elsewhere critiqued by Yamagami and Tollefson (2011). While the forces of globalization have obliged Japan to be more welcoming of foreigners into the country, whether as tourists or foreign workers and residents, this new-found 'openness' does not seem to extend to much of a recognition that these visitors or newcomers are not necessarily of the English-speaking kind. Foreign students coming to study in Japan come mostly from East Asian countries, with Chinese and Korean students accounting for the vast majority (Yamagami & Tollefson, 2011; Hashimoto, 2013), meaning too that plans for the globalization of education in the Japanese context should not be reduced to the simple 'matter of promoting the use of English' (Hashimoto, 2013, p. 27).

In the context of Singapore, curricular and classroom activities in IB which involve local Singaporean language varieties as well as translanguaging would qualify just as well as English to be included as *gaikokugo katsudo*. Just as relevantly, if one were to consider elementary and high schools in the Japanese homeland, Yamagami and Tollefson (2011) cite education ministry statistics which tellingly reveal that Portuguese, Chinese, Spanish and Filipino are some of the languages spoken or represented by non-Japanese students. English, while far from being the main language of these non-Japanese students, is nevertheless represented in official (albeit often elitist) discourse as the language of global opportunity. In the present case with IB, English's identification with social privilege plays into the hands (motivations) of astute parents who wish to capitalize on the school's elite status as an 'international' school situated in a major metropolis. The sole promotion of English is perhaps a clever strategy for containment, so that there is only the Japanese language with which the students can embed and entrench their Japaneseness and English against which they can juxtapose their Japaneseness. Any potential for greater possibilities for the promotion of diversity through languages other than English and through translanguaging opportunities may well be viewed as a threat (or nuisance) that will upset this simple juxtapositioning, and must therefore be contained and concealed within the same. Such containment and concealment would help ensure that narrower understandings of language, communication and identity would remain the order of the day. Communicative language teaching would only mean 'personal engagement with interlocutors from different cultures in one-on-one, one-at-a-time, face-to-face negotiations of difference' instead of being a means whereby new meanings and contacts can be made through '[the] surfing [of] diversity' (Kramsch, 2014, p. 302). Neither would it be possible or realistic to aim to engender the growth of 'multilingual individuals, sensitive to linguistic, cultural, and above all, semiotic diversity' within such a protective (or protectionist) ethos (p. 305). With the simplicity of this bespoken juxtapositioning safely and smugly in place, Japanese and non-Japanese, self and Other, elite and non-elite, expatriate and homebound (home-ridden), identity positionings can be maintained.

From simplicity in dichotomous juxtapositioning to a multiplicity of essentialisms

May (2003) draws attention to the pitfalls of what could be considered simplistic or acritical promotions of multiculturalism, which would in due course mutate or metamorphose into another form of racism. In such a development (or fomentation) of racism, 'race' as an all-too-common signifier is simply 'transmuted into [a] seemingly more acceptable discourse of "cultural differences"' (p. 202). Anglo-centric norms and essentialized representations of internationalization and multiculturalism in textbook content are duly reinforced by organized visits (those happy school excursions) to different 'cultural' sites in Singapore. The way in which these excursions are conducted is such that the children are put into tour coaches and led on guided tours of different local cultural sites. The left-unspoken effect of these guided tours is that the local Chinese population is made to come across as being reductively associated with Chinatown and its tourist attractions and with Buddhist or

Taoist temples where incense is burned and sacrifices offered piously to Chinese deities. The Indian community is then left to be associated with Little India and its Hindu temples and the Malay community with Friday prayers at mosques and with, what were once in history, authentic Malay kampongs. Kramsch's (2014, p. 307) observation that '[m]odernist pedagogies [tend] to restrict culture to customs and practices' comes across as having an element of truth in these cases. At the same time, such visits reinforce stereotyped understandings of race, religion and culture while normalizing what May (2003, p. 203) considers a 'naïve, static, and undifferentiated conception of cultural identity, and the allied notion of the incommensurability of cultures', which *nihonjinron*, not incidentally, also readily normalizes. For May (2003), such a fashion of naturalizing static 'group based identities appears irredeemably passé' (p. 203), as would be the manner in which 'totalizing narratives of ethnicity and nationalism' (p. 204) are liable to be used to remind the Japanese of how Japanese they are in the starkness of their difference from Singapore's Malay, Indian and Chinese populations. The 'contingent, the complex, and the contested aspects of identity formation' (May, 2003, p. 204) are left blissfully unrecognized and unexplored, almost as a matter of convenience, but reflecting what Kramsch (2014) considers an outmoded treatment of culture in foreign language education. While in foreign language education, culture 'used to mean mostly national culture, today … the link between one national language and one national culture has been significantly weakened' to the point of being unsustainable or untenable (Kramsch, 2014, p. 303).

Be this as it may, a school trip for IB's graduating class to one of Singapore's neighboring countries evinces the same sort of outmodedness and oversimplification. Besides visiting the usual places of religion and heritage, the tour actually includes a half-day homestay with a local family in a local house where students are supposed to learn about the ways different host families eat (durians, mangoes, rambutans and spicy food cooked in coconut juice, tamarind and prawn paste), play or pray. Prior to the start of the trip, the children are asked to learn basic words in the local language (see Horii (2015) on foreign language activities). These are useful words of politeness but learnt in truncated formulaic fashion and only for the fleeting superficialities of the occasion, suggesting the tokenism and exoticism of a whole exercise which serves to accentuate a sizeable (ideological, hence perspectival) chasm between host and hosted. It is in the planning and execution of such visits that a 'tourist's exoticized transactional approach', a 'totalizing tourist gaze on FL [foreign languages] and cultures' alongside an equally 'totalizing view of language as a formal symbolic system' are played out in the most affirming and conforming of ways (Kramsch, 2014, p. 306). All in all, 'essentialist racialized discourses are "disguised" by describing group differences principally in cultural and/or historical terms – ethnic terms, in effect', nearly all the time avoiding mentioning specifically the matter of race (May, 2003, p. 202). In activities of such a kind, there is evidence of 'an idealistic, naïve preoccupation with culture at the expense [or toward the blindsiding or obfuscation] of broader material and structural concerns', which are conveniently left unattended to (p. 200).

Hence and evidently, the sort of visits described above may not be promising indicators of cultural belief but strong, if (un)intended, reinforcers of cultural disbelief (see Holliday, 2013). Seargeant (2009) provides enlightening explanations of such a manner of culturalism in his description of what he calls a 'theme park' (*gakoku mura*) mentality, citing the example of the Murayama Shakespeare Country Club located in the small village of Murayama in Chiba Prefecture, one of a number of foreign theme parks created on Japanese soil. The park is described as having a formal garden in Elizabethan style, a farmyard, an orchard, a village green, a working windmill along with painstakingly replicated buildings in Stratford-upon-Avon at the time of Shakespeare, including his birthplace. Materials for these buildings are said to be imported from England and traditional methods of craftsmanship used to put them together (Seargeant, 2009).

Seargeant (2009) notes this *gaikoku mura*, 'despite the obvious international complexion' of the place, targets 'almost exclusively … Japanese visitors', the website being tellingly written in Japanese (p. 70). It is also an example of the (ostensibly autopoietic) way 'Japanese society processes images of international culture' (p. 71), recalibrating and (literally) refashioning the outside world according to Japanese expectations and/or internal specifications. Such is arguably the same sort of processing that must be done if yet another foreign culture presents itself, in this case, Singapore's (as if Singapore's cultures can be discretely essentialized), when children are put on tour coaches and taken to Chinatown, Little India and supposed versions of Malay homes and villages. Culture here is 'absorbed into a pattern of Japanese social expression' (p. 73) and specified within the circumscriptions of Japanese autopoietic schemas, while the sights (or sites) of the world are available for the seeing, but such sightseeing is only allowed to take place 'from within the security [and dictates or dictums] of one's own culture' (p. 72). Very tellingly in this connection, English classrooms in IB are given names after a parade of far-flung places, for example, Frankfurt class, Geneva class and Honolulu class. Other places whose names are drawn into this curious mode of nomenclature are Istanbul, Johannesburg, Kingston, Lisbon, Moscow and Naples. Outside each classroom is an evocative picture of each location. Fronting Lisbon is its scenic riverfront and old city; before Kingston town is an elegant looking ocean cruise liner; Honolulu is represented by its iconic sandy beaches and sailboats; while downtown Frankfurt is seen merrily decorated for Christmas. For good measure, the English notice board offers not only vocabulary relating to holidays and vacations, but features a poster capturing the Maldives complete with luxurious chalets and private pools.

The strategy is to make sure 'a predetermined path is navigated through the foreign culture [or textbook] to provide an experience that conforms to the expectations that have been cultivated by media representations [or more immediately and domesticatingly, textbooks and classroom wall pictures]' (Seargeant, 2009, p. 72). English can be about nice holidays, sandy beaches, luxury cruises and Christmas decorations, in short, perhaps anything else – except about being

Japanese. Visits to theme parks like the Shakespeare Country Park or those landmarked Singaporean religious or tourist sites duly allow 'Japan to regulate its image of the outside world' (Seargeant, 2009, p. 72). Such regulation, according to Seargeant, helps to 'refashion the image of the world according to subjective, home-grown standards' while symptomizing or epitomizing too 'Japan's attitude to international relations' (p. 72). For the Japanese, the image of the Singapore where they are domiciled, may just be another instance of the sort of refashioning or caricaturizing that is necessary for something unfamiliar to be reduced soothingly and timelessly into a theme park. Such a theme park can be viewed safely through the large polished windows of a tour bus and covered however superficially on a half-day trip, at the end of which, one can retire into the comforts of one's own inner cultural world. More importantly, a fixed and particularized image of the theme park must first be fully etched (in the mind) before it can be harnessed to conformingly serve the so-called 'education brief' referred to in Seargeant (p. 71). The intention for theme parks is ostensibly for them to serve as a didactic or disciplinary tool and 'a way to fulfil an education brief', alas to educate people on the cultures of others (p. 71).

English teaching and learning performed in gingerly manner

Having a Japanese institution teach the English language from an early age of six or seven, yet without the burden of having to defend or apologize for the teaching of something un-Japanese, is a precious opportunity of its kind. With even more subtlety, and within the recognizable auspices of a Japanese institutional domain, the social differentiation that comes with having one's children learn English much earlier than the rest of the country is a privilege to be (secretly) enjoyed. This privilege, which to be sure, is not enjoyed by children of Japanese workers who are not sent overseas with their families, may be viewed as a sort of betrayal of convention by the same, if they happen to look upon the circumscriptions of *nihonjinron* as an alibi to remain stoically or staunchly monolingual. Within this complex semiotic packaging, the teaching and learning of English is a way of marking out special identity, privilege and differentiation without the risk or vulnerability of having to admit to the waywardness of being un-Japanese or simply different.

For these privileged Japanese parents to be living overseas with their offspring and to be identifying with the benefits accruing thereof, one can say along with Blommaert (2003) that such nuanced 'forms of identity work could not be done [or possible] without the potential offered by globalization' (p. 610). Like Blommaert (2003), therefore, one might resonate with the fact that globalization gives rise to new packagings of sociolinguistic indexicalities, in this case, indexicalities relating to the subtle markings of privilege, albeit under the watchful eye of *ninhonjinron*-sponsored circumscriptions (prohibitions or inhibitions) marking preoccupations with Self (and not Other). In this connection, the more conservative of Japanese policy makers who take their part seriously will ensure that care is taken for English not to be allowed to undermine 'Japanese cultural identity and cultural values' (Hashimoto, 2007, p. 34), at least not within sight of those who remain in the homeland to hold the fort, while their expatriate counterparts are growing their careers and families overseas.

Teaching English within EFL-TESOL conventions as bulwark of defense of Japaneseness

As discussed, the English curriculum that is adopted by IB draws its inspiration and content from the likes of the *Family and Friends* series, which not unexpectedly, affirms an ideology of English language teaching that legitimates the circumscribing beliefs and practices of a TEFL-TESOL model (see Iino & Murata, 2016; Toh, 2019). Japanese students, even (or especially) when they reach university, continue to be identifiably positioned as EFL-type *learners* which is in diametrical contrast to their being potential ELF (English as a lingua franca) *users* (Iino & Murata, 2016). Treated perpetually as learners-in-deficit (see Toh, 2019), they are typically thought of as being uncomfortable with English, and unused to seeing it as a practical tool for real-life communication.

For Japaneseness to be maintained, the fact of the matter is that English teaching must remain within the narrow culturalist and native-speakerist confines of an EFL-TESOL model (see Holliday, 2005; Toh, 2019) precisely because the dictates of monolithic conceptualizations of language and culture must not be contravened, on pain of any consequent compromises with widely told myths of Japanese uniqueness. English teaching must be carried out in a way that Japanese learners must be made subjectively alien to the language, which to Pierce (1995) is a way of organizing and reorganizing who learners really can be, or in this case, who they should be. Textbooks chosen for the purpose must fulfil their role of naturalizing content that produces and sustains a subjectivity of alienation among such learners. The way English is taught must precisely be very much part of the maintenance if not the production of Japaneseness.

While English in Singapore is a localized, hybridized and pluralized multilingua franca (see Jenkins, 2015; Ishikawa, 2017; Toh, 2019), the English taught in a Japanese school, albeit (or especially) one remotely located in Singapore, cannot be allowed to assume the same hybridities and pluralities. The language must not be permitted to lose its symbolic (possibly snob) value as a language that must also remain decidedly foreign to (ordinary) Japanese (Stewart & Miyahara, 2011; Rivers, 2013). Following Allan's (2013, p. 59) observation that '[i]deologies assign language value', such a symbolic role arguably militates against or even precludes English taking on any practical role in terms of real-life communication, meaning making and identity formation (except to foster dis-identification or alienation). English can only remain meaningful to the Japanese if it remains (communicatively) *useless* to them. The English that is made available for learning by Japanese learners must be one that is guarded and indeed defended for its symbolic, ornamental and un-Japanese qualities (see Seargeant, 2009; Rivers, 2013) – precisely as a front-line defense of Japaneseness itself.

Ironic and oxymoronic incompatibilities with agency and transformation

The students' outsider status in relation to the world of the textbooks (carefully or otherwise) chosen for them is pre-emptively coupled with the fact that the identity options of Japanese students in Singapore are essentially regulated. Such regulation is made possible, not least, by dint of the fact that their very existence in Singapore (as determined by their immigration status) is that of 'accompanying dependent child' of an expatriate parent whose designation is that of an 'employment pass holder'. Such a parent is posted overseas for a designated period of time and is willy-nilly slated for re-deployment back to headquarters, sooner or later. The fathers' preemptive identity as an expatriate employee is superimposed preemptively on their children's. There are instances when expatriate parents decide after several years, to send their children back to Japan even before the father's (see Chapter 4) stint in Singapore is due for reconsideration or renewal, often for reasons to do with seamless transitioning between elementary and secondary education or between secondary education and entrance into university.

In none too subtle ways, these young people are subjects of discourses and hegemonies affecting their identity positionings and life trajectories. The reality of such hegemonies both conceals and unveils a web of contradictions and ironies if set against the optimistically transformative ideals put forth by concerned critical educators. Such contradictions and ironies become apparent if these critically transformative ideals are examined alongside the regularized situations facing children of Japanese expatriates (notwithstanding those suppositions of glamor often assumed to come with such an enviable status). However saddening examples of such ironies may be, the critically transformative ideals of well-meaning educators striving to pave the way for more humanizing approaches to educating the young, innocent and impressionable, are heavily contested by crass or harsher realities that stoke the very opposite.

Pittaway's (2004, p. 203) assertion that language learners are 'multidimensional being[s]' is very ironic in the face of strongly monolithic ideologies which encroach on the identity options and constructions of these learners, as would be Pierce's (1995, p. 16) even more laudable claims to the 'changing quality of a person's social identity' or the idea that 'the person might resist [any given] subject position or even set up a counter discourse'. For the identities of these students to be truly dynamic, multiple and subject to change (Pittaway, 2004), such liberating ideals would only ring true in a very perverse or inverted sense. Such inversion stems from ideological controls playing a significant part in actually regulating or regularizing student agency, preventing genuine change by rendering meaningless hopeful transformative ideals that regard student identities as *multiple* and *dynamic* (Pittaway, 2004). The element of hopefulness in these ideals is typically forced to give way to more cynical and hence oppressive (in)versions, including *malleable* or *manipulable* identity labelings. When their parents are sent elsewhere or sent home to Japan, these children will leave likewise. Within conceptions of social identity 'as a site of struggle' and subjectivity as a product of exposure to 'a variety of social sites', the human subject is, according to Pierce (1995) not normally 'conceived of as [one which is in any way] *passive*' (p. 15, italics added). In relation to the present discussion on the young people concerned, this observation may yet again be ironic or over optimistic.

According to Pittaway (2004), investment, as it can be applied in language learning, is what possesses the 'power to transform students to claim the right to speak and defend against obstacles' (p. 216). For teachers, engaging investment is meant to be a well-regarded 'process of leveraging learners' identities to help them achieve their goals and realize their potential for personal and/or [eventually] professional growth' (p. 216). In the case of the students in question, the leveraging of learner identities almost inevitably takes on a more pessimistic sense, even as their existence as 'multidimensional being[s] with a complex social history and equally complicated prospects for the future' (p. 203) undergoes what McVeigh (2006) would call an inversion (see McVeigh, 2006, for a parallel discussion on institutional inversion). Engagement with learners' multidimensional attributes becomes precisely an engagement with their monodimensional nature. The matter of learners' complex social histories takes on an oxymoronic affect (effect), in the sense that the very complexity of their social histories lies embedded within an acutely regulated form of (over) simplicity.

Pierce (1995) notes that the dynamic and multidimensional nature of student identity and subjectivity potentially 'opens up possibilities for education *intervention*' (p. 16, italics added), as opposed to *inversion*. If indeed such intervention is 'the crucial point for ... educators' that Pierce (1995) finds so promising, then the challenge to such a quest is a tremendously onerous one for the teachers of the students in question. This quest itself, if embarked on earnestly and honestly, will involve reflecting on the very tenets of the education their students are positioned at the receiving end of. Any teacher taking on this challenge will need to allow students to think, reflect and question, certainly at least the monolithic and monochromatic representations of life, personhood, living, being, behaving and becoming that are found liberally offered in the textbook pages they teach from. It seems a pity that children coming from such (perceivably or putatively) privileged backgrounds, and the potential they bring with them as young human beings to be nurtured into fine, open- and broad-mindedly globalized individuals, are that much subjected to powerful forms of monolithism, regularization and reductionism.

Perhaps this particular manifestation of a Japanese conceptualization (and dispensation) of elite education (see earlier discussion in this chapter as well as Yamagami & Tollefson, 2011; Stewart & Miyahara, 2011) is actually one which must remain loyal to manifestly conservative aspects of Japaneseness, and be subject to an invariable 'prescribing [of] particular subjectivities and values' (Allan, 2013, p. 59). Such loyalty must also, in one way or other, or in turn, translate to having students schooled and educated in a certain prescribed way. This might truly be regarded as the very least a Japanese system of schooling can be tasked to do for a burgeoning generation of future elites, so privileged at such a tender age to be having a fun and exciting time growing up in another country.

English teaching and betrayals of parochial concerns and behaviors

To continue the discussion, and not unaware that the manner of paradox or disarray in which stories like the one I am going to tell here will do to add to the complexity of issues just now discussed, I now turn to a matter which was first highlighted in Toh (2019). In (re)telling the story, I am helped by Norton and Early (2011, p. 423) who write about the 'particularly compelling way' stories are able to index social and power relations as well as investments in identity. The incident narrated here implicates social and power relations, professional behavior, personal comportment and conduct within a community. It also concerns matters relating to identity choice and positioning and serves as a way of gathering together the issues discussed in this chapter into one thought-provoking narrative.

In Toh (2019), I recount an actual occurrence involving the Head teacher of English at IB and her colleague in charge of the English Conversation program. These two teachers were referred to respectively as Teacher C (TC) who was Japanese, and Teacher D (TD) who came from a country in the northern hemisphere. As noted in Toh (2019), for our two children who were at that time new in Singapore and recently enrolled in IB, having curriculum time allocated for English lessons was going to be a promising novelty, given that they had, up until the time they left Japan, been schooled in the Japanese state system where absolutely no English was taught. Their experience of the English lessons at IB was, however, somewhat marred by the frequent change of teachers. My encounter as parent of our children with TC and TD was occasioned by the sudden and unexplained departure of an English teacher four weeks before the end of semester, a matter which would have given the children in her charge little or no opportunity for closure.

In the conference call I had with TC and TD to enquire about the sudden and unannounced departure of this teacher, it was TC who spoke first, beginning with 'repeated assertions that she could not hear me properly over the phone' while asking me to speak more clearly (Toh, 2019, p. 96). TC's response to my enquiry was both equivocal and evasive. When I sought clarity on how announcements were made about sudden changes of teachers as well as what was meant by answers like 'absent', 'on-medical-leave', 'yet-to-be-confirmed resignation', TD, the English conversation teacher, took over the call, while TC receded into silence. TD said that matters relating to my enquiry were handled by the school's senior administrators. As teachers, or so they avowed, they had no power to provide me with an answer. The conference call ended with TD's word that a school administrator would be contacting me about my enquiry.

As related in Toh (2019), my wife and I would receive a handwritten note from TC the next day, handed to us through our daughter. In the note, TC said that the reason she had not continued in the conversation was her recent bouts of nervousness whenever she had to speak to men with loud voices. Then turning to the matter of the sudden departure of the teacher, TC tried in her note to ameliorate the situation by highlighting the fact that the replacement teacher had many years of experience teaching English. This was quickly followed by her offering of words of praise to compliment our children, to the effect that they were nice children who were very polite to their teachers, always making it a habit of greeting her along the corridor each morning.

The message then took a personal turn. TC made a point of the fact that she lived 'very close' to us and that her own daughter was on the same bus as our children (see Chapter 5 for ideological and socially ramifying agendas with regard to bus routing). By virtue of being in the same vicinity (see discussion in Chapter 5 about conceptualizations of space in relation to bus routing), she expressed willingness to communicate personally with my wife about the matter of the teacher's sudden departure. TC's message ended with the following remark:

> I hope you'll understand the difference of (sic.) the ways (in various cases) between Japanese school (sic.) and other international schools, regarding how to announce information of anything (sic.) in school to parents.
>
> (Teacher C, in Toh, 2019, p. 97)

Norton and Early (2011) note that the matter of identity is implicated in investments of teachers, not just in their teaching practices within their own classrooms but also in the wider reaches of the community. TC's message is pertinent to the conduct of herself within the community that she imagines herself to be in, as both English Head in IB as well as the mother of her own child studying in the same school. It is evident that both bus route and neighborly proximity (actually a distance of a good four kilometers) feature greatly in her understanding of 'community' and this particular mode of understanding informs the way she attends to a matter that not incidentally pertains to her professional role as English Head (she chose to pen an undated handwritten note on absorbent color paper). Not as an aside, a distance of four kilometers is hardly proximal on a densely populated small island like Singapore. TC's sense of proximity appears more to be influenced by the school's exigent bus routing system and the fashion in which Japanese expatriate families tend to congregate in condominium clusters which in turn determines the planning of school bus routes (much about the spatial ideologies of which have been deconstructed in Chapter 5).

While a complete account and critique of the above encounter can be found in Toh (2019), the present commentary seeks to specifically notice significant points about delineations of space as well as identity investments within such delineations, staked by way of identification with a particularized social and spatial framing of 'community'. Within such a 'communal' framework marked out in this case by bus routing and condominium clustering, strictly professional spaces extend or elide seamlessly, indifferently and nonchalantly into private ones. Such flexibilities (or liberties taken to the same effect) derive and proceed from the advantages gleaned from being on the same bus route, as if being on the same bus route would mean being closer in (to) Japaneseness, in the most parochial of its senses. As seen in Chapter 5, the day-to-day running of these bus routes is routinely entrusted into the hands of a community of volunteer parents (mothers) who are not working, making up this bus 'community'.

No communication was received from the school's administrators, contrary to what was said by TD. A matter concerning IB's English program, at least to TC, was one that could have been better dealt with among the wives and mothers, in Japanese, on a Japanese-to-Japanese, Japanese-speaker-to-Japanese-speaker and mother-to-mother basis, even though this would have meant that TC would have had to speak to my wife in the context of her being more of a 'neighboring' Japanese-speaking bus-mother, rather than as the English Head per se. A non-Japanese male parent like me was not 'community'. My maleness and the loudness of my voice was another way of insinuating to me that I was peripheral to that 'community', being an English-speaking Singaporean-Chinese male, without her having to say as much. This was why TD, an English-speaker was tasked with speaking to me, the emptiness of her words notwithstanding. In the peculiarity of this case, English-speaking maleness became the alter ego of non-Japaneseness.

Given the way the matter unfolded, a clean and clear-cut professional solution could not somehow be achieved between the English Head and an enquiring (albeit non-Japanese) parent on a matter that affected the smooth running of English lessons. Proper closure for the children affected by the sudden change of teachers appeared not to be so much of a priority, as was the assertion of what was claimed to be 'the Japanese way'. Clear announcements to parents about the departure of a teacher, which TC admitted was presumably carried out in other international schools, was not something she said was done in the Japanese school she was speaking on behalf of, at least not from the way a handwritten note on absorbent paper was penned to explain 'the Japanese way' to a non-Japanese enquirer. One is reminded of Rudolph's (2018) account of the difficulties his Japanese students faced when challenged to think beyond essentialized discourses of Japaneseness. Apart from the student reflections seen in Chapter 2 on identity, globalization and discourses of Japaneseness which revealed struggles with hybridity and diversity in Japanese society, some other reflections cited in Rudolph (2018) are of relevance in the present connection:

> Student 14, for example, shared that, 'I defined Japan and other countries, and "we Japanese" and "foreigners" obviously. I did not try to respect other culture and custome. I though all things that Japanese doing was the correct and everyone should have to be like "us."' (sic) (Rudolph, 2018, p. 165)

There are of course recognizable differences between TC's implication (or insistence) that 'the Japanese way' of making announcements should be respected and the guileless loss of innocence that marks the above young person's admissions. TC's assertions would have been made with some consciousness that she was writing in her capacity as the English Head (notwithstanding her lack of clarity about this herself, in allowing this to be conflated with her part as neighboring mother) and that her remarks would likely carry more weight than if they had come from a budding neophyte clumsily insisting on their own special way (of being or doing Japanese).

To the institution's credit, there are good examples of situations where the people in charge have responded as promptly as might be expected (of Japanese or non-Japanese), perhaps more so in situations where the matter of the preservation of a Japanese way is less likely to factor in as a consideration or cause for concern. In such situations, it comes across that the school is indeed careful, thoughtful, efficient and proactive. Examples of such situations include timely preemptive warnings to parents about the possible spread of certain seasonal viruses, the threat or presence of certain tropical pests or vermin which might impinge on health and safety, or specific cases of intrusions by stray animals including one case of a monkey being found around the school compound. Such messages are very quickly and efficiently relayed to parents complete with appropriate precautionary instructions so that all concerned are kept apprised of the protective measures in place.

Inward turn towards talking about Japan in English

Drawing on the concerns raised by two contemporary nationalist scholars, Suzuki Takao and Tsuda Yukio, who have written critically on the (supposed) hegemonic influence of English and Western cultures on Japanese culture, Aspinall (2003) makes several important extrapolations about their views on 'reforming' foreign language teaching in Japan. Among these extrapolations are that the basic focus of foreign language teaching should no longer be about 'learning *from* foreigners' (Aspinall, 2003, p. 109). There should, in its place, be a purposed refocusing on Japan's domestic situation and more importantly, on the Japanese themselves, in order to find ways to 'help Japanese people express their ideas *to* foreigners' (Aspinall, 2003, p. 109, original italics). The above situation where an English head decides perforce to highlight alleged differences between how Japanese schools make their staffing announcements and the way the same is (presumed to be) done in other international schools, can be a case which exemplifies Aspinall's (2003) description of this refocusing on the self.

Aspinall (2003) further describes the nationalist position that '[s]ubjects such as "English for international understanding" should in fact be excluded' from the language curriculum (p. 110). The new emphasis, as is noticeable from the English Head's written note, is that 'the emphasis should be on *talking about Japan* in English' (Aspinall, 2003, p. 110, italics added), which is quite apparent with what was taking place with the note, referencing a Japanese way that needs to be explained to a foreigner. From this account, one might be justified in concluding that the teaching of English, as is acted out in the beliefs and actions of none other than the school's English Head, is both self-referential in terms of ideology and connately autopoietic in terms of internal specification. Hashimoto (2013) observes that Japan's resistance to globalization has meant that it has had to create 'its own version of internationalization', where internationalization positions the rest of the world as the Japanese Other, and its particular focus is more on 'promoting Japan to the international community, *not about becoming part of it*' (p. 29, italics added). Hashimoto (2013) explains this sort of parochialism or insularity using the example of what took place in the 2012 London Olympics when the Japanese team failed to win any gold medals in judo. A Japanese newspaper ascribes this failure to the implementation of a new points system and to the irregular judo styles of non-Japanese opponents. As noted in Hashimoto (2013),

> a retired Olympic gold medalist, Kaori Yamaguchi, made extensive use of the 'Japanese vs foreigners' rhetoric in her newspaper columns – such as 'foreigners do … but Japanese are the opposite'; 'when they compete against foreigners'; and 'it is a favorite trick of foreign athletes'. The generalization of Japan's opponents as 'foreigners' without any mention of names or nationalities indicates the assumption that Japanese do judo in a certain (proper) way and foreigners do not.
>
> (Hashimoto, 2013, p. 17)

One is reminded of earlier discussion in Chapter 2 (see '*Nihonjinron* and English language learning in Japan') that the teaching and learning of English among the Japanese is subject to their strong prefacing on a particularized version of internationalization influenced by *nihonjinron* beliefs. This version of internationalization epitomizes a line of reasoning which posits (or affirms) that the rest of the world (which includes non-Japanese English-speaking Singapore) needs or ought to better understand the Japanese way, whether it is about judo or making announcements, meaning that aspects of Japanese culture need to be explained particularly to those foreigners with whom the Japanese may choose to have some dealings (Kubota, 2002).

Moving from *critique* to *design* as a way of restoring voice, hope and dignity

As I write the concluding section of this chapter, I am reminded of a matter of epistemological importance by way of which notions of *critique* and *design* can be thought of as being part of one and the same (critical) praxis of action and reflection (Freire, 2000). If *critique* is a way of destabilizing ideologies and beliefs behind inequitable practices and structures, then *design*, according to Lillis (2003), is the impetus to move from such destabilization toward the construction of alternative discourses presenting fresh realities. By way of these fresh realities, the power to name, move and act is thereby (re)invested in those who have (once in time) been marginalized or silenced, students included. In other words, it might ideally be possible to think of *critique* and *design* as concurrent and coincident moves toward the overcoming of different forms of oppression (Lillis, 2003, also see Toh, 2017), both notions being potentially useful in restoring power, initiative and agency to those for whom education is meant to be the path to take in their quest for freedom, hope and change (Freire, 2000; 2014).

The reason I am so reminded of *critique* and *design* is the fact that in combination, both have the potential to nourish the sort of hope by which teaching and learning can once again build constructively on literacies, capacities, facilities and felicities as well as ways of acting and discoursing which students bring with them, that teachers should rightly reinforce. The hope and creativity needed for replacing what may once in time be a target for critique with something which students deserve better, is not without example or precedence. Hanson (2013) imagines a possibility where *design* assumes the form of a creatively multilingual and translingual approach to the teaching of writing, as opposed one which is stiflingly monolingual in character and fashion. Calling for teachers to indeed 'expand [their] expectations of students who self-identify as monolingual', Hanson (2013, p. 207) notes that teaching with (and towards) a multilingual orientation better reflects current linguistic realities and ecologies. Neither should English be regarded monolithically, where 'the presumption of English-language homogeneity in the midst of actual linguistic diversity' becomes decidedly a hindrance to having students become more capable of 'moving out of their monolingual comfort zone and into negotiating language differences in a multilingual world' (p. 207). If carried through with sincerity, students will stand the chance of becoming more confident in 'working across language differences' (p. 207) toward greater dexterity in 'negotiat [ing] language barriers' (p. 208). Kramsch (2014) points out in this regard that ongoing trends represented by the increased influence of technologies and information networks as well as by human and capital mobility are responsible for the emerging and changing conditions under which foreign languages need to be taught. The 'codes, norms, and conventions' which educators have faithfully (but quite inflexibly) relied on have been destabilized to the point that 'more reflexive, interpretive, historically grounded, and politically engaged pedagog[ies]' are now urgently called for (p. 302).

A good example of this sort of dexterity (first on the part of the teachers) is described in Iino and Murata (2016) which begins with pedagogical assumptions that rightfully acknowledge the plural nature of the English language. Like in the situation described in Iino and Murata (2016), it is possible for students, even or especially those from different backgrounds with respect to their experience with English (for example, Japanese returnee students from overseas, Japanese students who have learnt English in Japan, Japanese students who have studied in English-medium international schools in Japan, and overseas students who are not Japanese) to be eased away from the clutches of monolingual and monocultural approaches to English teaching and learning. Such easing away can become part of a concerted move from *critique* mode to *design* mode. *Design* in such a case would involve the opening up of space(s) where the negotiation of meaning as well as the norms of interaction and interpretation are actively supported (Kramsch, 2014; Iino & Murata, 2016).

The ultimate hope with such a challenge being to imagine beyond 'monolingualist assumptions of linguistic homogeneity' (Hanson, 2013, p. 213), schools placed in cosmopolitan multilingual situations like IB's can potentially tap on a *design* mode to enable students to become more aware of further possibilities in multilingual and translingual communication for signification and meaning making purposes (Canagarajah, 2013).

Dooley and Exley (2015) tell of a situation in Australia where school as well as teacher control of the curriculum, once a valued professional asset, became eroded as schools came under increasing external supervision by federal and state agencies. A national regimen of literacy testing was the cause of increased pressure to return to 'instruction in the print basics' while the inauguration of a national curriculum took place within a powerful resurgent 'back to basics rhetoric' (p. 46). A set of centrally produced work units brought about on this account put increased pressure on teachers to work closely along the guidelines in these units (Dooley & Exley, 2015). Objecting to the imposition of 'highly prescriptive, if not scripted, pedagogies' (p. 46), Dooley and Exley describe an instance in which the *design* mode is relied upon not only as a measure against prescription and obsessive prescribing, but also as a way of realizing critical consciousness and democratic experience. Dooley and Exley look deeply into various empowering dimensions of a critical literacy initiative aimed at skilling 9- to 12-year-olds from a high-diversity, high-poverty school environment as digital media production experts. The eventual aim was for these young people to mentor others in their classrooms, homes and communities. The successful outcome of this initiative meant that students were able to learn the skills to create their own media products, become agents of literacy development within their (largely migrant and indigenous) communities, apart from becoming more critically conscious of surrounding social inequalities and challenges.

Finally, in Pescatore (2015), the notion of *design* assumes its literal meaning in the author's account of the way a group of at-risk students in a small school district contribute to the creation of a blog to help parents and young people deal with the problem of bullying. For Pescatore, critical literacy's 'concrete result' as a form of pedagogy that 'strives for an empowering literacy' (p. 112) is a 'lifelong habit of approaching knowledge as a constructed affair' (p. 111). The latter, according to Pescatore is achievable by means of giving students a voice in the choice of classroom learning materials, assessments, and even due dates. Also, using materials like current events articles and also fiction, Pescatore describes her strategies of getting students to analyze bias, agenda, tone, diction and missing viewpoints as well as to write their reflections journals which she sees as 'a vital aspect to critical pedagogy' (p. 116). The outcome is the engenderment of a critical consciousness which enabled students to become all the more conscious of the 'relational and culturally based' nature of knowledge (p. 121). Citing the example of one of her students, John (pseudonym), Pescatore describes him as one who has experienced bullying, labeling and ostracism, but also one who responds positively in class and eventually becomes more critically conscious in his reading and writing:

> In February, John wrote on a worksheet for our novel, *Nothing but the Truth*, that no one can have the truth. With respect to Miss Narwin and Philip (characters in the novel), he said that 'They both have a perspective based upon what they have gone through and what has been experienced by the two individuals.' This shows movement from the phrase 'correct point of view' to a sentence that reflects a more developed understanding of a situated view of knowledge.
>
> (Pescatore, 2015, p. 119)

Moreover, as evidence of his shifting from *critique* to *design* mode, John takes it upon himself to journal actively beyond expectation, contribute regularly to the blog for parents and young people, and to even improve his self-image and 'redefine himself for the school community' (Pescatore, 2015, p. 118).

Thus, if to end the chapter on a note of hopefulness, it can be seen that through appropriate applications of *critique* and *design* (Lillis, 2003), one may, like in Pescatore (2015), begin to look ahead to having people become gradually more aware that it is possible to affirm voice, agency and self-understanding, even in situations which are initially or decidedly oppressive. Such affirmation can be achieved through facilitating a praxis of dialogic engagement with the challenging realities of one's surroundings, an important attribute of empowerment which rigidity, prescription, pretentiousness, self-centeredness and self-isolation are not likely to be able to bring forth.

References

Allan, K. (2013). Skilling the self: the communicability of immigrants as flexible labour. In A. Duchene, M. Moyer & C. Roberts (Eds.), *Language, migration and social inequalities: a critical sociolinguistic perspective on institutions and work* (pp. 56–78). Bristol: Multilingual Matters.

Aspinall, R. W. (2003). Japanese nationalism and the reform of English language teaching. In R. Goodman & D. Phillips (Eds.), *Can the Japanese change their education system?* (pp. 103–118). Oxford: Symposium.

Ben-Ari, E. (2006). The culture of Japanese business in Singapore. In Y. H. Tsu (Ed.), *Japan and Singapore: a multidisciplinary approach* (pp. 219–239). Singapore: McGraw Hill Education.

Blommaert, J. (2003). Commentary: a sociolinguistics of globalization. *Journal of Sociolinguistics*, 7(4), 607–623. https://doi.org/10.1111/j.1467-9841.2003.00244.x

Bolton, K., & Botha, W. (2017). English as a medium of instruction in Singapore higher education. In B. Fenton-Smith, P. Humphreys & I. Walkinshaw (Eds.), *English medium instruction in higher education in Asia-Pacific: from policy to pedagogy* (pp. 133–152). Cham: Springer.

Canagarajah, A. S. (2013). *Introduction. In A. S. Canagarajah (Ed.), Literacy as translingual practice: between communities and classrooms* (pp. 1–9). New York: Routledge.

Davidson, R., & Liu, Y. (2018). Reaching the world outside: cultural representation and perceptions of global citizenship in Japanese elementary school English textbooks. *Language, Culture and Curriculum*. doi:10.1080/07908318.2018.1560460

Donahue, R. T. (2002b). Guideposts for exploring Japaneseness. In R. T. Donahue (Ed.), *Exploring Japaneseness: on Japanese enactments of culture and consciousness* (pp. 3–27). Westport: Ablex.

Dooley, K., & Exley, B. (2015). Afterschool MediaClub: critical literacy in a high-diversity, high-poverty urban setting. In B. Yoon & Sharif, R. (Eds.), *Critical literacy practice: applications of critical theory in diverse settings* (pp. 41–56). Singapore: Springer.

Freire, P. (2000). *Pedagogy of the oppressed* (30th anniversary edition). New York: Bloomsbury.

Freire, P. (2014). *Pedagogy of hope: reliving pedagogy of the oppressed* [Bloomsbury Revelations Edition]. London: Bloomsbury.

Hanson, J. (2013). Moving out of the monolingual comfort zone and into the multilingual world: an exercise for the writing classroom. In A. S. Canagarajah (Ed.), *Literacy as translingual practice: between communities and classrooms* (pp. 207–214). New York: Routledge.

Hashimoto, K. (2000). 'Internationalisation' is 'Japanisation': Japan's foreign language education and national identity. *Journal of Intercultural Studies*, 21, 39–51. https://doi.org/10.1080/07256860050000786

Hashimoto, K. (2007). Japan's language policy and the 'Lost Decade'. In A. Tsui & J. Tollefson (Eds.), *Language Policy, Culture, and identity in Asian contexts* (pp. 25–36). Mahwah, NJ: Lawrence Erlbaum.

Hashimoto, K. (2013). 'English-only', but not a medium-of-instruction policy: the Japanese way of internationalising education for both domestic and overseas students. *Current Issues in Language Planning*, 14(1), 16–33. doi:10.1080/14664208.2013.789956

Holliday, A. (2005). *The struggle to teach English as an international language*. Oxford: Oxford University Press.

Holliday, A. (2013). 'Native speaker' teachers and cultural belief. In S. A. Houghton & D. J. Rivers (Eds.), *Native-Speakerism in foreign language education: intergroup dynamics in Japan* (pp. 17–28). Clevedon: Multilingual Matters.

Horii, S. Y. (2015). Creating a multilingual/multicultural space in Japanese EFL: a critical analysis of discursive practices within a new language education policy. In X. L. Curdt-Christiansen & C. Wenniger (Eds.), *Language, ideology and education: the politics of textbooks in language education* (pp.145–160). London: Routledge.

Hult, F. (2017). More than a lingua franca: functions of English in a globalised educational language policy. *Language, Culture and Curriculum*, 30(3), 265–282. https://doi.org/10.1080/07908318.2017.1321008

Ishikawa, T. (2017). Conceptualising English as a global contact language. *Englishes in Practice*, 4(2), 31–49. https://doi.org/10.1515/eip-2017-0002

Iino, M., & Murata, K. (2016). Dynamics of ELF communication in an English-medium academic context in Japan: from EFL learners to ELF users. In K. Murata (Ed.), *Exploring ELF in Japanese academic and business contexts: conceptualization, research and pedagogic implications* (111–131). London: Routledge.

Jenkins, J. (2015). Repositioning English and multilingualism in English as a lingua franca. *Englishes in Practice*, 2(3), 49–85. https://doi.org/10.1515/eip-2015-0003

Kramsch, C. (2014). Teaching foreign languages in an era of globalization: introduction. *The Modern Language Journa*l, *98*(1), 296–311. https://doi.org/10.1111/j.1540-4781.2014.12057.x

Kubota, R. (2002). The impact of globalization on language teaching in Japan. In D. Block & D. Cameron (Eds.), *Globalization and language teaching* (pp. 13–28). London: Routledge.

Lillis, T. (2003). Student writing as 'academic literacies': drawing on Bakhtin to move from critique to design. *Language and Education*, 17(3), 192–207.
May, S. (2003). Critical multiculturalism. In M. Peters, C. Lankshear & M. Olssen (Eds.), *Critical theory and the human condition* (pp. 199–210). New York: Peter Lang.
McVeigh, B. (2006). *The state bearing gifts: deception and disaffection in Japanese higher education*. Lanham: Lexington Books.
Norton, B., & Early, M. (2011). Researcher identity, narrative inquiry, and language teaching research. *TESOL Quarterly*, 45(3), 415–439. https://doi.org/10.5054/tq.2011.261161
Pescatore, C. (2015). Developing critical literacy in a tenth grade English class. In B. Yoon & R. Sharif (Eds.), *Critical literacy practice: applications of critical theory in diverse settings* (pp. 111–128). Singapore: Springer.
Pierce, B. N. (1995). Social identity, investment, and language learning. *TESOL Quarterly*, 29(1), 9–31. https://doi.org/10.2307/3587803
Pittaway, D. S. (2004). Investment and second language acquisition. *Critical Inquiry in Language Studies*, 1(4), 203–218. https://doi.org/10.1207/s15427595cils0104_2
Risager, K. (2006). *Language and culture pedagogy: from a national to a transnational paradigm*. Clevedon: Multilingual Matters.
Risager, K. (2011). The cultural dimension of language teaching and learning. *Language Teaching*, 44(4), 485–499. https://doi.org/10.1017/S0261444811000280
Risager, K. (2018). *Representations of the world in language textbooks*. Bristol: Multilingual Matters.
Risager, K., & Chapelle, C. A. (2013). Culture in textbook analysis and evaluation. In C. A. Chapelle (Ed.), *The encyclopedia of applied linguistics* (pp. 1–5). Oxford: Blackwell.
Rivers, D. J. (2013). Institutionalized native-speakerism: voices of dissent and acts of resistance. In S. A. Houghton & D. J. Rivers (Eds.), *Native-speakerism in foreign language education: intergroup dynamics in Japan* (pp. 75–91). Clevedon: Multilingual Matters.
Rudolph, N. (2018). Education for glocal interaction beyond essentialization and idealization: classroom explorations and negotiations. In A. F. Selvi & N. Rudolph (Eds.), *Conceptual shifts and contextualized practices in education for glocal interaction: issues and implications* (pp. 147–174). Singapore: Springer.
Seargeant, P. (2009). *The idea of English in Japan: ideology and the evolution of a global language*. Bristol: Multilingual Matters.
Stewart, A., & Miyahara, M. (2011). Parallel universes: globalization and identity in English language teaching at a Japanese university. In P. Seargeant (Ed.), *English in Japan in an era of globalization* (pp. 60–79). Houndmills: Palgrave Macmillan.
Thang, L. L., MacLachlan, E., & Goda, M. (2006). Japanese women working in Singapore. In Y. H. Tsu (Ed.), *Japan and Singapore: a multidisciplinary approach* (pp. 186–218). Singapore: McGraw Hill Education.
Toh, G. (2001). Primary school English textbooks in Singapore across the decades: an examination of the cultural content of the Oxford Series, PEP and PETS. In J. Tan, S. Gopinathan & W. K. Ho (Eds.), *Challenges facing the Singapore education system today* (pp. 140–157). Singapore: Prentice Hall.
Toh, G. (2006). Native gurgles and conference giveaways. *Asian Englishes*, 9(2), pp. 104–111. https://doi.org/10.1080/13488678.2006.10801194
Toh, G. (2012). Having English as a resource for multicultural understanding: exploring possibilities in Japanese ELT. *Journal of Multilingual and Multicultural Development*, 33(3), 301–311. https://doi.org/10.1080/01434632.2012.655248

Toh, G. (2016). *English as medium of instruction in Japanese higher education: Presumption, mirage or bluff?*London: Palgrave Macmillan.

Toh, G. (2017). Japanese graduate school students' writing in English: facilitating pathways towards 'design'. *Writing and Pedagogy*, 8(3), 550–573. https://doi.org/10.1558/wap.29241.

Toh, G. (2019). *Effecting change in English teaching: exposing collaborators and culprits in Japan*. London: Palgrave Macmillan.

Xiong, T., & Qian, Y. (2012). Ideology of English in a Chinese high school EFL textbook: a critical discourse analysis. *Asia Pacific Journal of Education*, 32 (11), 75–92. https://doi.org/10.1080/02188791.2012.655239

Yamagami, M., & Tollefson, J. (2011). Elite discourses of globalization in Japan: the role of English. In P. Seargeant (Ed.), *English in Japan in an era of globalization* (pp. 15–37). Houndmills: Palgrave Macmillan.

7 Interrogating 'Singapore-as-technology' in the reproduction of Japaneseness

I began this book with a consciousness that lived histories are often able to find their extension and elaboration in praxis, an observation from Freire (1985) which reminded me that my own praxis was a necessary and integral part of the extension and elaboration of concatenated events (which included my nine-year stay in Japan and my return to Singapore with family, as well as an earlier attempt to write about this topic) that became part of the backgrounding of the present discussion. My seeking a way of understanding how Japanese residing in Singapore have sought to envision and administer their lives and futures, particularly through insights gleaned from the manner in which they educate their children, became part of the furtherance of both history and, consequently, praxis.

Simon and Dippo's (1986, following Sartre, 1963) meaning of 'project' as being veritably determined both by *real* and *present* conditions' while interest and energies are being directed toward 'how people are *implicated* in the *regulation and alteration* of the terms of how they live together and how they *define what is possible* and *desirable* for *themselves* and *others* (p. 196, italics added), assumed an added significance of registering for me key areas of concern that needed to be attended to in a discussion on human interaction and relocation of the present nature. Specific aspects of relocation and interaction or what Goosseff (2010) would call out in his discussion on autopoiesis as a challenge of structural coupling were seen to be concerned with: (1) investments in (and enactments of) Japanese identity among the Japanese domiciled in Singapore, bearing in mind powerful ideological discourses of Japanese homogeneity much discussed in *nihonjinron* literature; and (2) outworkings of Japanese identity enacted or played out in Singapore's English-speaking cosmopolitan multiracial multicultural setting, such outworkings since observed to be part of a bid for assertion and affirmation of certain (particularized but rather ethnocentric) forms of Japaneseness, ultimately seen (or deemed) to be highly necessary for the continuation or preservation of the same.

My discussion was also guided by a broader organizing problematic on the nature of criticality (Simon & Dippo, 1986), not only as a way of appropriating the narrative data which benevolently facilitated the various critical discussions, but also as a way of dealing with concerns over inequality, mendacity and domination found within the same. This storied data also revealed matters of important overarching professional (and variously, ethical and moral) concerns. These were concerns which related to (and as has been seen, impinged on) the production and articulation of critical discourse, the sustenance of the credibility of critical academic practice, ultimately implicating seminal challenges to criticality itself. As I have sought to reflect in my discussion, these were concerns of an inherently professional and ethical nature, which at the same time demonstrated that they also resonated with issues and struggles over identity and identity investments, ways to signify, mean, make meaning and become meaningful, as well as ways of being, behaving and becoming (more or less human or humanized).

A nurturing and naturalizing of elitism and exclusivity through schooling

While attending to the educational experiences, identities and subjectivities of the children being schooled in the particular institution (IB) and system discussed, it soon became fairly clear that the roles, identities, subjectivities and culpabilities of attendant and answerable adults were also implicated in the beliefs and practices characterizing (or epitomizing) the system. Additionally, it became observable that these characterizing beliefs and practices were mirror reflections of the autopoiesis and stasis that inhered and helped organize (maybe circumscribe) both institution and system, constitutively. In this way, it became apparent that schooling was not entirely for its own sake, but served or lent itself not incidentally as both tool and project of Japaneseness, while the systemic technologies that supported its running also served to host other ideologically self-reproducing self-preserving self-referencing agendas.

In terms of the shaping of identity not just of the students of the school in question, but by association, the Japanese community in its entirety, assertions of superior and exclusive identities invoking a 'bourgeois capitalism' that fetes the self-concept of a 'conservative mercantile class' (Clammer, 2000, p. 216), were seen to be an important aspect of identity production and formation. For a community like this, conceptions of self, while linked to consumption styles at one level, is keenly reliant on Japanese capitalism as 'being the major contemporary source of cultural nationalism' and very importantly, 'the primary shaper of what it is to be Japanese' (p. 217). The legitimating and reifying of elite expatriate identity positionings were therefore a necessary and naturally evolving aspect of the courting and manicuring of privilege and exclusivity. Such privilege and exclusivity would in turn lend access to social entitlements (e.g. colonial clubs; children's playgroups and birthday invites; wives' and mothers' luncheons or afternoon tea gatherings in exclusive places) preserved only for people in the well-heeled upper echelons, quite out of the reach of average Singaporeans or other foreigner working types.

Ironically, such foreigner working types, as has been seen in Thang et al. (2006), include those individual (usually unmarried) Japanese working women employed in Singapore on local contracts which do not afford them the same privileges and exquisite lifestyles enjoyed by their better advantaged counterparts. As has been noted in earlier discussion, these working women are able to form much closer relationships with their local Singaporean colleagues than their counterparts who are identifiable by their loftier status.

The symbolic aspects of the abovementioned schooling arrangements, where schooling is not entirely for its own sake, are a variation or inversion of Dale and Hyslop-Margison's (2010) worries precipitated by the 2008–2009 economic crisis. The authors describe the particular fashion in which education institutions have taken to a 'business operation model at the direction of the managerial class', in their race to offer training geared 'to meet neoliberal market demands' (for workers) (p. 6). Such demands, as they acutely observe, 'have far less to do with actual labor market readiness or needs ... than they do with the ideological manipulation of students as future workers' (p. 6). In Freirean terms, IB, the institution in question, feeds into neoliberal discourses and agendas as described in Dale and Hyslop-Margison (2010), but more so towards meeting the demands for personnel in the privileged managerial echelons that are conformant and compliant to Japanese conceptualizations (constructions) of such a type of ('human') resource. In this case, compliance pertains to the creation or cloning of an obedient and conformist but staid if unimaginative form of elitism that will hopefully power Japanese mercantilism into a promisingly distant future. So while it remains veritably true that education itself has continued to play its part as 'the chief tool in shaping national uniformity' (Reischauer, 1988, p. 217), there is also an aspect of education that is not quite so obvious to the untrained eye which aligns it with the culpabilities of subtle promotions of elitism and, quite possibly, cultural superiority.

Such subtle alignments with elitism run contrary to commonly averred to beliefs that Japan remains a uniformly egalitarian society (see Lie, 2003). In such a manner, schooling potentially becomes a way of sowing the seeds of a form of elitism or privilege that is identified with and anchored particularly on tenets of Japaneseness, while nurturing (naturalizing) from a very innocent and tender age an ideology of difference and entitlement. Dale and Hyslop-Margison's (2010, p. 6) rendition of teaching then becoming 'restricted to passive neoliberal compliance', given any truth in it, can only spell a matter of extremely serious concern to do with hidden but no less potentially worrying forms of differentiation or divisiveness.

Schooling as a moral, ideological, identity-laden and identity-charged project

Singapore constitutes an overseas location where Japan, Inc. continues to command and assert its palpable economic as well as social-cultural influence while generating its quantum of cultural capital and corporate profits, in the course of contributing to the continued growth of Singapore's economic miracle (or bubble). Meanwhile, the rest of the world, as keen observers like Risager (2006) and Peters and Roberts (2012) may view it (i.e. the world itself), is one that is increasingly open and borderless and where information as well as linguistic and cultural practices intermingle and spread dynamically through a differentiated plethora of social and business networks (Risager, 2006). In addition, the differential, partial and virtual nature of these routes and networks trace and inhere notably complex transnational patterns, shadowing the paths of human migration and trends in commodity markets (Risager, 2006; also see Douglass & Roberts, 2003). As noted earlier in Chapter 6, Japanese businesses drawing on their sharp acumen must know very well the ebbs and flows of these global fluidities, as much as enterprising seafaring itinerant merchants of yesteryear must have known intimately the directional changes of the trade winds they depended so much upon to grow their fortunes.

While Japanese ventures into Singapore continue to demonstrate the sharpness of Japanese business foresight, the sophistication of Japanese technical expertise and the qualities of dedication and commitment within Japanese work ethic, there nevertheless remains to be recognized, the matter of the continued legitimation of characteristically (and rather parochially) one-truth forms of Japaneseness (see Befu, 2009), even in cosmopolitan overseas locations like Singapore. These monolithic forms of truth persist in the cultural and institutional outworkings and practices of entities linked even to overseas Japanese populations alike, despite such (mostly transient) populations being once removed from the cribs and chancels of the Japanese homeland. The persistence of such assertions of Japaneseness on foreign soil has in turn attracted critical observations about their influence and bearing on Japanese conceptualizations of internationalization and multiculturalism, while affecting (deleteriously) the manner in which these two notions are bought forth and represented to school students, sometimes in artlessly reductive fashion.

One would be reminded of a point made in Seargeant (2009) about the way in which experiences or occurrences that are considered un-Japanese are treated. Things deemed un-Japanese undergo a form of schematic reduction, like the way theme parks (or *gaikoku mura*) are made to host reduced or caricaturized forms of anything foreign or unfamiliar. In this connection, the rest of Singapore (and neighboring Southeast Asia) outside the protective sanctums of IA to ID, are liable to be similarly reduced, and be viewed through equally caricaturizing lenses that would have them schematized within a theme park framework. This is not least reflected in the way in which school excursions are planned around schematized or stereotyped representations of Singapore's ethnic cultures. The truth about a visit to Chinatown is the fact that 'the two- and three-storey Chinese shophouses were cleared from urban areas of Singapore' as part of urban redevelopment initiatives in the 1970s. As also noted in Trocki (2006), Chinatown was effectively, if ruthlessly, relocated to government-built tenements in Singapore's mainly working class suburbs, to the ubiquitous multi-storey HDB (Housing and Development Board) flats, as part of attempts to re-profile Singapore's sophisticated downtown urban skyline. If indeed '"Chinatown" and its people were moved [or diverted] to the HDB flats in the various "new towns" around the island' (Trocki, 2006, p. 155), then a school excursion to 'Chinatown' might more appropriately and authentically be planned around a visit to a housing block in a suburban Singaporean neighborhood, where in fact, the multicultural nature of Singaporean life is more to be savored and appreciated, authentically at that. Significantly too, a certain *omiyage* [souvenir] item produced by the school has embossed on it meme-like pictures depicting what seems to be iconic (or ironic) captions of Singapore. Featured pictorially are Singapore's Merlion and Ferris wheel called the Singapore Flyer both standing prominently by the seafront, tall buildings depicting Singapore's lofty skyline, but also orientalized images (Said, 1978) of the local flora and fauna seen in the images of a durian fruit, a coconut palm, a house lizard or wall gecko, a garden snail, and a mangrove crab. These images prove to be useful not only in revealing the manner in which Singapore is specified autopoietically, but also in reflecting the school's approbation of the same revealing specifications.

Distancing and reductionism

Japan's love-hate relationships with things or matters deemed to be un-Japanese on its part, reflect the complexities, subtleties and anomalies which continue to characterize 'indigenous trajectories of desire and fear with global flows of people and things' (Appadurai, 1990b, p. 3). We are reminded in this case of the tendency for things foreign or unfamiliar to be placed at a safe psychological distance as a way of self-preservation or maintenance of the status quo (Donahue, 2002b; Befu, 2009). This tendency is one that continues to be the case despite current expectations (possibly slightly premature with reference to the Japanese situation) for researchers of social and anthropological phenomena to conceptually assume 'erosion of the spatially marked cultural home' and to focus their energies on 'phenomena of homelessness, multinationalism [and] deterritorialism' (Lebra, 2004, p. 262). Lie (2003) provides vivid reflections of the fact that the Japanese may not be anytime ready for such assumptions to be realistic. Discussing social-territoriality in the Japanese mind in relation to a very narrow range of identity positionings for migrant workers, Lie (2003) notes the following:

> Asian migrant workers' significant diversity of educational attainment or class background is ignored in the dominant Japanese view. A Bangladeshi construction worker may be a college graduate, a Filipina bar maid a professionally certified nurse, an Iranian telephone card seller a son of a medical doctor. Upper and lower class, college educated and illiterate are all lumped into the category of foreign workers.... Underlying the contrast between the lower-class foreign workers and the middle-class Japanese is the widely diffused belief in Japanese affluence and Third World poverty.... Class and nation are ... fused in the prevailing Japanese social view. (pp. 74–75)

In the school classroom meanwhile, the reduction of *gaikokugo katsudo*'s wide choice of possibilities to only English speaks of an essentialist understanding (perhaps a deliberate one) of internationalization which suggests its indexing to an equally narrow range of meanings and identity positionings. Hashimoto (2013) notes that in Japan,

> the Japanese language has the status of the national language and its dominance is not open to question [while] the notion [of] bilingualism is an attribute that belongs exclusively to foreigners or 'Others'. (p. 29)

At the same time, Hashimoto (2013) reveals that this particular 'absence or denial of bilingualism among the Japanese people in the Japanese education system has shaped the so-called English-only practices in curricula' (p. 29). An internationalization that involves languages other than English (Mandarin, Malay, Tamil are but a few possibilities in Singapore) or more hybridized translanguaging practices (Garcia & Li, 2014; Li, 2018) is thereby rendered far-fetched and thus practically unattainable or undesirable. In this connection, Hashimoto (2013) points out that Japanese children like the ones in IB who have lived overseas are relegated to being 'treated as Others' (p. 29). Attempts are felt to be necessary 'to "de-Other them" by transitioning them' through exposure to 'Japanese-only environments', usually on an 'as soon as possible' basis (p. 29).

Moral and ideological project accented on Japaneseness

As noted, IB, the school itself and the world views and educational trajectories it sets out to represent to (and see reproduced in) children of Japanese families demonstrate signs of their being part of a moral and ideological project in Japaneseness, with the curriculum tendered as both tool and technology. Within this curriculum, English teaching, with its reduced, essentialized and stilted curricular content, can be counted on to be a particularly potent and reliable technology in the attested quest to keep students (and those English teachers who are operating or tarrying under the same influence) on the short leash of the same moral and ideological project. In this way, the institution itself becomes qualifiable as a strategically remote overseas base for educating a next generation of smartened future elites, exposing them to a world beyond Japanese shores (albeit a curated or manicured version), without fears of being observed and envied by the pryingly curious eyes of those who are left back home. While this is happening, those left back home continue trustingly and obliviously in the myth of egalitarianism (Lie, 2003), a myth which must remain enduringly (alas mistakenly) undisturbed and untampered with among the Japanese.

The short lease (and leash) of a typical expatriate posting to Singapore serves as a mark and reminder of its very temporality and ephemerality, nice condominiums, spas, swimming pools, exotic living and servile domestic helpers, not excluded in the attractive packaging of overseas sojourns. The galvanized reality for these sojourners of the privileged kind lies doubtlessly in their eventual return or repatriation to Japan at the conclusion of an expatriate posting. Only a lucky few may yet be sent to another exotic location to carry on being called or sidled up to as white-collar elites. Many will simply go back to the jobs they had before they went overseas on their hiatus. Yet even within such temporality and ephemerality, the 'soft power' of Japanese institutional ideology and its 'capillary effects' (in the words of Duchene et al., 2013, p. 10) find (and wind) their way inescapably into the lives and 'moral sel[ves]' (p. 11) of these men and their families. Institutions A to D may well furnish some comforting or reassuring reminders of the homeland they have rather lately left (for an interim), but their disarming displays of Japaneseness also masks their 'other work of governing those who come within [their] ambit' (p. 10). These institutions serve as a moral beacon and emotional support to the Japanese over the period of their Singapore stint or domicile, ever faithful cuckoo-clocks which remind them of the timed and temporal nature of their stay, but which 'also shape them' and their progeny (p. 10) over the period of time spent away from the watchful eye of head office.

Harnessing Singaporean technologies and Singapore-as-technology towards reinforcing Japaneseness

As far as education is concerned, the highly competitive Singaporean environment with its reverence for quality and academic excellence is one that is reputedly highly conducive to disciplined and regulated approaches to the nurturing of a next generation. Singapore has in place a comprehensive education system (and ethic) founded unapologetically on coldly meritocratic principles envisioned to support and reward only the smartest and the best.

IB's registration with Singapore's Committee of Private Education can be regarded as a benchmarking that speaks of sterling quality, trustworthiness and unquestionably high standards, enabling the school to ride proudly on the same back (badge) of reliability. Yet what has been witnessed of IB in the previous chapters does not seem to be suggestive or representative of any manner in which international and transnational spaces can be effectively harnessed for purposes of education, certainly not in the sense of the expansiveness of Waters & Brooks' (2011) description of the creative potential of emergent educational spaces. This possible or apparent lack of appreciation for education's expansive international, transnational and policy spaces happens in spite of the fact that Singapore is one very place where energies and resources are channeled or funneled readily into innovative undertakings geared toward the schooling of future generations of global talent.

While Singapore's global connectivity is appreciated much for what it offers in terms of opportunities for business, the same does not seem to be in terms of harnessing the former for international and transnational education. Instead, the Singapore environment (practically in theme park fashion – see Chapter 6) is arguably and perhaps opportunistically reconstituted as tool and technology for the production of certain identities and subjectivities, all of which are directed towards the furthering of agendas legitimating statist and culturalist constructions of Japanese identity. If not usefully (re)choreographed as a Lilliputian theme park, Singapore has to be refurbished to recreate a miniaturized or microcosmic Japan, overseas. In the case of the Japanese kindergarten discussed in Chapter 2, the Singaporean environment had to be forcibly re-spaced to simulate a Japanese one (Chew & Thang, 2006). Artificial cherry blossoms had to be used to evoke the cheeriness of spring in Japan and equally artificial maple leaves had to be used to recreate autumn. For good measure, winter had to be literally flown to Singapore on a Japanese airliner, arriving at the doorstep in the form of a real but refrigerated snow man (Chew & Thang, 2006).

This production of certain particularized subjectivities depends heavily on the engenderment of super-structural and institutional spaces and hegemonies which make such engenderment and production possible (McVeigh, 2002). As observed in Chapters 2 and 5, McVeigh (2002) links the institution and constitution of Japanese politeness and the practice of civility to statist mercantilist agendas towards the production of certain subjectivities of compliance, all but making politeness a vacuous form of social conformity or complaisance. By the same token, Japanese schooling in Singapore can, arguably, be just as culpably reconstituted for (re)alignment with statist identities and agendas. Singapore by dint or contingency of its very hosting of an instantiated version of Japanese schooling thereby helps to constitute and produce certain identities and subjectivities among those schooled within such a system, an arrangement which would not otherwise be repeatable, certainly not even within Japan itself. Singapore becomes an (un) intended part of the production and preservation of particularized forms of Japaneseness, albeit Japaneseness forged and deputed overseas.

English language education

As noted in Chapter 1 and following Williams (2010), much of the writing I have done in this book has been part of what can be regarded as a creative process of 'learning by doing' (p. 141) as well as a form of cognitive storytelling which Barkhuizen (2011) refers to as 'narrative knowledging' (p. 396). Where fixity and intransigence have many a time wormed their way into the (inner) workings of both the knowledge economy and academic meaning making, a recourse or resort to learning by doing, learning by telling and learning by writing, can prove to be a humanizing and cathartic strategy in the challenging bid toward the discovery, realization and appropriation of new knowledge. Learning by doing, moreover, may (arguably) be harder even for professional or ideological regimes to put a despotic stop to, except perhaps for the most oppressive of such regimentations.

Nevertheless, it remains entirely possible that some other book, if it gets written on the very same topic, may view education (particularly English language education, which comes within my area) in a similar schooling situation quite differently. English language education in the way it has been seen meted or carried out in this present discussion could well (or otherwise) be viewed as the availing of a wonderfully rare and perfect opportunity for young and impressionable Japanese learners to be exposed to a powerful international language, mastery of which will present many golden opportunities for future career advancement (see Aspinall, 2003; Stewart & Miyahara, 2011). The outcome of such good fortune must be that children so opportunely exposed to English will become worthy ambassadors for Japan in the international arena of business and diplomacy when the time eventually comes for them to shine in their chosen careers (this is *not* in the light of my own sworn reservations over matters to do with curriculum and pedagogy). If to enjoy comprehensive schooling in the Japanese system in an overseas location is a sterling badge of privilege, part of the icing over such privilege must certainly be to have weekly curricular time set aside specially for English language instruction right from a child's very inaugural year in elementary school. In Japan, this is simply not possible, logistically and ideologically (Oda, forthcoming). It might even be thought of that IB, the elementary school in question, and others like it in other global mega-cities where the proliferation of Japanese conglomerates and multinationals justifies a demand for Japanese schooling, are beacons and epitomes of an openness and commitment to globalization. Children at IB have yearly get-together sessions with nice and friendly children from Singaporean schools – to practice English and have a memorable time together. The adoption of such textbook series as *Family and Friends* complete with Anglo-centric norms, would in addition, be an even more revealing sign of a ready willingness to assume an international outlook. The use of textbook materials put out by major international publishing companies outside of Japan must be favorably considered against the fact that schools back home remain heavily dependent on the bespoken *Eigo Nooto* (see earlier discussion in Chapter 6) for their obligatory *gaikokugo katsudo* activities en route to the holy grail of international understanding (Horii, 2015). If globalization is, moreover, to be eagerly taken hold of as a golden opportunity for the cultural and economic advancement of the Japanese nation, then Japan must be wasting no time in 'develop[ing] new skills (especially in technology and English) in order to meet the challenges of globalization' (Stewart & Miyahara, 2011, p. 31). Based on such an understanding of globalization, IB, and Japanese schools similar to it, must be (app)lauded for doing a splendid job of giving Japanese students a brilliant head start in the learning of a language that can only augur the promise of greater things to come for them, their future employers and for their country.

As has been seen, the experiences which qualify my own humble opinion do not permit me to agree with such a triumphalist viewpoint on the teaching of English in an institution like IB. The teaching of English is in large part a tool for the production and commission of Japaneseness and the maintenance of Japanese identity. The teaching of English in this case is not even about tendering a hackneyed or muted response to 'the privileging of language and communication skills in the "new economy"' (Allan, 2013, p. 59).

Observations relating to truly liberating pedagogies beyond regulated or hackneyed forms of didacticism

I have written the chapters of this book ever conscious that knowledge is neither static, mechanistic nor 'something to be transferred and deposited in … students' (Freire, 1985, p. 92). In contrast, knowledge is said to inhere in 'relationships between human beings and the world' (p. 91), its relational nature making it dynamic and negotiable, open to 'a constant searching' as well as 'invention and reinvention' (p. 93). Neither is it about transforming living subjects into passive objects, 'docile and passively accept[ing] the contents others give or impose' (p. 93). In this vein, truly liberating pedagogies are perhaps also not about going to 'another part of the world' to 'normalize it' according to a particular 'way of viewing reality', nor should they be about transmission, mechanical transfer, depositing, handing over, manipulation or cultural invasion (p. 89). For Freire, these terms indicate a denial of 'true action and reflection' while implying and insinuating 'actions which transform people into "things"' thereby 'negat[ing] their existence as beings who transform the world' (p. 89). By the same token, identity like education, is not fixed, prescriptive or preexistent, but situated and produced in interactions between people and in the context of broader social processes (Norton & Early, 2011), as already noted in the way elite expatriate identities among the Japanese can only be forged and composited in a uniquely overseas situation like Singapore's.

If this should be said here, therefore, I am obliged think and write with a strong consciousness that true education, as it is for Freire (1985), involves 'educational action of a liberating nature' (p. 91) and 'incarnates [a] permanent search of people *together with others* for their becoming more fully human in the world in which they exist' (p. 90, italics added). My writing, moreover, is also in no small part motivated by the hope that in situations where the operations of dominant ideologies and discourses spawn and perpetuate unfair and outmoded practices, misperceived, misappropriated or simply dehumanized meanings can be changed for purposes of greater fairness and equity. Such fairness and equity are vital with respect to education as Freire (1985) sees it, in its quest for those involved to become more fully human or less crassly dehumanized (see Freire, 1985; 2000; Dale & Hyslop-Margison, 2010).

Epistemologies and nature of criticality in Japanese education

Not apart from this quest for humanization and greater meaningfulness in education, I have sought from early on in my discussion to frame the concerns I raise within a problematic that facilitates questionings about the nature of criticality and critical practice as they relate to Japanese education, in the hope of making out a way to highlight the challenging aspects of both concerns that are not normally so apparent or visible. As noted in Chapter 5, the matter of epistemologies relating to criticality and critical practice will be further addressed here in this final chapter, hopefully, as a way of not just paying due attention to power asymmetries and incommensurable policies and practices, but to consider how these same asymmetries resulting from ideologized policies and practices can be surfaced, denaturalized and resisted. Matters referencing criticality and critical practice where they concern Japanese education have already been the subject of close examination. Such close examination has, from among a range of issues, sought to highlight for notice ones related to: (1) inconsistencies arising out of internationalization initiatives and their outcomes; (2) questions over the ways in which English is taught, treated, tested or otherwise appropriated in different quarters and domains of Japanese society; and (3) identities and subjectivities of Japanese students living overseas with their expatriate parents. In these instances, as well as in matters referencing ideology and identity negotiation discussed in Chapters 5 and 6, the demands on criticality and critical practice have come across as being ones that are steeply challenging in nature, begging the question of the sort of criticality which would truly commensurate with such challenges.

To answer this question, the particularity of such a call to criticality mandates a fairly unique understanding or appreciation of the same, insofar as my concerns here relate to education, especially language education, in Japan, or at least within a Japanese ethos of schooling. This call to criticality is one that needs to contend squarely and honestly with the autopoietic aspects of a status quo of intransigence, certainly if meanings referencing *nihonjinron* specify the nature of organizational closure (see Goosseff, 2010). In the case of Japanese expatriates and their families, if moving or being posted overseas has to be treated autopoietically as an external form or source of perturbation (Goosseff, 2010), then criticality itself must on this very account, be honestly admitting and confronting of such a perturbation *as a perturbation* and not something else in pretense (for example, a euphemistic paraphrase or parody of some form of petty, paltry or sanitized irritation). Criticality in this sense, is about calling the proverbial spade by its avowed name. It is also an uncharacteristic form of honesty and gallantry as it applies to the academe, or even parrhesia, if one is brave and principled enough to answer Rivers' (2015) call to candidness as a fundamental attribute of criticality.

In an example given in Chapter 2, the way in which nature and the four seasons are interpolated synecdochically to represent a putative Japanese trait, the conflation of Japan's four seasons with nature places a monopoly on nature's associations with Japaneseness. Criticality in this case must not just be about calling out the unreasonableness of such an attempt at monopolizing the meaning of nature, but about the more powerful (but less apparent) ruse of using something as naturally innocuous as nature to monopolize, categorize and marginalize, for the mere sake of insinuating one's uniqueness. While it is true that it is not expedient for assertions of uniqueness to be expressed so blatantly lest it turns into chauvinism, where criticality is concerned, it is the subtlety of such forms of monopolization of meanings that must surfaced and singularized for questioning.

Autopoiesis and the challenge to (for) criticality

If the monopolization of meanings appears as an outward manifestation of autopoiesis, the latter's associations with the internal environment of operationally closed entities and organizational closure (Goosseff, 2010) suggests that criticality must be patently alert to different forms and symptoms of operational closedness. In this regard, one would imagine a form of criticality that is admissive of and sensitive to the (mostly recalcitrant or mischievous) outcomes of self-referencing and self-specification, which happen by dint of autopoiesis. Conceived of in this way, criticality assumes a didactic role in the way it focuses attention on asymmetries or monopolies of whatever epistemology or ideology, while not discounting the possibility of willful ignorance, intransigency, obstinacy, hypocrisy or mischief, when it comes to specifications of meaning.

In this connection, one is reminded that autopoiesis and the Bakhtinian concept of the dialogic nature of communicative acts, both recognize the fact that 'the someone [who is] primarily addressed [in a communicative act] is *internally generated* and faithful only to the maintenance of the autopoiesis of the author' (Goosseff, 2010, p. 150, italics added). Thinking about textbooks, their authors and Bakhtin's internally generated addressee (also called a superaddressee), the case can be made for criticality to include a critical consciousness of this subjective superaddressee among textbook and materials writers. Given a critical consciousness that materials play self-referentially to an autopoietic superaddressee, criticality potentially raises awareness of the possibility (likelihood) that authors (including myself as I write), are liable to be caught in a circuitry of a tail-chase, of this vaunted superaddressee. Criticality, in this case, would provide the motivation to both be conscious of, and to allow one's dialogic imagination to extend beyond, this monologic tail-chasing circuitry – for the betterment of undertakings in curriculum writing and materials creation. One can arguably foresee in reductionist textbook materials the reality of a caricatured superaddressee (or worse, a putative learner), possibly one that personifies or epitomizes the sort reductionist stereotyping of non-native speaker learners, nicely critiqued in Kumaravadivelu (2003c).

Addressing my superaddressee

Finally, criticality (if I may be allowed to directly address my superaddressee who I trust is also my valued reader) will require a willingness and open mindedness to take a strategically humorous view of human hypocrisy and foible. The superaddressee I address in this regard is someone who personifies the sort of open-heartedness, sensitivity and intelligence to embrace such a possibility. Given that closedness, intransigence or sheer obstinacy (academics not spared) mandates a pretentious or pompous dissembling and dissimulation of the very ideologies that belie the same sorts of miscreance, exposures of such miscreance mandates a criticality that sportingly bears (with) an element of tolerance for the sorts of humor attracted to (or tantalized by) the critical questioning of such hypocrisies and foibles. Such critical expository questioning should take place regardless whether the hypocrisies and foibles (and of course, their underlying ideologies) in question are uniquely of a Japanese, or otherwise and more generously, a human, nature.

May it never be the case that hypocrisies and/or foibles become the proprietary monopoly of one uniquely defined group(ing) of people, whoever they are, or whoever they set themselves up to be.

References

Allan, K. (2013). Skilling the self: the communicability of immigrants as flexible labour. In A. Duchene, M. Moyer & C. Roberts (Eds.), *Language, migration and social inequalities: a critical sociolinguistic perspective on institutions and work* (pp. 56–78). Bristol: Multilingual Matters.

Appadurai, A. (1990b). Disjuncture and difference in the global cultural economy. *Public Culture*, 2, 1–24. https://doi.org/10.1215/08992363-2-2-1

Aspinall, R. W. (2003). Japanese nationalism and the reform of English language teaching. In R. Goodman & D. Phillips (Eds.), *Can the Japanese change their education system?* (pp. 103–118). Oxford: Symposium.

Barkhuizen, G. (2011). Narrative knowledging in TESOL. *TESOL Quarterly*, 45(3), 391–414. https://doi.org/10.5054/tq.2011.261888

Befu, H. (2009). Concepts of Japan, Japanese culture and the Japanese. In Y. Sugimoto (Ed.), *The Cambridge companion to modern Japanese culture* (pp. 21–37). Cambridge: Cambridge University Press.

Chew, D. K., & Thang, L. L. (2006). The Japanese kindergarten of Singapore: 'internalization' and 'internationalization'. In Y. H. Tsu (Ed.), *Japan and Singapore: a multidisciplinary approach* (pp. 240–258). Singapore: McGraw Hill Education.

Clammer, J. (2000). Received dreams: consumer capitalism, social process, and the management of the emotions in contemporary Japan. In J. S. Eases, T. Gill & H. Befu (Ed.), *Globalization and social change in contemporary Japan* (pp. 203–223). Melbourne: Transpacific.

Dale, J., & Hyslop-Margison, E. (2010). *Paulo Freire: teaching for freedom and transformation*. Dordrecht: Springer.

Donahue, R. T. (2002b). Guideposts for exploring Japaneseness. In R. T. Donahue (Ed.), *Exploring Japaneseness: on Japanese enactments of culture and consciousness* (pp. 3–27). Westport: Ablex.

Douglass, M., & Roberts, G. S. (2003). Japan in a global age of migration. In M. Douglass & G. S. Roberts (Eds.), *Japan and global migration: foreign workers and the advent of a multicultural society* (pp. 3–37). Honolulu: University of Hawai'i.

Duchene, A., Moyer, M., & Roberts, C. (2013). Introduction: recasting institutions and work in multilingual and transnational spaces. In A. Duchene, M. Moyer & C. Roberts (Eds.), *Language, migration and social inequalities: a critical sociolinguistic perspective on institutions and work* (pp. 1–21). Bristol: Multilingual Matters.

Freire, P. (1985). *The politics of education: culture, power, and liberation*. Westport Connecticut: Bergin and Garvey.

Freire, P. (2000). *Pedagogy of the oppressed* (30th anniversary edition). New York: Bloomsbury.

Garcia, O., & Li, W. (2014). *Translanguaging: language, bilingualism and education.* Basingstoke: Palgrave Macmillan.

Goosseff, K. A. (2010). Autopoiesis and meaning: a biological approach to Bakhtin's superaddressee. *Journal of Organizational Change Management*, 23(2), 145–151. https://doi.org/10.1108/09534811011031319

Hashimoto, K. (2013). 'English-only', but not a medium-of-instruction policy: the Japanese way of internationalising education for both domestic and overseas students. *Current Issues in Language Planning*, 14(1), 16–33. doi:10.1080/14664208.2013.789956

Horii, S. Y. (2015). Creating a multilingual/multicultural space in Japanese EFL: a critical analysis of discursive practices within a new language education policy. In X. L. Curdt-Christiansen & C. Wenniger (Eds.), *Language, ideology and education: the politics of textbooks in language education* (pp.145–160). London: Routledge.

Kumaravadivelu, B. (2003c). Problematizing cultural stereotypes in TESOL. *TESOL Quarterly*, 37(4), 709–719. doi:10.2307/3588219

Lebra, T. S. (2004). *The Japanese self in cultural logic.* Honolulu: University of Hawai'i.

Li, W. (2018). Translanguaging as a practical theory of language. *Applied Linguistics*, 39(1), 9–30. https://doi.org/10.1093/applin/amx039

Lie, J. (2003). The discourse of Japaneseness. In M. Douglass & G. S. Roberts (Eds.), *Japan and global migration: foreign workers and the advent of a multicultural society* (pp. 70–90). Honolulu: University of Hawai'i.

McVeigh, B. (2002). *Aisatsu*: ritualized politeness as sociopolitical and economic management in Japan. In R. T. Donahue (Ed.), *Exploring Japaneseness on Japanese enactments of culture and consciousness* (pp. 121–145). Westport, CT: Ablex.

Norton, B., & Early, M. (2011). Researcher identity, narrative inquiry, and language teaching research. *TESOL Quarterly*, 45(3), 415–439. https://doi.org/10.5054/tq.2011.261161

Oda, M. (forthcoming). Behind the sandcastle: implementing English language teaching policies in Japan. In X. Gao (Ed.), *Second handbook of English language teaching.* Dordrecht: Springer.

Peters, M. A., & Roberts, P. (2012). *The virtues of openness: education, science, and scholarship in the digital age.* Boulder: Paradigm Publishers.

Reischauer, E. (1988). *The Japanese today: change and continuity.* Cambridge, MA: Harvard University Press.

Risager, K. (2006). *Language and culture pedagogy: from a national to a transnational paradigm.* Clevedon: Multilingual Matters.

Rivers, D. J. (2015). The authorities of autonomy and English-only: serving whose interests? In D. J. Rivers (Ed.), *Resistance to the known: counter-conduct in language education.* London: Palgrave Macmillan.

Said, E. W. (1978). *Orientalism.* New York: Random House.

Seargeant, P. (2009). *The idea of English in Japan: ideology and the evolution of a global language.* Bristol: Multilingual Matters.

Simon, R. I., & Dippo, D. (1986). On critical ethnographic work. *Anthropology and Education Quarterly*, 17(4), 195–202. https://doi.org/10.1525/aeq.1986.17.4.04x0613o

Stewart, A., & Miyahara, M. (2011). Parallel universes: globalization and identity in English language teaching at a Japanese university. In P. Seargeant (Ed.), *English in Japan in an era of globalization* (pp. 60–79). Houndmills: Palgrave Macmillan.

Thang, L. L., MacLachlan, E., & Goda, M. (2006). Japanese women working in Singapore. In Y. H. Tsu (Ed.), *Japan and Singapore: a multidisciplinary approach* (pp. 186–218). Singapore: McGraw Hill Education.

Trocki, C. A. (2006). *Singapore: wealth, power and the culture of control.* London: Routledge.

Waters, J., & Brooks, R. (2011). International/transnational spaces of education. *Globalisation, Societies and Education*, 9(2). 155–160. https://doi.org/10.1080/14767724.2011.576933

Williams, G. (2010). *The knowledge economy, language and culture.* Bristol: Multilingual Matters.

Index

Made in the USA
Las Vegas, NV
29 October 2024

ecb46abc-8871-4bd3-913d-323fa75f0629R01